Relationship Development Intervention with Young Children

Companion volume

Relationship Development Intervention with Children, Adolescents and Adults
Social and Emotional Development Activities for Asperger Syndrome, Autism, PDD and NLD
Steven E. Gutstein and Rachelle K. Sheely
ISBN 1 84310 717 1

of related interest

Asperger's Syndrome
A Guide for Parents and Professionals
Tony Attwood
Foreword by Lorna Wing
ISBN 1 85302 577 1

Playing, Laughing and Learning with Children on the Autism Spectrum
A Practical Resource of Play Ideas for Parents and Carers
Julia Moor
ISBN 1 84310 060 6

Giggle Time – Establishing the Social Connection
A Program to Develop the Communication Skills of Children with Autism
Susan Aud Sonders
ISBN 1 84310 716 3

Addressing the Challenging Behavior of Children with High-Functioning
Autism/Asperger Syndrome in the Classroom
A Guide for Teachers and Parents
Rebecca A. Moyes
ISBN 0 84310 719 8

Relationship Development Intervention with Young Children

Social and Emotional Development Activities for Asperger Syndrome, Autism, PDD and NLD

Steven E. Gutstein and Rachelle K. Sheely

Jessica Kingsley Publishers
London and Philadelphia

First published in the United Kingdom in 2002
by Jessica Kingsley Publishers
116 Pentonville Road
London N1 9JB, UK
and
400 Market Street, Suite 400
Philadelphia, PA 19106, USA

www.jkp.com

Library of Congress Cataloging in Publication Data

Gutstein, Steven E.
  Relationship development intervention with young children: social and emotional development activities for Asperger Syndrome, autism, PDD, and NDL / Steven E. Gutstein, Rachelle K. Sheely.
    p. cm.
  Includes index.
  ISBN 1 84310-714-7 (v. 1 : pbk) -- ISBN 1-84310-717-1 (v. 2 : pbk.) -- ISBN 1-84310-720-1 (set)
  1. Autistic children--Rehabilitation. 2. Asperger's syndrome. 3. Social skills in children. 4. Developmental disabilities. 5. Friendship in children. 6. Handicapped children--Attitudes. 7. Child   development. I. Sheely, Rachelle K., 1942- II. Title.

RJ506.A9 G88 2001
618.92'898203--dc21

2002021905

British Library Cataloguing in Publication Data

A CIP catalogue record for this book is available from the British Library

ISBN-13: 978 1 84310 714 9
ISBN-10: 1 84310 714 7

Printed and Bound in Great Britain
by Athenaeum Press, Gateshead, Tyne and Wear

"Two are better than one; because they have a good reward for their labour. For if they fall, the one will lift up his fellow: but woe to him that is alone when he falleth; for he hath not another to help him up."

Ecclesiastes 4:9–10

This book is dedicated to Oliver Lapin who blessed us by sharing his experiences with us for a too-brief time.

Contents

Activities

I

Introduction

"Friendship is unnecessary, like philosophy like art. It has no survival value; rather, it is one of those things that give value to survival."

– C.S. Lewis

"Things would be so much better if I could just find him one friend." Heroic parents desperately search for a peer who will accept and play with their son and daughter with Autism, Asperger Syndrome, Pervasive Developmental Disorder (PDD) or Non-Verbal Learning Disability. They dream that an understanding friend will serve as a crucial relationship bridge.

The sad truth is that you cannot acquire friends as if they were objects or possessions. And you cannot just place a child with severe social deficits in the presence of a typical peer or in a normal social setting and assume he will gain the skills and motivation to be a friend. Many people do not realize the complex integration of skills required for friendship. Unfortunately there are no shortcuts or easy solutions. Friendship, even for the most capable of us, requires hard work in order for us to obtain even minimal payoffs. And for those born with Autism, Asperger Syndrome or PDD, the odds are stacked against them from birth.

This is a collection of exercises based on the Relationship Development Intervention model (RDI). Our previous book *Autism / Aspergers: Solving the Relationship Puzzle,* described the intervention model and theory of RDI. The goal of this volume is to provide a comprehensive program for developing relationship skills with children with Asperger Syndrome, PDD, Autism or Non-Verbal Learning Disabilities. A second volume *Relationship Development Intervention with Children, Adolescents and Adults* contains exercises suitable for adolescents and adults with similar problems. This volume is designed for younger children, typically those from the age of two, up to age eight or nine. It emphasizes foundation skills such as social referencing, regulating behavior, conversational reciprocity and synchronized actions. The activities are specifically written for younger children and cover Levels I – III in our six-level system. If you complete the activities in this volume and are ready to move on, you can purchase the volume for older children and adults and begin at Level IV. The second volume is written for those working with older children, adolescents and adults. While we provide activities that cover Levels I – III for older individuals, we emphasize the advanced friendship development and maintenance skills found in Levels IV – VI.

We are often asked why we use a developmental model that begins with basic relationship exercises. Why not work only on "age-appropriate" social skills? Our response is to ask the person if they would recommend teaching calculus to someone just because they happened to be of college age, even if that person was unable to comprehend addition and subtraction. When we use the mathematics analogy, people quickly recognize the absurdity of such an endeavor. But, when it comes to friendships and social development in general, many people continue to teach advanced friendship skills to persons lacking relationship fundamentals. Friendships, like mathematical ability, depend upon a foundation of many skills built upon previously acquired skills. You cannot do higher math until you've mastered the more basic skills. Friendship is like the most complex calculus. You cannot open the text to advanced friendship and expect much success if you have not mastered the earlier chapters.

The second similarity to math is evident when we recognize why many of us have forgotten most of the math we were taught. The response, as we know all too well, is because we did not have a use for it at the time we were learning it. Because it had no function, no meaning to us, we could not learn it effectively. Learning friendship skills requires that the learner understand the function of that skill on a personal level. We learn best when we can understand the application to us of the skills we are being taught.

How to use this book

We have included many objectives to plan and evaluate your program. An important implication of this objective-based system, is that the program is designed so you can easily evaluate a child's progress. Objectives are listed in the Progress Tracking Form. Each one is related to a specific exercise, or series of exercises in one or both of the manuals. This means that you will always know why you are doing an activity.

The Topic Index of Activities provides a cross-referenced index of activities and objectives. Most activities are presented in developmental progression. If you wish, you can move in a systematic fashion from one objective to the next, by progressing through the activities in the order they are presented.

If you would prefer to work on specific topic areas, rather than following the progression we have laid out, again refer to the Topic Index of Activities. Here you can choose a topic such as Conversation, or Emotional Regulation and find activities corresponding to it, listed in developmental order.

As RDI is a developmental program, it is often helpful to begin working at the correct stage. Of the two, it is more important to not start too high than it is to begin too low. At The Connections Center, in Houston, we always begin by administering the Relational Development Assessment (RDA) – a two-hour-long series of sample activities that we observe, videotape and carefully rate. We have begun training clinicians in different areas of the USA to use the RDA. Keep watching our website to see if there is anyone trained in your area.

But what if you cannot access a clinician who administers the RDA? Does this mean you should not go on with the program? Of course you should! Use the Progress Tracking Form. Read the stage descriptions and objectives for each stage. Try out the exercises of the stage that seems to be representing the developmental level of the person you are working with. Make sure you have not skipped any critical developmental steps. For example, it astonishes us to see how many "High Functioning" people come to us with deficits in basic Social Referencing, a skill we address in Stage 2 of our 24-stage model. Do not bypass these foundational skills in a rush to get to more "age appropriate" exercises.

Who should use this book?

Parents

Parents can implement most of these exercises at home. We have written this book to take the mystery out of social development. Many activity instructions are provided in a step-by-step manner that should not require a professional. By Stage 8, when peer partners are needed, we do recommend finding a suitable counselor, therapist or other "Coach" and carefully matching peers.

Teachers and Special Educators

Teachers and Special Educators should enjoy using this manual. The Relationship Development Program is designed for easy implementation in school settings. In fact we use it at our own therapeutic day school in Houston, Texas. This, alongside the second volume, provides a comprehensive curriculum for relationship development that can be used with all students, whether they have specific disabilities or not. These volumes should make developing an Individualized Educational Plan – an IEP – a much simpler process, as the program provides clear objectives which are connected to specific exercises and activities.

Therapists

Therapists should also greatly benefit from using these manuals. Our evaluation protocol and intervention exercises are already in use by therapists in various disciplines throughout the USA and Canada. Added benefits for clinic and managed care providers are the clear objectives, which can help when obtaining insurance coverage and when demonstrating effective utilization of resources.

Using the website as a companion

Although this is a self-contained manual, our website, *www.connectionscenter.com*, can be used as a companion to the book. It should serve as a major support to implement RDI. On the site you will find ways to contact clinicians from different areas who have been trained in our evaluation method – the Relationship Development Assessment. We also list professionals whom we have trained to serve as Relationship Coaches, using the RDI model. Our message board allows parents and professionals to exchange tips and ideas for new and modified activities. It also provides a place where people from the same area can find one another to set up dyads and groups of partners at a similar stage. On the site you will find links to purchase all of the materials and supplies needed for the program. Finally, we are in the midst of videotaping and producing most of the RDI activities. Activity CDs and DVDs will be available for order on the site. All purchasers will receive a free limited time subscription to view videotaped segments of many of the activities described in the book. They will also have free, unlimited access to the activities archive and to the activities exchange message area.

What is the end product of RDI?

As you implement the RDI program, you will shortly notice significant changes. The child will be more fun to be with. Both adults and other children will approach him or her more and desire to interact. He will smile and laugh more. He will dramatically increase the amount of time he spends looking at you and other people in a meaningful way – not just making eye contact but also trying to figure out how you are feeling. He will appear more "alive" and natural and show more enthusiasm and joy. In the months and years to follow, you should expect to see the following social changes:

- He will make true friends who genuinely appreciate him

- His communication will become less scripted and more creative, as will his humor

- He will receive more invitations from peers and have more desire to accept them

- He will become a good collaborator and a valued team member

- He will make meaningful contributions to others' lives

- He will be much more fun to teach

- You will feel less like an "object" and more like he sees you as a real person

- His actions will be less governed by scripts and rules and more by the needs and feelings of those around him.

His thinking will change as well:

- He will act in a more flexible manner and be more accepting of change and transitions

- He will be more curious about discovering new features of his world

- He will be more creative

- He will consider several alternative solutions to problems

- He will think in terms of "gray" areas and not just "right or wrong, black and white" terms

- He will seek out and value others perspectives and opinions

- He will be more aware of his unique identity.

Who is RDI for?

We are frequently asked if one age group, one disorder or people at a certain level of severity are suitable for RDI. The answer is that RDI is a very broad-ranging program. The only group of people that we consider might not benefit from RDI are those for whom we must first address severe aggressive, oppositional or non-compliant behaviors prior to working on relationship skills.

- RDI Activities are designed for the entire range of AS, PDD and Autism, from low to very high functioning children and teenagers.

- The program can also be used with children who are not AS or autistic but who have relationship development problems, like ADHD, Bi-polar Disorder, Tourette Syndrome and Learning Disabilities. At higher levels, it is an excellent relationship development curriculum for typical children.

- Activities are presented which can be useful for children from age two onward.

Where did RDI come from?

Those who read my first book know that I [Steve] spent over 20 years studying relationships as a child, marital and family therapist, academic researcher and program developer. After years of working intensively with people in the Autism Spectrum, Rachelle and I grew dissatisfied with the limited results we obtained using the methods that were available. We believed that many people in the Autism Spectrum were capable of participating as true partners in authentic emotional relationships, if only we provided a means for them to learn about and experience them in a gradual, systematic way. For the past ten years we have been developing and refining our assessment and intervention methods based upon this belief.

In the next chapter we will discuss the essential skills of friendship and how relationship skills are different from other social skills. The third chapter provides you with information about how to get started in our program. Beginning with Chapter 4 we describe activities for the first three levels and twelve stages of our program. Each chapter covers the activities for that level.

2

Friendships are Relationships

In preparing this book, we reviewed the extensive research done in Developmental Psychology over the last 25 years, on the development of friendships. We distilled our findings into ten skill areas that encompass the qualities of children and adolescents who are successful in finding and maintaining friendships. These skills progressively build upon one another over a period of many years. The skill areas are: Enjoyment, Referencing, Reciprocity, Repair, Co-Creation, We-go, Social Memories, Maintenance, Alliance and Acceptance. As you progress through our exercises you might find it helpful to return to this section to reference which of the areas you are targeting. Below, we provide a brief description of each area:

Enjoyment

Friends must be enjoyable, exciting companions. Children with enthusiasm and an upbeat mood are valued, even if they have other deficits or limitations. Friends strive to find ways to make positive emotional connections with their peers. The nature of the connection changes developmentally, with collaborative play giving way to conversations involving humor, shared interests, emotions and problem solving about relationships.

Referencing

Children who develop friendships are adept at using the feelings, ideas and actions of their social companions as a critical reference point for determining their behavior. What our friends do matters to us a great deal and we are constantly "referencing" them. In its earliest stages, "referencing" involves basing your actions on the immediate emotional reactions of your social partners. Referencing rapidly moves to the "inside" world and becomes a continual discovery of the minds of our friends and family. Good friends develop mental "reference maps" of the interests, favorite activities, strengths and weaknesses of their pals.

Reciprocity

Friends must "pull their own weight." Reciprocal, "give-and-take" relationships begin when young children learn to become equal partners and maintain the shared meaning and enjoyment of their social encounters. At a later stage, reciprocity becomes focused on mutual appreciation and support. The child who is responsive to a friend's needs and interests has the right to expect responsiveness in turn. Good friends expect that at times they will choose to give up doing something they want in order to satisfy a strong desire of a friend.

Repair

Friends must be able to manage disagreements and discuss their complaints and conflicts without doing permanent damage to the relationship. Individuals who disagree more than they agree are unlikely to become friends. But you cannot have unrealistic expectations of friends and friendships. Many people encounter difficulties because they expect their friends never to disappoint them, to know everything about them, or to be their friend exclusively. Hurt feelings and disappointments are an unavoidable part of close friendships. The person who is unwilling or unable to forgive others and seek to "repair" the relationships will have difficulty forming close friendships. A friend must be able to separate the intentions of an act from its consequences and be ready to understand that the motivations of friends sometimes are not clearly demonstrated in their actions. Finally, a friend must be willing and able to look within himself and see his own responsibility for causing the difficulties that will inevitably occur. The technical term for these skills is "Relationship Repair." Without well developed repair skills even those relationships which begin well are rapidly destroyed.

Improvisation and co-creation

One of the major payoffs of a friendship is the enjoyment of finding special ways to share our perceptions and ideas in offbeat or novel ways that produce our own unique products. Others may not appreciate our "inside" jokes. But they bring good friends who have shared unique experiences to their knees with laughter every time.

We-go

Being a friend means that you experience yourself as an essential part of a greater unit than just yourself. Friendship implies the concept of a "We-go." When close friends are together, they may intensely share the same feelings and ideas to the point where they experience themselves as operating with one shared mind. The term "We-go", coined by the developmental researcher Bob Emde, is a shortened version of "We-Ego" and connotes the experience of operating as a "group mind." This is a group Ego that allows friends to accomplish things that they could never do alone.

Social memories

Successful and stimulating experiences contribute to a sense of shared history, joint fate and a perception of investment in the relationship. Friends jointly record and love to re-tell about funny, sad or powerful experiences that they have shared. These "re-tellings" serve as the essential glue that cements friendships together. Memories of sharing joy and overcoming adversity remain with the friendship forever and serve to rekindle it in times of adversity or after periods of inactivity.

Maintenance

One of the hallmarks of friendship is the desire to commit free time to one another in the absence of pressures or external rewards to do so. Good friends think about each other, even when apart. They keep in contact on a regular basis. They maintain contact just to stay connected, without any other agenda or ulterior motives. The statement "I just wanted to hang out with you" or "I called for no reason at all" have familiar variants in every culture in the world.

Alliance

Friends rely on one another as critical allies at times of adversity. The knowledge that you can have a reliable friend who will be at your side whenever needed, provides us with the courage to face up to almost any adversity. Friends keep confidences, stick up for one another and remain honest and loyal. A person who violates confidences, acts disloyally with a friend when others are around, or engages in deception is perceived as unreliable. As children get older they judge friends based on consistency between words and deeds. You must be willing and able to help your friends when they are in need.

Acceptance

People are at ease with their friends because they feel liked and accepted by someone familiar with their strengths and their weaknesses, their charming as well as their irritating qualities. When you succeed at difficult endeavors, your friends are expected to recognize these achievements with congratulations and express admiration. By contrast, failure and negative events provide equally important opportunities for functioning as a source of support, with displays of acceptance, affection, caring and concern. Friends are called upon to provide help, advice, comfort and emotional support. Criticism must also be rendered tactfully, but only when it is needed and specifically requested.

Relationship Skills

Reading the above descriptions, you may be struck by how the essential skills of friendship differ from the typical "social skills" taught in classes or social skills groups. We are accustomed to thinking of social skills as teaching behaviors such as making eye contact, waiting your turn, smiling, asking good questions and similar behaviors. In fact, this is because there are two very different types of social interaction and, in almost all cases, children are only taught one of these. Unfortunately the type that is taught, called "Instrumental Skills", does not lead to success in friendships and other relationships. Instrumental skills are mainly about getting what you need and about fitting in. Scientists refer to them as "instrumental" because, when we employ them, we tend to use people like instruments to get our needs met. When they use the term Social Skills, most people are really thinking about Instrumental Skills. But the set of attributes that lead to friendships do not fall into the Instrumental category. Rather they belong to a second group we call "Relationship Skills." Both types of skills are important. But, only Relationship Skills lead to the ability to have friends and intimate relationships. The following diagram provides a simple illustration of this distinction:

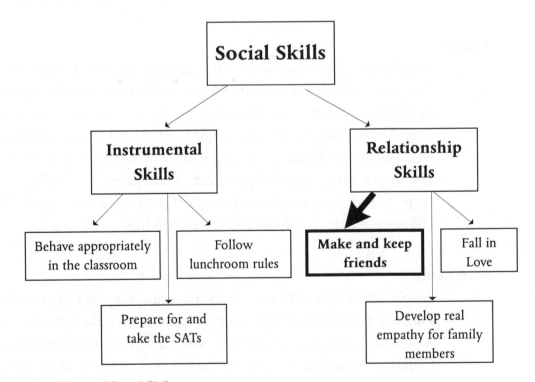

Two Types of Social Skills

Instrumental Skills are applicable to situations in which people typically behave in predictable, scripted ways. Relationship Skills are used when social contact is an end in itself. Relationship Skills have a very different purpose. They are used to create and deepen connections between people, share excitement and joy, and participate in joint creative efforts. Relationships, like friendships and children's play encounters occur in a rather unpredictable, non-scripted improvised manner. Flexibility and creative thinking are valued, along with remaining co-ordinated.

Relationships teach us about multiple perspectives. They provide the experience to show us that there is more than one right way of thinking, feeling, solving a problem and behaving. Through relationship encounters, we see the world through another's eyes and notice it is not identical to our own. Relationships teach us to think about the world in a "relative" and not absolute manner. In a relationship our actions cannot be interpreted as "right" or "wrong." Rather, they are meaningful or not depending on how they impact the individuals involved in the relationship. Rather than pushing a button or following a script as is possible in an Instrumental encounter, relationships require us to constantly evaluate and re-evaluate the state of our connection to one another and make ongoing adjustments.

We have found that the two types of skills require very different learning methods. This fundamental difference is the reason we developed Relationship Development Intervention. It is also why many of the exercises in these volumes may appear different from those you have encountered in other approaches to Social Skills.

When we teach Instrumental Skills we work with memorized scripts, employed in a specific manner to reach a desired endpoint. We teach people to recognize the proper context to perform a particular script, such as a lunchroom, or a supermarket. Instrumental Skills are best learned in natural environments, so that you will recognize the context and connect the script with the specific setting. They are best taught through direct instruction, social stories, behavioral shaping and modeling. The partners we choose for learning Instrumental Skills are typically more competent people. Often we will assign a more capable buddy to serve as a role model. The curriculum for Instrumental Skills involves learning a set of rules and expecting that everyone will follow them. The progression of learning entails accumulating a large repertoire of discrete scripts for as many settings as possible. Skills are selected based upon the age of the person and the daily settings he must encounter. The reason we teach instrumental skills is to help people learn the relatively unchanging social rules that govern non-emotional interactions. Whether they are happier, experience greater enjoyment, or feel closer to another person is not the point. The main objective is to help the person cope with day-to-day problems and situations that he may face in routine situations.

Relationships do not rely on pre-selected scripts. Actions we choose to take in a relationship encounter depend heavily upon what our partner is doing at that instant. Therefore the "right" response will change from moment to moment. We seek out relationships to add new ideas, to integrate ideas and to collaborate and co-create. Therefore, relationship encounters are filled with novelty and variation. Because they involve the ongoing introduction of novelty, relationship interactions require constant evaluation and regulation. We have to make sure that there is not so much variation that the interaction degenerates into confusion and chaos. But, on the other hand, if there is too little novelty and creation we lose the purpose of the encounter. The relationship becomes stilted and boring. Success requires learning to continually monitor and regulate a "Relationship Balance" of creation and predictability. It is like an ongoing juggling act, where we wish to add as many balls as possible and at the same time prevent any ball from dropping.

Because of their complexity and need for full attention, Relationship Skills must first be learned and mastered in simple environments. In RDI, as in typical development, the first relationship coaches should be adults, who act as both guides and participants. They function using a model that noted theorist Lev Vygotsky termed "Guided Participation." Initially the best teachers are adults who act as both guides and participants. Gradually, they can lead the child on a path of learning to a point where they can manage more complex environments. When the child is ready to work with a peer, reserach again clearly tells us that it is best to find someone who is at the same level of development. More competent children tend to delay the development of regulation and referencing skills that are necessary for relationship competence. They tend to inadvertently do the important evaluation and regulation "work" of the relationship for the more impaired child, leaving him or her in a highly dependent and incompetent position. Even the best juggler will add too many balls or become distracted for a moment and the same is true with relationships. No matter how skilled we are, relationships are always becoming disconnected and so participants must learn to monitor for breakdowns and quickly effect repairs. They will not do this if more competent partners are taking care of problems for them.

Relationship competence requires a careful, systematic layering of skills. They must be taught with increasing complexity carefully added. Each step we take in constructing relationship competence, serves as the scaffolding for the next step in a carefully crafted manner.

3

Relationship Development Intervention (RDI)

RDI is the first systematic intervention program designed specifically to help children born with obstacles that prevent them form attaining relationship competence in the natural environment. It is based on the premise that relationships are self-motivating, ends in themselves. When typical children engage in encounters with playful, caring adults and children, they obtain an immediate increase in positive excitement and joy, or a sudden decrease in anxiety or distress. Unfortunately, most of the children we work with do not initially obtain the same degree of satisfaction from their relationships. Throughout our program, you will notice that we work hard to provide children with samples of the potential payoffs in enjoyment and positive excitement they can obtain from social encounters. As quickly as possible we want the child to observe his social world, not because he is expecting a material reward, but because he is curious and excited about what he might see around him. We want him to be thinking, "Let me see what is going on. It might be fun."

RDI is an invitational model. You will not be coercing or bribing. Rather, you will invite the child to allow you to guide him to new and exciting meanings and involvement with the world. This means introducing new things to see, hear and touch, and new ways to act but in a very gradual and systematic manner. You will become the safe, trusted guide to an infinite universe, that can either be seen as terrifying or exciting.

Unlike their instrumental cousins, relationship skills are wonderfully portable and generalizable form one person and setting to another. Anyone who learns to be a real good friend will almost certainly know how to be a good son, brother, father, teammate, husband and co-worker. Relationship skills are almost all interchangeable. Friendship skills are the same attributes that make you a good family member, boy scout and teammate. All of these relationships develop together. You cannot learn to be a good friend and not also work at being good at all of these other relationships.

Relationship Coaching

You will become the child's trusted guide to the social world. We hope to teach you how to add small bits of novelty, mixed with predictable elements, in such a way that they are not disturbing but rather exciting, creating a very positive natural "addiction" for more social noverly and variation. Guided participation means that you will be acting in a type of partnership with the child. But, it is a partnership that initially you will tightly control. It makes no sense to allow a person who is severely impaired and learning disabled to be in the lead with you, the more expert guide following. That would be like allowing a severely dyslexic child to teach himself to read with you following his lead no matter what mistakes and misperceptions occur. You will take as many elements as possible from what the child provides and integrate them into your activities and phrases, but you will decide which elements to choose. Remember, that as you guide you must also pace.

Pacing means adjusting elements of your behavior to the child's unique needs. For example, matching the child's need for movement, action and language. It means determining how rapidly you walk, or move, so as to allow the child to remain at your side, given his motor limitations. It means incorporating his words, phrases and even some of his activities, as long as they do not interfere with your guidance. It means carefully determining how quickly you can add new activities, modify existing ones and chain them together. It means determining how many times you can repeat an activity before he grows bored. When you are successfully pacing, you create the experience of safety and predictability for the child that remains even when you add novelty to the interaction.

We have chosen the term "Coach" to describe your role. The term can apply whether you are a parent, teacher, therapist, or other involved person. The designation of "Coach" moves us away from a medical "pathology" model. Being a Coach requires learning to be a careful observer of both the child and yourself. You are going to become skilled at walking a tightrope of guiding and pacing, always trying to maintain the interaction at a peak state, where the child feels intense excitement and challenge, yet still experiences himself as a competent junior partner. Your objective is to try continually to enjoyably surprise the child but not to shock him. This is akin to going to an amusement part where you are pleasantly startled and continue to want to go on the next ride. You will inevitably make mistakes. Even our most trained clinicians err on the side of too much variation or predictability. The key is to rapidly learn from your mistakes and modify what you are doing.

Pay careful attention to the need to dramatically alter your role as the child progresses through the different stages and levels. At Level I, you function as the center of the child's attention: a highly directive but fun guide, who is exposing the "Novice" to the basic elements of a relationship for the first time. You may turn his head, not to force him to make eye contact, but to show him where an exciting face is so that he can enjoy it. But you will not continue to turn his head to "make him" look. That is coercive and he will develop an aversion to looking. Instead, you may make a loud noise that startles him in to looking. But you will not continue to startle just for the sake of upsetting him. Over time your role will shift. By the close of Level II you will have become an activity partner, and finally in Level III you will be moving into the role of Facilitator. By the time the child reaches the close for Level III, you will have the pleasant experience of being able to fade into the background during a peer interaction, knowing that the children are now able to sustain the encounter through their own efforts and are no longer heavily relying on you. Changes to your role are gradual and subtle, but critical.

The Relationship Curriculum

As readers of our first book know, the complete RDI "curriculum" is composed of six levels and 24 stages. Each level in turn has four stages. Each of the six levels represents a dramatic developmental shift in the central focus of relationships. As we move up levels, the number and complexity of skills necessary for success increases exponentially. In this book the following chapters begin with brief summaries of Stages and Levels I – III. For those of you not familiar with the RDI system we present a brief outline of the entire six levels below:

Level I: Novice

Level I is structured around teaching the pre-requisites for becoming a good Apprentice in the world of learning about relationships and feelings. At this initial level, students are referred to as "Novices" and are not expected to do much of the work of regulating relationship encounters. As such, it sets the stage for all future guidance. At this level children learn to make adults the center of their attention. They develop the skills of Social Referencing, literally using other people as their primary reference points.

Level II: Apprentice

Our second level introduces to the student, who has now earned the rank of "Apprentice," to the responsibilities of shared regulation and communication repair. We also emphasize learning to enjoy variation and rapid transition. At the end of Level II we begin working with partnered peers, whom we refer to as "Dyads."

Level III: Challenger

This middle level introduces children, who are now referred to as "Challengers," to the enjoyment of improvisation and co-creation. In this level children experience what it means to have a "We-go," a group Ego that allows us to accomplish things we could never imagine achieving on our own. In Level III, children begin for the first time to practice their relationship skills in small groups. This book ends with Level III activities.

The stages below are aimed at older children and adolescents. Exercises related to these stages can be found in our companion volume, *Relationship Development Intervention with Children, Adolescents and Adults*.

Level IV: Voyager

This pivotal level celebrates the movement of relationship focus to the world of perceptions and subjective experience. Here, the relationship student, now known as a "Voyager," is introduced to different perspectives and the use of imagination to enhance his joint voyage through the world. In Level IV, Voyagers come to grips with a world that is not defined by absolutes. It is a world where your point of view is just as important as what you see.

Level V: Explorer

In Level V the "topic" of relationships again transforms, this time to the inner world of ideas, interests, beliefs and emotional reactions. Conversation takes on a whole new richness and depth as partners seek to share each other's inner worlds. The child, now known as an "Explorer," is now capable of exploring his and other's pasts and futures and is able to put himself in another's shoes; an important step in developing empathy.

Level VI: Partner

Our final Level focuses on the partnerships we develop for lifelong relationships. Partners re-examine their relationships with their family and groups in a new more sophisticated light. They develop a coherent sense of personal identity and they seek out more mature friendships based on trust and personal disclosure.

An Overview of Activities

Just skimming through the activities in these volumes, it may appear that we have covered the "terrain" and left no relationship stone unturned. Nothing could be farther from the truth. While the breadth of the program appears huge compared with a typical text on social skills or emotional development, there is much more work to be done. Many of the exercises we present are models or representative of many others that should be added for a truly comprehensive curriculum. A number of additional activities are suggested or described in the Variations section of each activity. We also encourage you to develop your own variations and share them with others on our website.

The exercises are laid out in what we hope is a user-friendly manner. Each one begins by describing "Highlights" which are a quick way of identifying the main themes or objectives of the exercise. This is followed by a brief summary which provides a more in-depth overview and rationale as well as tying the activity to those exercises that come before and after it. The next sections are the "nuts and bolts" of the activity. "Participants" describes the optimal number of persons who should be involved. Typically Stage 7 is an ideal time to expand the social unit and include a matched peer partner. However, most of the earlier activities can easily be done in a classroom or a small group setting, as long as the Coach recognizes that he or she is not attempting to get the children to interact with one another, but rather that the Coach is still the primary practice partner for each child. "Getting Ready," describes the materials and preparation needed. "Coaching Instructions" are just that: step-by-step directions for implementing the activity. Following this, the "Variations" section describes or suggests activities that we feel would be excellent extensions and/or complements of the "main attraction." The final section, "Obstacles/Opportunities," describes critical points to look out for in both positive and potentially negative domains.

Exercises are designed for repeated practice. Many require a good number of hours to complete. Several of the exercises are actually strong recommendations for changing the way that you and others communicate. Others are activities that can be confined to specific practice periods. Some activities will take months to reach a level of proficiency and others weeks. How long an activity should take will depend upon the child you are working with and the time you have allotted to practice. We urge you not to rush! We recognize that this requires a high level of commitment but we have found that when we move too rapidly, the child can never experience a sense of true partnership and competence.

You are free to use whichever activities you wish. We have no objections to your skipping any exercises you find unappealing or that work on objectives you believe have already been mastered. We do caution you against working on exercises that may be significantly above the person's developmental level. This can lead to a frustrating experience for both Coach and child.

Activities are presented in order of their level and stage. For those who choose not to follow the RDI model, the Topic Index of Activities provides a handy Activity reference. All activities are listed along with their objectives, and primary and secondary "Topic" areas. Topics include the following areas: Collaboration, Communication, Conversation, Emotional Functioning, Flexibility, Executive Functioning, Family, Group, Problem Solving and Self Development.

For those in schools and other professional settings where objectives must be clearly specified prior to authorization of intervention, the Progress Tracking Form provides an index of activities that correspond to each objective. You can pick your target objectives and immediately reference the exercises that correspond to each.

Friendships require many skills not usually thought of as "social." Our curriculum encompasses a number of non-social objectives, including flexible thinking, rapid attention shifting, behavioral self-regulation, reflection, planning, forethought, preparation, emotion regulation, improvisation, creativity, mistake management and problem solving. Along with these areas friendships also require more familiar Social Skills. Among these are reciprocal conversation, collaboration, and teamwork.

Tips for Relationship Coaches

Before we move on to the actual activities we want to briefly outline some of the basic principles of being a RDI Coach. We hope you will return to this section frequently and use it as a reference point for your work.

Focus on competence

We cannot overly emphasize how important it is for children to learn that they can be active participants in the relationship process. To maintain the effort that relationship skills require, children must experience a sense of competence along with enjoyment. When they know they can be equal partners it dramatically increases their motivation to work. This is a good reason to begin at a simple stage. This is also a reason to match peers carefully when the time is right, rather than placing a person with relationship deficit with someone who is much more competent.

Spotlight

As you work through the activities, you will learn to make sure that you keep the child's focus trained on emotional information. We call this "spotlighting." Emotions are communicated primarily through the visual medium. You will learn to limit your language and emphasize facial expressions. You will "amplify" emotional communication through exaggerated facial expressions and gestures and a slow, deliberate and emphatic manner of speaking.

Keep it simple

Relationship skills have to be developed in a careful, systematic progression, with one set of skills serving as the scaffolding needed in order to master the next level of complexity. In the beginning you will keep the environment simple. You will also keep your objectives simple, making sure you work on one thing at a time. You will also simplify activities and begin with activities where objects do not compete for the child's attention.

Create a space for RDI

When we talk about "space," we are referring to both the physical and mental dimensions. You cannot limit relationship skills to a specific time in the day. There should be a "lab" time when you get to practice and modify activities. However, if you cannot generalize the skills into the rest of the day, they will just fade away. On the other hand, make sure that your efforts do not become all work and no play. Watch out for burnout. This is a marathon not a sprint. Doing these activities must be genuinely fun for everyone. If it seems like work, this is a sign you may be doing something wrong. If this happens, take a break, re-think how you are approaching the exercises and return to them with new excitement and a commitment that they will be fun for everyone involved.

Balance enjoyment with responsibility

Try to keep things fun and lively, but do not allow the child to introduce too much variation and novelty before he can function as a partner in regulating the interaction. We always teach children to function as regulating partners first, before allowing them to improvise and participate with us in adding new elements to activities. One of our constantly repeated "mantras" is "No co-variation without co-regulation."

Make sure skills are meaningful

As you move through the exercises, you will notice that we take great pains to ensure that there is a value and meaning for any skill being taught. Of course you can teach skills without their functions – their intrinsic payoffs – but do not be surprised if they are not used. Years ago, we taught social skills without much consideration for developmental readiness and meaning. Our patients learned complex skills such as joint attention, but never used them outside of the treatment room.

Work towards self-efficacy

Interacting with typical children is not a good way to first learn relationship skills. They take over too much, or they create too much complexity. There is nothing harmful about the child spending time in the day with typical peers, as long as they are well-meaning. But the child will never learn to be a desired relationship partner from such encounters. Children in the Autism Spectrum learn best with peers who have the same tempo and need for slow pacing and carefulness along with functioning at a similar stage of relationship development. Evenly matched peers create a requirement that each child acts as a partner to regulate their activity. Children who have a history of having succeeded together, helped each other and shared common rituals develop very close bonds. They become emotionally close, true friends, way before we would typically expect. In a similar vein, we ask that you not prematurely worry about larger groups and close friendships. Do not put the cart before the horse.

Find the edge of development and stay there

None of us has the motivation to persist in an endeavour that results in our feeling incompetent. We do not want to put people in situations like that. We should not raise false expectations that placing a child in a complex social situation will provide many payoffs. The boundary area where the child can understand and independently carry out their part of an activity under the tutelage of a Coach is the place where the most excitement lies, but only if you provide the scaffolding. The correct stage to work on is one that is not too low to be boring or too high to be overwhelming. Unfortunately, many people in the Autism Spectrum "burn out" and avoid the social world, because they have been forced to do too much for too little payoff.

As you journey through the following pages, we want you to remember the most important principle of RDI, which we refer to as "Joyful Collaboration." When developing relationships it is critical that everyone experiences a great deal of joy. Furthermore, the source of joy must be seen as the product of a unique collaboration. The child must perceive that joy emanates not from a game or toy, but from sharing a special experience with a social partner. If you keep the concept of Joyful Collaboration in mind, the following activities will reward you as they come to life for you and your child.

LEVEL 1: NOVICE

LEVEL 1: NOVICE

Introduction

Summary

The goal of Level I is to develop a core relationship between you and the child. The child begins the program by learning to be a Novice, which literally means one who recognizes he is in need of guidance by a Master. In Stage 1, the face and gestures of the Coach become the center of the child's attention. The Novice learns in Stage 2 to use this non-verbal information as a critical reference point for guiding his own behavior. Stage 3 provides children with a primer on following the guiding actions of the Coach. Stage 4 introduces the child to a world of coordinated actions, which he will inhabit for the remainder of his life. Coordinating your actions requires a new form of information processing. The crucial data is derived from comparing your actions with your partner's to determine the best way to create and maintain a connection.

Level I skills are like the foundation of a house. They are essential to support the entire structure. There is often a tendency to rush through, or bypass, these critical skills, especially when working with older or more verbal children. But time and time again, insufficient practice at Level I has resulted in later dead-ends in development.

We are often asked if there are any precursors to beginning RDI. While our activities in Stage 1 are geared towards a very basic level, they cannot be successful with a Novice who is unwilling to comply with instructions, or one who is highly defiant. These Novices are candidates for initial behavioral approaches that emphasize compliance and acceptance of direction and instruction, hopefully using positive reinforcement approaches. While not essential, it is also helpful if the Novice has some experience with Structured Teaching approaches which involve following a simple activity schedule. However, we typically can work on this simultaneously with our efforts in Stages 1 and 2.

Participants

The Coach and Novice are the sole participants in Level I. The child is not yet ready to manage a relationship with peers, nor can he handle interaction with more than one person. In fact the Coach is doing almost all of the work needed to maintain the relationship. Initially it is important to have a single, main Coach who becomes the center of the Novice's attention. But as we move to the end of Stage 1, we are already interested in expanding the list of persons who qualify as a Coach so that the child learns to accept the guidance of several adults.

Settings

The first few activities of Stage 1 are designed to teach you to change your style of communication with the child. Later activities are designed as specific exercises to be conducted within controlled settings. In Level I we expect children still to be highly distractible. We do not want constantly to compete for attention with objects and noise. Therefore, we seek to limit potential visual and auditory distractions. The degree to which we set up a minimal stimulation environment is wholly dependent upon the distractibility of the Novice. With some children we have to begin in an almost completely bare room. Others may require a careful consideration of objects that serve as attention competitors.

Language

Language in Level I is used to enhance facial referencing and not distract from or compete with it. Vocalization is used for enhancement of excitement, directing attention to our faces and celebrating our simple successes. Ritualized song segments, often repeated "chants" and phrases and silly words are used for their relationship binding and enhancement elements. We often take phrases that the Novice enjoys and repeat them, with slight changes in emphasis or rhythm. We find that this significantly increases his or her fun. We may pick up on stereotypical language, modify it and add it contextually to the activity we are setting up. For example one of our young children was repetitively saying "Blue bubbles" during a marbles activity. We turned this into "Bubbles please, bubbles please" and then "Big blue bubbles please." The following is a short list of how language is used in Level I:

- Repeat the phrase in a silly voice and then change the voice

- Repeat a common phrase, but first very slowly and then very rapidly

- Vocal noises provide rhythmic accompaniment for play with motion (humming or chanting while hopping or banging on some object)

- Purposefully fail to complete an often-repeated phrase or sentence and observe as the Novice completes it

- Pause at a crucial word in a frequently used phrase and allow the Novice to fill it in

- Add or substitute just one word to increase the silliness of a phrase but still leave the phrase recognizable

- Language used for celebration:
    - We did it!
    - That was great
    - Good work!
    - Yeah!
    - Give me five!
    - Wow!
    - Cool!
    - That's funny!
    - That's silly!

Coaching Points

- Remain firmly in charge of the structure of all activities. Novices are allowed to introduce only small amounts of variation.

- We are usually combining a number of Stage 1 and 2 activities in a ritualized but fast pace in the initial stages of intervention.

- Stage 1 may take a great deal of energy. If you are a parent trying to do the work yourself, consider finding students and other helpers to relieve you.

- Carefully observe and make a list of which language, objects and other elements enhance, which distract and which are neutral as agents of focusing the Novice's attention onto you.

- It is critical for activities to be exciting and produce happiness. They should never be done when you or the Novice is tired or in a bad mood.

- Prepare to be very exaggerated and dramatic with your face, gestures and voice tone. You must be continually varying your voice tone, pitch, volume and phrasing in exciting, enjoyable ways.

- Take a short break about every ten minutes to evaluate whether the child will spontaneously invite you to play and visually reference your face.

- Watch out for a tendency for the Novice to try and control the interaction.

- It is important to distinguish between interactions where the Novice experiences pleasure from being entertained by you (Instrumental) from those encounters where the enjoyment is derived from sharing a common experience (Relationship).

- Don't project how you are feeling onto the Novice. Because you think you are sharing the same experience it doesn't mean he is. If the Novice tries to do the activity by himself without you, it means that he has not learned that you are a crucial part of his enjoyment.

- Referencing should increase dramatically after the first 30 hours of practice.

- There is no need to teach eye contact as a discrete skill. When we work in RDI, children learn to gaze at our faces not because we provide some external reward, but because they are curious about our expressions and eager to share our emotions. In fact teaching eye contact in a rote manner will confuse the child and detract from progress in RDI.

STAGE 1: ATTEND

Goals and objectives

The activities in Stage 1 are designed to create sufficient motivation for the Novice to orient toward Coaches as the center of attention. The main objective of this stage is to eliminate, or drastically reduce, the need to cue, or prompt a child in order to get his attention. When a child is focusing on your face and actions, it is much simpler to invite him to participate in increasingly more exciting and enjoyable activities.

Activity Summary

The stage begins with activities that provide guidelines for conducting communication with a child in the Autism Spectrum. The initial five exercises train you to simplify and amplify the communication environment. You will learn to use fewer words and to use your words more meaningfully and powerfully. You will work on reducing the amount of energy spent prompting the child to respond. You will "spice up" your communication with unexpected actions and sounds. Finally, you will learn to Spotlight and amplify your expressions, in order to magnify the importance of non-verbal facial communication for the child.

Following these initial activities, we turn to exercises that emphasize excitement and fun. Curiosity and a desire to share enjoyment will hopefully replace prompting and external reinforcement as the major reason why the child pays attention to you. Due to this new motivation we typically observe significant increases in facial expression and emotional communication. We expect increased shared smiles and laughter, appreciative communications and requests to initiate and continue enjoyable activities.

Due to the fast pace of activities and the degree of uncertainty, we introduce children to the importance of keeping their eyes on their guides, who become critical "reference points." The children learn that activities are exciting and can provide a sense of mastery, but only as long as they continue to monitor the important emotional information you provide. This prepares children for the next stage, where we concentrate on Social Referencing.

Critical Tips

- Limit verbal communication and spotlight your facial communication.

- Communicate verbally only when the Novice is watching your face.

- Use "indirect" cues when the Novice is not paying attention to your communication.

- Emphasize the excitement and fun of interacting over demands for interaction.

- Observe carefully to determine proper activity length and pacing.

- Observe carefully to determine objects that interfere with social attention.

- Remain clearly in control of activities.

- Introduce sufficient unpredictability in your actions that the Novice is motivated to continue monitoring your actions and whereabouts.

- Take frequent breaks to rest and provide an opportunity for the Novice to communicate with you.

My Words are Important

ACTIVITY HIGHLIGHTS
° Developing attentiveness to communication
° Teaching the child to value your words
° How to speak so you are listened to

Summary:

How often do you become frustrated because you have to repeat yourself over and over again? Many children in the Autism Spectrum do not listen well. They are easily distracted and require the speaker to repeat himself and do all the work of making sure that the communication is received. In this exercise, we emphasize, in a subtle way, that both the speaker and listener have responsibilities during communication. If the child regularly shifts his focus and attends to your speech, you can skip this exercise.

Children learn to use indirect cues to increase their attention to the speaker. It is important for children not to rely on prompts ("Pay Attention! Look at me! Are you listening!"), to know when to pay attention. Such Direct prompts result in the child becoming more "prompt dependent;" always waiting for someone to cue him that he must listen, before shifting attention to the communicator. The Indirect prompts we use in this activity do not create the same type of dependency. The child perceives himself as voluntarily choosing to take an orienting action, rather than being requested or told to do so. The perception of voluntary action leads the child to be less prompt dependent and more likely to pay attention in the future without any cues or prompts. The emphasis on developing voluntary action is a theme that you will find in all of our exercises.

You will notice that the first several activities in this initial stage do not fall under the heading of "exercises." Rather they are changes in your communication style that we would like you to implement. Think of these activities as new communication habits we would like you to develop.

Participants:

This exercise requires participation from all of the significant persons in the child's environment.

Getting Ready:

Remember that this is not an activity to reserve for a specific time or place. It is an ongoing method of communication you should employ, until the child pays attention to your communication without prompts.

Coaching Instructions:

There is no formal explanation provided to the child. You will be observing the child's level of attention when you are speaking and gauging your actions based upon whether he is listening carefully and visually watching you. There are three basic steps in this exercise:

☐ STEP 1   DELIBERATE SPEECH

The first step requires everyone communicating with the child to slow their rate of speech and speak with more deliberate pauses between words and sentences. This will take extensive practice and feedback. Do not underestimate the importance of changing your language style, even for very verbal Novices. By speaking slower and with clearer enunciation, you increase the value of each of the words you do speak and also make it simpler for the child to process the information.

☐ STEP 2   BALANCING

The next step is to keep your communication in "balance" with the child. "Balancing" your communication has two elements. First, try not to use more words in any utterance than the child uses. This means that if the child normally speaks in two or three word phrases, keep your own phrases at this length. If the child is completely non-verbal, use very short phrases. The second part of "balance" entails not adding further words until the child provides a meaningful response to a first set of words that you have spoken. We ask you not to continually repeat yourself and not to add more information if your initial information has been ignored. If we are aiming to make our words valuable to the listener, it is important that we do not continue to provide more words, if our initial words are not attended to. If you do, it will "de-value" your words.

☐ STEP 3   SPOTLIGHTING

The third step is to insert "spotlighting" elements into your speech. Such an element is an indirect but powerful signal to the child that some important information is present that requires his attention. Spotlighting helps the child to perceive the words that stand out and are most critical. Spotlighting is much more effective than "cueing" in creating generalization and the perception by the child that he has "chosen" to shift his attention. You will need to experiment with what alterations in your speech pattern produce the most effective "spotlights" and have the most impact on the attention of the child. We may insert a deep breath, a sigh, or a "stutter" when come to a critical point in a sentence. We may get "stuck" on one word, repeating it, as if stuttering for about five seconds or so. Stuttering at critical moments usually results in a gaze shift and rapidly increased focus. If a stutter on its own does not work, we often will make a significant shift in voice volume to accompany the stutter.

Variations:

Other options for providing indirect cues include, changing voice tone, slowing down your rate of speech, pausing, coughing and clearing your throat.

Obstacles/ Opportunities:

A small group of children with autism appear oblivious to these methods. They may monitor their communication environment so poorly that they do not even notice your highly emphasized, indirect prompts. These children require an initial behavior modification approach where they initially learn to respond to direct prompts. In these cases this exercise should be applied as a second step.

LEVEL I, STAGE I, ACTIVITY 2

I Lost my Voice

ACTIVITY HIGHLIGHTS

° Develop attentiveness to facial expressions
° Increase the importance of non-verbal communication

Summary:

This activity is similar to "My Words are Important" in that it emphasizes that other people's communication should be the center of the child's attention. The difference is that now we emphasize paying attention to faces, rather than words. Many highly verbal children attend to much of the language directed at them, but are oblivious to the non-verbal communication that accompanies our words. They continue communicating while looking away, walking away and even out of sight of others. They devalue non-verbal communication and unwittingly train us to do likewise when we are with them. Unfortunately, research tells us that over seventy per cent of a speaker's intent is communicated through non-verbal channels. This exercise is a critical training experience for anyone wishing to be a Coach.

Participants:

Once again, we will need the cooperation of all the important persons in the child's environment.

Getting Ready:

This activity requires that the Novice seek out your non-verbal communication for fun, excitement and needed information. If the Novice can simply seek out another person in the immediate vicinity to talk to, your efforts will be futile.

Make sure to explain that the intent of this activity is not to give the child "the silent treatment" or to create a negative experience. We are not recommending that anyone ignore the child, or not pay attention to his speech. Rather, we are requesting that everyone de-emphasize their own verbal responses and rely on rich and clearly exaggerated non-verbal responses.

Decide upon a period of time in which you will act as if you have lost your voice. Make sure that nobody else "fills in" for you at that time. Make sure that your speaking loss occurs at times when communication is important to the Novice. This includes making sure you have some periods of time with the Novice in areas where you have removed any competing objects that would distract the Novice, such as computers or video games. The exercise will not accomplish much if the Novice does not even realize that something is different. If you believe that the Novice will understand, explain that you are losing your voice as an exercise. You have been instructed to only use your face and your body to communicate. You can invite the Novice to play along with you and pretend that he/she has lost their voice as well.

Coaching Instructions:

When you are ready, stop responding verbally to the child. Maintain an animated, inviting expression during this period of time. Stay very involved with the child. Be highly responsive to his communication attempts. Use lots of pointing, gesturing and amplified facial expressions. Stay very emotionally animated. Invite the Novice to interact in exciting ways when possible. But don't spend time watching TV, or playing games that do not require any speech. And do not allow anyone to become a "substitute" communicator for you.

Variations:

This is an excellent activity for home and small classroom settings. We also employ several similar important variations. One is called "I Lost my Hearing!" In this exercise you can speak, but pretend not to be able to hear the child, who must then find non-verbal ways to communicate. You can tell the child who understands, that you can lip-read and so they have to find your face in order for you to "see" their words.

Obstacles/Opportunities:

Like the previous exercise, this activity will not be effective with a child who does not have a strong need to communicate with you. If this is the case, you should first employ a behavior modification "shaping" approach to develop the desire to communicate. We do not believe this activity should be continued if it causes undue upset. However, many children initially protest these communication activities and such attempts should not deter you from persisting.

Unexpected Sounds and Actions

ACTIVITY HIGHLIGHTS

° Maintain attention to speakers

° Staying focused on partners during interaction

Summary:

Trying to talk with someone who "drifts away" after you begin speaking, is just as irritating as having to prompt them to pay attention in the first place. We include this activity to address problems of children who might initially orient to people they interact with, but then quickly become distracted and do not maintain their attention. The simple premise of this exercise is that many children do not stay focused on the speaker because they lose interest, or are distracted by something in their environment with more novelty. The child may randomly focus on some object, return to some prior activity, or simply "tune out" the speaker.

Participants:

This exercise is not as dependent upon the cooperation of everyone in the child's environment. However, the more people who engage in it the better!

Getting Ready:

This is another activity that cannot be done effectively in a specific time period. You have to be ready to take unexpected actions whenever you observe the child displaying difficulty in maintaining attention while you are communicating with him. We once again feel the need to provide an important caution: If you want children to pay better attention to your words, you must learn to use fewer words and to talk with much more emphasis and deliberation with the words you use. If you do not make your words valuable, do not expect them to be valued. Remember, the way we increase the worth of any commodity is to make it more precious to the consumer!

Coaching Instructions:

First, decide on which unexpected actions you are going to use. We have provided a sample list at the end of the exercise description. You will need to be a good observer during this exercise. Watch for signs that the child is not paying close attention to you. As soon as you see attention flagging, stop what you were saying and take one of your unexpected actions. Then observe the result. It is important to keep a positive, enthusiastic attitude and expression during this activity. Actions should be dramatic. They can be "startling" without being frightening or threatening to the child. We provide a short list of possible actions at the end of the exercise. Feel free to add your own.

Variations:

"Unexpected Actions" is a great way to add some "spice" to activities that have started to become "stale" but still contain skills that we would like the child to practice. Some children fail to maintain their gaze on those speaking to them, but assume that when it is their turn to talk, all eyes will be upon them. For these children a truly unexpected action is to suddenly turn away in the middle of their attempts to communicate. Of course you should only do this if you believe the child will notice and attempt to get you to shift your gaze back to them.

Obstacles/Opportunities:

Once again, we want to be careful to distinguish between actions that might surprise or even startle a child and those that are truly upsetting.

Unexpected Actions:

- ° Looming in close while talking and/or walking
- ° Placing a meaningless word in the midst of a sentence
- ° Grabbing your head with your hands dramatically, while opening your mouth silently, in an expression of great surprise
- ° Moving from whisper to shout and back to whisper in the course of a sentence
- ° Taking off your shoe and placing it on your head (or a similar type of action)
- ° Taking out a handkerchief and placing it over your face or as a barrier between you and the Novice while you are talking
- ° Suddenly falling down in the midst of a sentence.

LEVEL I, STAGE I, ACTIVITY 4

Chant

ACTIVITY HIGHLIGHTS
° Enhancing language development
° Use language as a creative medium
° Use language to enhance excitement and joy
° Language is used to help "bind" actions together

Summary:

Language is a critical tool, if used correctly, to enhance a child's sense of excitement and interest in participating in his social world. It is also a means to "bind" our activities and actions together in a meaningful way, so that the child will perceive the coherence and organization of activities. In typical development, language is used playfully and creatively from its onset. In this exercise we work on developing language as an organizational binding element, an excitement-enhancing element and a playful element in its own right.

Participants:

Coach and child.

Getting Ready:

Begin by learning a few of the child's characteristic phrases, if you do not know them already. In addition, you must learn how to speak in very limited and careful ways, even if the Novice is extremely fluent. We are going to be using a very ritualized form of language more akin to "chanting" than to conversational speech.

Coaching Instructions:

Begin this exercise by developing simple repetitive phrases that you chant while you are doing routine actions together with the child and alone in the child's presence (yes, we want you to chant out loud to yourself!). Keep the phrases simple no matter what the language capability of the child. If you are walking to the kitchen try chanting, "Walking, walking walking to the kitccchen," with the last word being drawn out and the each repetition of "walking" chanted in greater volume. Direct your eyes to the child. Nod and smile broadly, inviting the child to join in. Walk in cadence with your chant, using it as a type of military march. After repeating the phrase verbatim a number of times, alter different elements one at a time in an enthusiastic manner. For example, as you are walking to the kitchen enthusiastically chant, "We are going, going, going to the Kitccccchen." Change the emphasis on different words, the speed of movement as you go and any other elements. As the child gets accustomed and enjoys these chants add even more playful elements to them. For example, as you drive in your car try chanting, "We are riding our horsssses." Do not be surprised if the child quickly joins in as a partner to your chants.

We would like you to continually use chants in this manner for the remainder of activities in Level I. For example, when doing the "Building a Mountain" activity, as we are carrying our beanbags over to the "Mountain" we are chanting, "We are building a mounnntain, a mountain, a mounnntain. We are building, building, building a mounnnntain!"

A second step is joining into the child's phrases and gradually modifying them. This entails learning and repeating phrases the child is already using, often in a rote fashion. When you repeat the phrase, you should do so with a slightly different, but highly exaggerated, intonation and emphasis than the child. Once the child acknowledges that you have joined in (typically by visually referencing and smiling at you), you know you have a phrase that you can play with. Try and add a single word to the phrase. For example, if a child is looking at a cup of marbles and saying "300 bubbles" you can add "300 giant bubbles." As you "take over" the phrase, do not wait for the child to initiate it. Begin to function as the initiator of the phrase and non-verbally invite the child to join in with you. As you do this, pause at different points in the midst of the chant and have the child anticipate and finish the phrase. Continue to add variations of words, emphasis, speed and even melody. Use extremely silly and playful pretend voices that continue to change without warning.

Variations:

For children that ask irrelevant repetitive questions try to preempt them with a chant of "Ask me another question," repeated several times. When the child asks a question repeatedly, respond by repeating the question in a chant-like fashion and stating, "What a great question! What a wonderful question! Ask me another one please!" Once again you inviting the child to join you in being playful, rather than focusing on the information element of his speech.

Obstacles/Opportunities:

You will be startled to find that when you incorporate some of the child's familiar repetitive phrases into your chants, they become much easier to modify and vary in an enjoyable manner, without any protest whatsoever from the child. Similar to prior activities, we are recommending that you practice this exercise frequently throughout the day. But it is especially important to do it in conjunction with the activities that we are presenting throughout Level I.

Unexpected Labels

ACTIVITY HIGHLIGHTS

° Using novelty for shared humor
° Pretending skills
° Flexible thinking

Summary:

This exercise is a great way to introduce humor to the child, outside of a highly verbal and scripted context. It is also important in its emphasis on flexible thinking. There is no great sophistication to the humor of this exercise. Be prepared to act downright ridiculous! But despite its simplicity, "Unexpected Labels" can be a great deal of fun for children of all ages. Remember, you can do this in small amounts all day long. Don't try to restrict this activity to limited periods, or it will ruin the surprise element.

Participants:

You can perform this on a one-on-one basis or in a small group or class setting, if behavioral limits can be maintained.

Getting Ready:

You can begin this exercise using a box full of small, everyday objects. You and the child can sit, facing each other, several feet apart, with a box in front of you. If you are working with a small group, seat all participants in a circle with the box in the center but ensuring that it is closest to you.

Coaching Instructions:

This activity has two steps:

☐ STEP 1

Pull any object, like a shoe, from the box and pretend it is something else, "I've got a new hat." Put the shoe on your head and say, "Doesn't it look elegant?" For more emphasis use an exaggerated facial expression and voice tone. Remember to meet the gaze of the child and laugh together. Repeat this several times until you believe the child is ready for a turn. Try and do an equal number of non-verbal "slapstick" activities using mime.

☐ STEP 2

After several trials of the initial exercise, respond in a new way to the child's substitution. When the child removes an object and says it is another, reply as if it were yet a third object. For example, if the child removes a safety pin from the box and says, "Look I've got a sock." You should say, "Right, you've got some ketchup."

Variations:

Make sure you continue to add things to the box, so there are always new surprises. We want you to gradually move away from reliance on a "prop box" for this activity. You can and should find your props anywhere, all day long. After a while you can pick up almost anything, smile and say, "What do you think this is?" If the child guesses something silly you can say, "That's right!" If he provides a conventional response you can say, "No, it's a _____", making sure to smile and exaggerate your voice so that the Novice knows you are pretending.

Obstacles/Opportunities:

People worry that when we first teach language to a non-verbal child, he may become confused if we begin to change labels. We have never seen this happen. In fact we note that this playful approach to language significantly increases children's willingness to experiment with new words and phrases without the typical "demand" pressure that adults place on language-delayed children. However, if this is a concern, you can stick with non-verbal varieties of the exercise. You can put the shoe on your head and mime that it is a hat without a single word. We find that practicing these types of silly labels actually aids in language acquisition. You will be able to tell immediately whether the child appreciates your humor, rejects it or is confused. Initially, if participants are impulsive and cannot wait their turn to grab things from the box, keep the box behind you and give it to the child only when it is his turn.

LEVEL I, STAGE I, ACTIVITY 6

Two Coach Approach

ACTIVITY HIGHLIGHTS
- Rapid gaze shifting
- Enjoying the novel actions of social partners
- Anticipating exciting actions

Summary:

"Two Coach Approach" or its "One Coach" variation, should be one of several activities included in an initial "schedule" of fun, exciting exercises conducted daily with a Stage 1 child. It should be conducted in a setting that does not present significant distractions. This is an environment where distractions are minimized so that you are the most interesting things in the child's environment, rather than competing with the child's favorite objects or games. The one difficulty of this activity is that, as the name implies, it requires the participation of two Coaches.

Participants:

It is best to have two Coaches (there is a "One Coach" variation if needed).

Getting Ready:

Make sure you have chosen the proper setting where there are few if any objects or distracting stimuli. We want people to be the center of attention.

Coaching Instructions:

First, Coaches need to agree on their joint strategy – what each will do when it is his or her turn to be in the "spotlight." Next they determine, if possible with the child, which type of action he would like them to take when they finally reach the child's side and are signaled to "go." Then they provide a simple "go" signal for the child to use, when they get close. We prefer for the signal to be either a head nod, meaning "go ahead," or a headshake, meaning "do not proceed." Make sure the child knows how and when to use the signal – when you have both moved very close and are poised to take an action.

As the game begins, Coaches each stand about four feet away and to either side of the child. Each coach takes his or her turn taking one "giant" step towards the child. The coach who takes the step should "grab the spotlight" by taking some dramatic and silly action, likely to result in the child's shifting his gaze and hopefully engaging with you in a bit of laughter. Immediately after the child engages with one Coach, the other Coach initiates an action to shift attention over to him or her. When you both finally reach the child, which should occur at the same moment, loom over him and give him exaggerated head nods, waiting for the "go" signal from the child. When the child gives a head nod, begin some type of safe, enjoyable rough-and-tumble play like tickling, or tossing the child onto a pile of beanbag chairs. If the child gives a headshake, then you should retreat to the starting position and begin approaching again.

Variations:

If you only have access to one Coach, you can still do this activity. Play a variation of the "freeze" game that we will discuss in the next stage. Approach the child slowly. Periodically make a dramatic noise and action. When the child shifts gaze to you "freeze" in place until he shifts his gaze away, then approach again doing the same thing until you are directly next to him. Some children really enjoy, as the climax of the activity, being picked up by two Coaches, who count to three and gently swing him onto a large pile of beanbag chairs.

Obstacles/Opportunities:

You will notice that in this activity we try to provide an active communicative role for the child. As quickly as possible, we want to provide children with a sense of healthy control in their social interactions. We believe that the feeling of "social self efficacy" is critical to both enjoy and "own" social interactions. Some children may fail to communicate at all. If they do, let them know that failure to communicate will be taken as a "go" sign, with the Coaches then deciding which type of action they will take on their own.

LEVEL I, STAGE I, ACTIVITY 7

The Tunnel

ACTIVITY HIGHLIGHTS
° Increased visual referencing
° Increased emotional attunement

Summary:

We stumbled upon the idea of using cloth tunnels years ago. We saw a six foot long collapsible tunnel in a store and intuitively felt it would have some use. We have found that the tunnel is an indispensable object for our young children who are not attending to parents and emotionally referencing, even for security. This exercise rapidly increases the young child's visual referencing, as well as his level of emotional attachment and attunement to the adults in his environment.

Participants:

Two Coaches and a child are typically required. One of the Coaches should be someone with whom the Novice is emotionally attached.

Getting Ready:

You will need a five or six foot long collapsible fabric tunnel.

Coaching Instructions:

This activity has four steps:

☐ STEP 1

Position one Coach at the exit of the tunnel. The other Coach should take the child's hand and gently move him to the entrance of the tunnel. If he resists going in, give him a beginning nudge, but do not force him in against his will.

☐ STEP 2

Once the child enters the tunnel, the "Entrance Coach," should move away from the child's sight. But, make sure that the child knows he cannot crawl back out the entrance. You may have to elevate the entrance a bit to clearly communicate to the child that he has reached a "point of no return" and must go forward. Have the "Exit Coach," appear and disappear at the exit, so that the child notices her appearing and disappearing as he crawls through the tunnel.

☐ STEP 3

For added excitement the "Entrance Coach" can move to the outside of the tunnel and gently rock it back and forth to give it some of the qualities of an amusement park ride. Stop doing this if you notice that it makes the child prefer to stay in the tunnel for long periods of time. While there is no harm in this, it does get boring for the Coaches.

☐ STEP 4

As the child approaches the tunnel exit, the "Exit Coach" should peek in with a very silly face and emphatic sound effects. When he emerges, the Coach should pick up the child and give him a face-to-face hug and then quickly proceed to a second exciting activity. We typically add a "table walk" component. For example, the Coach quickly places the young child on one end of a nearby sturdy, long table and moves to the other end. The "Entrance Coach" acts as the child's "spotter," walking just behind the child, but not touching him, as he proceeds to walk the length of the table and fall into the "Exit Coach's" arms. We find that children will stay raptly focused on the adult at the end of the table.

Variations:

The tunnel has many uses in later activities. A Coach can get inside of it in an upright vertical position and play "Peek-a-boo" as a human Jack-in-the-Box. Apprentices can also use it as an entrance to their clubhouse. We highly recommend you purchase one, especially if your child is of pre-school age.

Obstacles/Opportunities:

Sometimes a child will become voluntarily "stuck" in the middle of the tunnel and will refuse to come out. In such cases we do several things. Because it is collapsible we can decrease the length of the tunnel. We can also elevate one end, thus providing an incline that "suggests" to the child that it is time to exit. Finally, we can rock and roll the tunnel a bit too much so that the child decides it would be more comfortable to continue on through. This rarely presents a problem after several trials.

LEVEL I, STAGE I, ACTIVITY 8

Climbing and Jumping

ACTIVITY HIGHLIGHTS
° Increased excitement and laughter
° Heightened awareness

Summary:

Arnold and Eileen Miller, founders of the Cognitive Development Center, an innovative therapeutic day school for children with autism in Boston, Massachusetts, discovered years ago that placing children with autism on elevated structures immediately heightened their attention and referencing. We all know that children love to jump from a small height, as long as it is safe. Years ago we combined the two elements into a very basic exercise called "Climbing and Jumping." We have used this activity for over ten years. Inevitably when we discuss or show this exercise at a workshop, someone will critically wonder how we could be encouraging children to climb and jump off of things, thus creating the danger of injury. We have not had a single child injured either at our offices or at home while climbing and jumping for all of these years. However, we must add this caveat: If you have any concerns in this regard, please do not attempt this activity!

Participants:

Initially we like to use two Coaches and one child. One Coach acts as the "spotter" and holds onto the child, or keeps within "grasping" distance, depending upon the motor skills and wariness of the child. The other Coach lies or sits on the pile of beanbag chairs directly underneath the edge of the table and act as the "receiver," catching the child when he leaves the elevated platform. As children learn the activity and as Coaches determine that they are going to respect their limits for the activity, you can easily practice this with just one Coach.

Getting Ready:

You will need a sturdy platform about the height of the child and at least six sturdy beanbag chairs or similar cushions. Place a good pile of beanbag chairs directly adjacent to the platform on a carpeted surface. We know that you will use good judgment in determining height and safety issues related to the particular child.

Coaching Instructions:

There are three steps outlining the progress a child can make:

☐ STEP 1

Directions are very simple. With a young child we initially lift him and place him on the elevated platform. Once on the platform we never let go of the young child. Very slowly we swing his arms and ours and count to three with our voices becoming more excited on each number. At three we guide the child off the platform and into the arms of the Coach who is awaiting him on the cushions. Without any prompts or cues, the child's eyes will be clearly fixed on the Coach below. The Coach meets his eyes as the child falls. She grabs the child and engages in some brief face-to-face rough-and-tumble play or tickling before beginning again.

☐ STEP 2

As the child progresses, or with an older child, place a small sturdy stepladder adjacent to the platform and guide the child up the ladder and onto the edge of the platform, making sure to continue to act as a spotter while he does this.

☐ STEP 3

As the activity progresses even more, we can often allow more independent action from the child, such as climbing by himself, walking onto the edge of the ledge and jumping into our arms while we are on the cushions

Variations:

If the platform is sturdy enough and you are in shape, you can practice climbing and jumping alongside the child. But only attempt this after the child has mastered Step 3. Allow the child to climb first, while still holding his hand. Move together to the edge of the platform. Count together and fall together while still holding hands and meeting each other's gaze. Get up together and move to the ladder as a coordinated team. We practice this activity on platforms of varying heights. For example, you can do it outdoors with a deck or a porch, but never at a height that would pose a physical danger. This is also a natural activity for children who like to swim.

Obstacles/Opportunities:

Make sure that you never lose the leadership of this activity no matter how proficient the child becomes. You are in charge of the sequence of actions and of the cadence of the count. The child does his jumping or falling only on your signal and never using his own initiative! Make sure that the child understands that this activity is done only with an adult "spotter" and only in a special setting. Never let the child practice this activity on his own! Discontinue immediately if you have even the slightest suspicion that the child will not respect the limits you have set for climbing and jumping. Obviously, this is a "fun" activity. It is not intended to terrify the child and should immediately be discontinued if not enjoyable. We have found that by carefully varying heights and the role of the two Coaches, even the most fearful child can enjoy and safely engage in this exercise.

LEVEL I, STAGE I, ACTIVITY 9

Affection Sharing

ACTIVITY HIGHLIGHTS
- ° Attending to verbal and nonverbal communication
- ° Responding to facial expressions
- ° Shifting body position and gaze to share affection

Summary:

It is human nature to desire affectionate touch from persons with whom we feel close. For some children, the ability to respond to physical cues for the appropriate exchange of affection may be highly impaired and result in awkward or, in some cases inappropriate behavior. This activity helps children learn to better read and respond to simple verbal and nonverbal affection sharing communication. We will describe how to work with both a preschool and older child.

Participants:

For the pre-school child you will once again require a "spotter" and "receiver" Coach. One Coach will suffice with an older child.

Getting Ready:

This activity requires one rectangular table of sufficient height to bring the pre-school child's eyes level with those of the Coaches. The Coaches should stand at opposite ends of the table. No props are necessary for older children.

Coaching Instructions for Pre-School Children:

This activity has four steps:

☐ STEP 1

The "spotter" Coach places the child in a standing position on top of a table facing the "receiver" Coach. Carefully spot the child to channel his movement and ensure his safety.

☐ STEP 2

The "receiver Coach" extends her arms to the Novice but does not touch him. She waits for him to shift his gaze toward her face. Once he has done so, even momentarily, she quickly fills her cheeks with air and pulls his hands to her face. This ensures that their eyes will lock for the sharing of excitement. The "receiver Coach" pops the air out of her cheeks, exaggerating both facial expression and sound.

☐ STEP 3

The "receiver Coach" lifts the Novice into her arms and sings the syllables "Mama" to the tune of "Row Your Boat."

☐ STEP 4

The "spotter" Coach places the child on the floor and walks with him to the "receiver Coach" who kneels at eye level to receive him. The "receiver Coach" returns the child to the "spotter" and the previously described pattern is repeated.

Coaching Instructions for Older Children:

There are two steps to this activity:

☐ STEP 1

Parent and child at sit eye level. The parent slowly moves his or her face toward the child until their heads gently. The parent says " I love you" and the child, if verbal, replies, "I love you, too."

☐ STEP 2

Three or four family members sit in a circle with the child in the middle. Randomly, each calls the child's name. The child walks toward the person who called. They slowly move their heads towards one another, lightly touch foreheads and repeat the script stated above. Standing on all sides around the table, family members can now randomly turn the child, to move him between them, for hugs.

Variation:

You can provide further variety for the pre-school child, by moving him from the table to the floor and surrounding him with beanbag chairs. Not only will the child be able to move between Coaches, without the structure of the table, but he will be able to visually orient and move independently between them.

Obstacles and Opportunities:

Once again, if you are concerned about placing the young child on a table or platform, you can still do this activity by lowering yourself to his eye level.

LEVEL 1, STAGE 1, ACTIVITY 10

Now You See Me, Now You Don't

ACTIVITY HIGHLIGHTS
° Anticipating a social partner's next action
° Communicate for continuation of exciting actions
° Shifting body position and gaze to attend to novelty
° Initiating nonverbal emotion sharing

Summary:

"Looking" is one of the easiest behaviors to teach a person. We often see children taught to respond to the cue, "Look at me" by making eye contact. Unfortunately, the necessity for this verbal prompt is a sign that the child may not have learned the natural reasons why we visually "reference" each other's faces so frequently. Through this activity, we try to provide the child the same reasons his typically developing peers have for "looking." The game of peek-a-boo reminds not only children, but also ourselves, that relationships are fragile and that, if we ignore them, we quickly lose our ability to remain connected with those we care for.

Participants:

Coach and child.

Getting Ready:

To begin this activity, Coach and child sit at a small table in immediate proximity, either directly across from each other or at a 90° angle. You need a small towel, and a table cloth.

Coaching Instructions:

This activity has three steps:

☐ STEP 1

Gently pull both of the child's hands toward your eyes to orient the child's gaze on your face. Now cover your eyes with the child's hands. Quickly follow this by covering the child's eyes with your hands. Now go back and forth, with each of you covering the other's eyes with your hands at a rapid pace. Remember to continue to hold onto the child's hands.

☐ STEP 2

With the child's hands covering your eyes ask, "Where's (name)?" Remove the child's hands so that you can see and say, "Peek-a-boo" while laughing with the child. Now cover the child's face with your hands and again say, "Where's (name)?" Remove your hands to reveal the child's eyes and again say, "Peek-a-boo!"

☐ STEP 3

Obtain the child's attention and place a small towel over his face. In an exaggerated voice ask, "Where's (name)?" Wait for the child to remove the cloth. If the child does not do so, gently pull the cloth from his face, while laughing with excitement. Now places the cloth over your own face and reverse the activity. Once a child has mastered peek-a-boo with a small towel, cover him with a tablecloth to make the game more challenging and exciting.

Variations:

Moving this game outside a playroom and into other settings will increase the likelihood of generalization.

Obstacles/Opportunities:

An inability to sit independently may need to be addressed within the context of this activity. Setting up a movement routine can be an efficient and easily generalized method for doing so. Begin with a "table walk." After walking across the table, quickly seat the child on a chair, count to ten and return to the table walk activity. Once the child is independently moving between table and chair, introduce this activity. Although we've not personally experienced it, masks could frighten children. Making sure that the child sees the mask before your face is covered usually removes the obstacle of fear.

LEVEL I, STAGE I, ACTIVITY II

Swing and Fly

ACTIVITY HIGHLIGHTS
° Gaze shifting from one person to another
° Communicating to continue exciting actions

Summary:

"Swing and Fly" is an activity originally created for the very young child. Relying on pause and hesitation to build excitement, the child typically references your facial expressions as he "flies." As the game evolves, it will develop to include the component of swinging. The child will then find that the demands of the game require he shift his gaze between both Coaches who will alternately pause and hesitate prior to swinging the child onto a beanbag chair.

Participants:

Two Coaches and a child. It is important to note that this activity, although written for a very young child can be modified for older children as well.

Getting Ready:

Eight good-quality beanbags are needed for this activity. Beanbag chairs are staples for many of our activities and will most likely be worn out and replaced several times before a child reaches Level III. To prepare for this activity, two piles of bags are placed six feet apart. Eventually, this distance will be increased to the furthest parameters of the room. One beanbag on each stack will provide comfortable seating. The other two will cushion your backward fall.

Coaching Instructions for a Young Child:

This activity has four simple steps:

☐ STEP 1

Coach 1 sits on a beanbag with the child on her lap, facing Coach 2 who is seated facing the child, no more than a foot or two away on her own beanbag chair.

☐ STEP 2

Coach 2 holds out her hands and counts in an exaggerated, slow fashion: "one, two, three." Coach 1 should release the child at the count of "three" and gently push him toward Coach 2.

☐ STEP 3

As the child approaches Coach 2, she extends her legs to support the Novice's trunk and shouts, "Let's fly." She firmly grasps his forearms and swings the child into the air using her arms and legs, so that their eyes are level. Then she lowers him onto the beanbag chair.

☐ STEP 4

Both Coaches firmly grasp an end of the beanbag chair and gently lift the child off the ground. They swing the chair back and forth while counting to three. At the count of three they carefully toss the beanbag-with-child onto a large stack of beanbag chairs. This never fails to produce glee and demands to, "Do it again!"

Coaching Instructions for the Older Child:

This activity has three simple steps:

☐ STEP 1

Coach 1 sits on a beanbag chair, with the child standing directly in front of him, facing Coach 2. Coach 2 stands facing the pair, right next to an empty beanbag chair. Coach 1 counts to three in an exaggerated manner and gently pushes the child into a slow run towards Coach 2.

☐ STEP 2

As the child approaches, Coach 2 guides him to fall on the beanbag chair right beside him. He looms over the child and hesitates to create suspense. Then he tickles him (or takes some similar action if he does not enjoy tickling).

☐ STEP 3

As in the younger activity, both Coaches toss the child and beanbag onto a pile of beanbag chairs.

Variations:

Using the same configuration, the child should learn to run between both Coaches before falling on one of the beanbag chairs. Coaches assume positions on either side of their respective beanbag chairs. They keep the child running back and forth until, unexpectedly, one of the Coaches guides the child down onto one of the beanbag chairs.

Obstacles and Opportunities:

We have known children who panic and attempt to bolt the first few times they are picked up on the beanbag chair. This is not necessarily a reason to give up the activity but it does communicate a need to ensure the child's safety so that he can enjoy swinging. For a fearful child, you can first practice raising and lowering the beanbag, saying, "Up, down, up, down." Once this sensation becomes familiar, it will be easier to play the game as described. Following this activity, take an opportunity to slow down the pace and simply lie on the beanbag next to the child. While you are lying side by side, you may wish to engage in a playful activity such as taking turn touching each other's nose and laughing. This also provides the child with a chance to invite you to play again.

LEVEL I, STAGE I, ACTIVITY 12

Masks On, Masks Off

ACTIVITY HIGHLIGHTS:

° Increase excitement

° Develop referencing

Summary:

Masks are a means for creating excitement and novelty and developing the basic function that motivates children to gaze at faces. The purpose of this activity is to encourage the child to reference faces without needing specific prompts.

Participants:

Coach and child

Getting Ready:

You will need a variety of different masks. Avoid frightening masks. Masks should be under the table covered by a cloth so that the child cannot see them. You should be seated on the floor at a 90° angle to the child and within easy reach of the masks.

Coaching Instructions:

The activity has three simple steps:

☐ STEP 1

Cover your face with the first mask and make an appropriate animal sound. The child will usually touch the mask fairly close to your eyes and visually orient toward it. Allow and encourage this but for no longer than 30 seconds.

☐ STEP 2

Remove the first mask and place a second mask on the table. If the child tries to take the mask, simply say, "No. Mine!" Show the child how to put the new mask on and take it off your face. The removal of the masks signals a point for shared laughter. If the child does not share laughter, you can bring the child's hands to your face and laugh in an exaggerated manner.

☐ STEP 3

Place the mask first on your own face and then on the face of the child. The excitement of shared laughter should always follow the removal of masks.

Obstacles/Opportunities:

If children are unable to sit independently on a chair they should be taught to do so. Setting up a motor routine can be helpful. We have found the following to be efficient and easily understood. Begin with the table routine, followed by swinging, then lead the child to the chair. Count to ten. Continue with this routine until the child independently moves through the motor routine with limited assistance from an adult.

This activity provides an opportunity to prepare children for Halloween. It also introduces at a very elementary level of understanding the relationship between reality and fantasy. Many children in the Autism Spectrum have great difficulty in understanding deception, especially as it relates to humor and inconsistencies between words and the delivery of those words. While this activity does not address this difficulty directly, it does set the stage for later work.

LEVEL I, STAGE I, ACTIVITY 13

Push/Pull with Sound Effects

ACTIVITY HIGHLIGHTS:
° Experience of coordinated movement
° Increased visual referencing for enhanced excitement

Summary:
This is a very simple activity that children of most ages find pleasant and fun. It is an easy introductory activity for them to join in as partners providing shared motion and sound. It is a sure-fire way to increase visual referencing. It also provides a nice introduction to the pleasure of coordinated movement.

Participants:
Coach and child.

Getting Ready:
Sit on beanbag chairs directly across and facing each other.

Coaching Instructions:
This activity has two simple steps:

☐ STEP 1

Grasp the child's arms in a manner that allows him to be pulled safely. Begin a gentle but firm back-and-forth, pulling–pushing, rocking movement. Push and pull in a series of small steps so that moving the child all the way back into his beanbag takes a series of three or four small pushes. Each time you push make the same very distinct sound effect noise, such as "Ugha, ugha, ugha." Do the same thing when you pull the child back to you in stages, but use a different noise like, "Ahoh, ahoh, ahoh." Do not confuse the noises. Add a third "ending" sound when you reach the endpoint of a pull and push, such as, "Whack." So you should be pushing four times chanting Ugha, ugha, ugha, ugha", then pulling four times while chanting, "Ahoh, ahoh, ahoh, ahoh" and finally ending the action by saying, "Whack!"

☐ STEP 2

Vary the speed of movement and then the number of stages. After this, begin to add new sounds each time you go back and forth. But, make sure that there are clearly different, distinct sounds for pulling and pushing. Encourage the child to join in with the sound effects if they have not already done so.

Variations:

You can add as many different sound effects as you like. You should also add a number of variations to break up the predictability and increase the excitement, to prevent the activity from becoming "stale" too quickly. Among the variations you can use are sideways and angled movements, hesitations, speed variations and circular movements.

Obstacles/Opportunities:

Some older children may perceive this activity as "babyish." If so, you might try telling them that you want them to learn it, so that they can do it with a younger sibling or a younger child that you need help with. Once begun, they love the activity and want to repeat it.

LEVEL I, STAGE I, ACTIVITY 14

Fast Paced Actions

ACTIVITY HIGHLIGHTS
° Enjoying fast-paced social interactions
° Referencing partners for shared excitement and joy
° Rapid attention shifting from objects to social partners
° Eye–Hand coordination

Summary:

Now we focus on activities that provide a great deal of excitement, while teaching the child to rapidly shift focus. These activities also allow the child to function as a more active participant in creating the action. "Hot Potato/Trade Me/Overload" is the first activity we introduce that has several different elements – rapid passing, trading, and bombarding – combined into a single activity. In addition, "Trade Me" practices rapid attention shifting. While we have chosen a combination of three activities, there are countless more. The key factor is that the activity be fast-paced, easy to do, require the child to rapidly shift gaze from object to person and involve no objects that would distract the child.

Participants:

Coach and one or two children.

Getting Ready:

For "Hot Potato/Overload/Trade Me" choose the objects you will use for the "potato" as well as for trading. We prefer soft balls as "potatoes" and small soft stuffed animals for trading. You can trade any small object that is soft and moderately interesting to the child. Initially, try not to use any object that will distract the child. Place the "potatoes" and trading objects into a box from which you can easily retrieve them as needed.

Coaching Instructions:

This activity has three steps:

☐ STEP 1

This activity begins by teaching the child a rapid passing game. The objective of the "hot potato" part of the activity is to establish a rapid pace. Pretend with an exaggerated voice and gestures that you have a "hot" object in your hand. Pass the object over to the child while indicating that they are to pretend that it is hot and quickly pass it back, so as not to be burned. Keep at this until you can maintain a rapid back-and-forth exciting pace that can last several minutes.

☐ STEP 2

After a few minutes, when the excited, rapid pace is established, switch to the second part of the activity. Instead of passing one of the "potatoes," quickly reach into the box in which your passing objects have been stored, take out a new object and use it as the "potato" and pass it to the child. Do not let the child pass it back. Quickly remove a second object for yourself. Now, immediately say, "Trade me," and exchange the objects with the child. If the child balks, take the object from the child and quickly make the trade. Then increase your pace even more. Discard your object and quickly take a third object from the box. Rapidly make another trade. Continue in this fashion for several minutes.

☐ STEP 3

Now the game shifts to "Overload." Begin taking soft objects out of the box and rapidly passing them to the child. Do not give him time to examine any, or give them back to you. Rather keep taking balls and soft objects and "piling" them onto the child's lap, while laughing and inviting the child to laugh with you. Of course the key is to "overload" the child so that he does not focus on any one particular object. When you have taken out all the objects, you and the child can fling them up in the air for added excitement (again, making sure that all objects are soft!).

Variations:

Tessa Sandlin, a teacher, plays a game called "Hot Potato with Referencing." A small group forms a circle and begins rolling a ball to each other rapidly. Then the rules shift. You can only roll a ball to a group member if you gaze at them and they smile at you. When this gets too easy, she introduces more balls with the same rules. As you might imagine, there are an infinite number of fast-paced activities that will yield similar results. Remember to be careful about introducing objects that will distract from the human interaction.

Obstacles/Opportunities:

This is a great opportunity to determine whether a rapid pace increases the child's ability to shift focus and stops them becoming "stuck" with any one object. Make sure to keep the pace of "Trade Me" rapid enough so that the child does not have sufficient time to get involved with any one object. Even though we emphasize the rapidity of the pace, observe carefully to determine the optimum pace for each child.

LEVEL I, STAGE I, ACTIVITY 15

Jack-in-the-Box and Spike the Dog

ACTIVITY HIGHLIGHTS
° Referencing adults for safety and security
° Referencing for reassurance

Summary:

The Jack-in-the-Box toy has become a staple for young children. It provides children with engaging music, along with the surprise of the sudden opening and appearance of the figure inside the box. Prior to the "pop" it is natural for children to move closer to a coach

Spike the Dog, complete with spiked collar and a big bite provides a similar experience for older children. Spike is a diminutive plastic dog replica that seems good for only one thing, but he does that one thing very well. Spike has a mouth with a set of fake "teeth" that do not look very scary and cannot hurt anyone. But, when you open his mouth it starts a mechanical action leading to his jaws suddenly shutting. The game Spike was designed for is to put your finger in his mouth and see if you can pull it out before he chomps down! Partners take turns being brave. This activity never fails to induce lots of emotion sharing and gaze shifting. Of course you must demonstrate that Spike is harmless and should never coerce a child into playing. Children and even teens seem to love playing this game!

Participants:

Coach and child.

Getting Ready:

Younger children can use a traditional musical Jack in the Box. Older children can use Spike the Dog, or any similar toy that has a surprising emergence.

Coaching Instructions for Jack-in-the-Box:

The activity has three steps:

☐ STEP ONE:

Begin the activity by engaging the child with a social smile. Slowly wind up the music box, stopping just before the "Jack" pops out.

☐ STEP TWO:

Touch the child, smile excitedly in anticipation and pull the child close.

☐ STEP THREE:

Once the tension has built, complete the cycle, grab the child, share the excitement as the "Jack" finally pops out.

Coaching Instructions for Spike the Dog:

This activity has four steps:

☐ STEP ONE:

Begin the activity by engaging the child with a social smile. Now demonstrate Spike's bite by placing your fingers one at a time on Spike's teeth, feigning exaggerated excitement, but no pain, when his mouth unexpectedly clamps down.

☐ STEP TWO:

Put your fingers inside Spike again, but this time say, "I hope he gets me this time" followed by, "Oh Rats!" each time Spike does not bite.

☐ STEP THREE:

Once the child understands that excitement is obtained from Spike's "bite," take turns placing a finger inside Spike's mouth. Each time, prior to the placement of a finger on Spike's tooth, meet each other's gaze, act scared and then place a finger in Spike's mouth.

☐ STEP FOUR:

Once Spike bites, scream, laugh and grab each other.

Variation:

Using the melody of a familiar song with different words, can create hesitation, surprise and a safe wariness.

Obstacles and Opportunities:

The child who is truly frightened should not be forced to play either game. It is important to remember that, if a child is frightened, it is not simply enough to tell him that it will not hurt. He will need to see another person overcome the fear he is experiencing. By including a second Coach with whom the child is familiar, the child can watch that person overcome his fear.

LEVEL I, STAGE I, ACTIVITY 16

Beanbag Medley I

ACTIVITY HIGHLIGHTS

° Rapid increases in visual referencing

° Participating in highly motivatiung interactions

° Meaningfully chaining activities together

Summary:

As you may have realized by now we love to use large, durable beanbag chairs in our activities. They are like amoebas and have no real shape of their own. Children of all ages love them and together we find hundreds of different uses for them. Many of our younger students begin their mornings by jumping together onto a giant pile of 45 beanbag chairs we have placed in their "community" room. It certainly wakes them up for their first class! This exercise presents a typical "medley" of five simple beanbag chair activities that get chained together into one fluid exercise that most children find quite exciting. If you live in the USA you can have a look at our website for information about how to get good quality beanbag chairs at a reasonable price.

Participants:

Coach and child.

Getting Ready:

All you need is lots of energy and about eight sturdy beanbag chairs. Remember to take enough breaks so that you do not wear out!

Coaching Introduction:

There are five separate activities which are chained together in a fast pace to complete the exercise:

■ **ACTIVITY 1   HOT BEANBAGS:**

In this version of "Hot Potato", we pretend that the beanbag chairs we are seated in are hot, so we have to get up and switch chairs frequently. We chant, "Hot Beanbag. Help!" This serves as the cue for Coach and child to quickly move to another chair. We begin the game with two chairs and switch from one to another. Then we add three and eventually four chairs and begin moving in first a clockwise and then a counter-clockwise motion, doing our, "Hot beanbag. Help!" chant together.

■ **ACTIVITY 2   BEANBAG SANDWICH:**

This is a great follow up activity when both Coach and child are a bit tired from "Hot Beanbags." At the end of the first activity, you and the child will typically be lying on a beanbag chair. After resting for a minute, get up and stand over the child. Tell him excitedly that you are going to make a sandwich out of him. He is the meat and you are using "beanbag bread." Cover him with a beanbag chair, first making sure he is lying on a beanbag chair. If you like you can put a piece of large red construction paper on top of him prior to placing the top beanbag and tell him, "That's the tomato." A green piece can be the "pickle." You can pat the top beanbag down and tell him you are making the sandwich and spreading the mustard. If he would like, the Novice can then make you into a sandwich.

■ **ACTIVITY 3   COVERED UP:**

With the Novice in the "down" position, you can begin piling beanbag chairs over him while excitedly chanting, "Where is ____? I can't see him? Where did he go? Are you in there? Come out! Come out!" While you are chanting, continue to keep piling the beanbags on, unless you hear any sign of fear from the child. When the child emerges from the pile, congratulate him with, "There you are. You made it!" Then lie down and let the child pile the beanbags on top of you.

■ **ACTIVITY 4   BEANBAG BARRIER:**

Play a game of "Trap the Novice." Play a short game of chase with the child until you can "corner" him in one corner of a room. Begin placing beanbag chairs around the child to form a barrier around him. While you are doing this, smile broadly and chant, "I'm building a wall! I've got you trapped! You can't get out!" Pretend that you are trying to keep the Novice from escaping from this "jail." Allow the child to begin trying to climb over the barrier. Make a "feeble" (but not too obviously feeble!) attempt to keep him from escaping. When he does escape, congratulate him for being strong enough to "defeat" you. If he would like, he can build a barrier and trap you. This time you will not be able to escape, until he decides to free you. What a great feeling of power!

■ ACTIVITY 5   BUILD A MOUNTAIN:

In the final activity you will pile all the beanbag chairs in one corner of the room in preparation for building a beanbag "mountain" in the opposite corner. You will do all the work of coordination at this stage. Choose a beanbag, take the child's hands and place them on one side of the chosen bag. Grasp the other side and, rapidly carry the beanbag chair over to the location of the mountain. While you are carrying, you should chant, "We're building the mountain, a beanbag mountain." When you reach the corner of the room chosen for the mountain, place the beanbag chair on the ground and see if you can get the child to join you in carefully patting it down. Initially, you may have to keep the child from running off. Use one hand to hold onto the child and take his other hand in yours and together pat down the bag.

When sufficient beanbags have been placed in a pile, creating a small tower, it is time for the child to climb the mountain and become the "King" of the mountain. Make sure to "spot" the child carefully, holding onto to him firmly while he climbs. You may need a second Coach during this part, to keep everything safe and secure. When he gets to the top, allow him to sit on the topmost beanbag for a short while, enjoying being the "King" and then gradually help him climb or slide down.

Variations:

If you have two Coaches, you can end "Building the Mountain" by providing an amusement park-like ride. With the child firmly seated on the topmost bag, Coaches should each firmly grasp one side of the beanbag he is sitting on with one hand, while using the other hand to firmly grasp the child's arm under his armpit. At the count of three, Coaches pull the topmost bag from the mountain with the child seated upon it. Then slide it down the pile and onto the ground, making sure they hold the child tightly.

Obstacles/Opportunities:

We have never had a single accident in over 12 years of playing these exciting beanbag chair activities. The key is to be cautious and always carefully "spot" the child. "Beanbag Medley" almost never fails to be a thrilling activity for Novices. Be careful to watch that the Novice is not getting over-stimulated. Remember to slow the pace when you notice this. Take frequent breaks so you both do not become exhausted.

Simple Participation

ACTIVITY HIGHLIGHTS

° Enacting a simple role with proper timing
° Conduct rapid gaze shifting from objects to people
° Anticipating your social partner's actions
° Communicating to continue exciting actions

Summary:

In this exercise, the child is an active participant in simple, exciting activities. Along with beanbag chairs, balloons, paper airplanes and marbles, are a few of the objects we find useful during the early stages of intervention. Certain objects appear to strongly compete for the attention of children in the Autism Spectrum. We find that these objects, when used correctly, actually foster gaze shifting between objects and people. This is partially due to the difficulty most children have blowing up balloons by themselves and recreating the enjoyable sequences we introduce. For these reasons, balloons and paper airplanes are valuable tools for visual referencing and non-verbal communication. There are numerous enjoyable ways for playing with them, and the elements of surprise and unpredictability do not overwhelm most children. Everyone likes to play with marbles. When properly controlled, our marble game provides a fast paced activity that can be varied in interesting ways.

Participants:

Coach and child.

Getting Ready:

Sit facing each other at a small table. You should have six balloons and three paper airplanes placed outside the child's visual range. You will also need two plastic cups, one of them half-filled with marbles.

Coaching Instructions for Balloons:

This activity has three steps:

☐ STEP 1

With the child seated facing you, blow up the balloon and slowly release the air onto the child's neck, knees or hands. Lay the now deflated balloon on the table and wait for the child to return it to you or to communicate in another fashion such as moving it to your lips, that he wants you to repeat the game. If the child does not do so, place your hand over his hand and retrieve the balloon. Once you have the balloon, hold it up at face level while drawing the hand of the child to your face, thus shifting his or her visual gaze to your eyes.

☐ STEP 2

Now, blow up the balloon again and this time release the air onto the child while stretching the mouthpiece so that it makes a screeching sound. Use the child's natural tendency to touch the balloon as a signal to continue or stop the noise. For example, if the child touches the balloon it should screech until he removes his hand. The balloon should gently be moved in and out of the child's visual range to encourage visual referencing and emotion sharing. If this does not happen spontaneously, hold the balloon level with the child's face until the he shifts his gaze to your face.

☐ STEP 3

Blow up the balloon and count to three. Engage the child with anticipatory laughter. Release the balloon so that it flies around the room. Typically, a child will return the balloon to you to maintain this play. So long as the child is not putting the balloon in his mouth, give him time to come back to you. If his body language shows that he has become focused on the balloon, retrieve it and once seated you should make sure he knows how to initiate this play by handing it back to you.

Coaching Instructions for Paper Airplanes:

Place a paper airplane on the table within the child's visual range but not within arm's reach. Say, "Time to fly" and launch the airplane. Wait 30 to 45 seconds for the child to retrieve the airplane and return it to you for launching. If the child does not do so, launch the second and third airplanes. With each launch, provide 30 seconds for the child to independently retrieve and return the airplane for a new launch. If, by the release of the third airplane, the child does not return the airplane, it will be necessary to help him understand his role in the activity. Hold his hand, walk to each airplane and hand-over-hand retrieve each one with him. After returning to the table, place an airplane on the table for launching. This process should become ritualized using hand-over-hand guidance until the child shifts gaze between you and the airplane, retrieves the plane, and returns with it independently for the next launch.

Coaching Instructions for Marbles Please:

Begin the activity by holding two cups; one cup filled with marbles and an empty cup. If you believe the child may have difficulty holding a cup of marbles without flinging or dropping them, you will need a second Coach to hold the child's cup along with him. Now hand the child the cup of marbles and start the game. Quickly say, "Marbles please!," hold out your empty cup and with your other hand, take the child's hand holding his cup and pour his marbles into your cup. Now quickly ask, "Marbles please?" and without waiting for an answer, pour the marbles back into the child's cup. Keep the pace fast so that the child is not tempted to play with or toss the marbles. Get into a good rhythm of back-and-forth marble passing and then gradually allow the child more independent action, until he is successfully engaging in his role without help. The

1

final verbal "script" for the activity entails one partner asking, "Marbles?" and the other saying, "Yes, please."

Variations:

As children become more accomplished with "Marbles Please," you can add more complexity by providing three different cups, each filled with a different substance such as marbles, pennies and paper clips. In addition there is one empty cup. You and the child then take turns holding out your empty cup and requesting one of the three substances: for example, "Clips please," or "Pennies please."

"Hats on, Hats off" is another simple activity that younger children enjoy. You and the child each have a floppy hat. Stand in front of a mirror. Chant, "Hats on!" and both partners put your hats on. The chant of "Hats off" leads to both removing your hats in unison. Then move to glasses, gloves, shoes and anything else you can think of. Eventually this can become a fast-paced activity that you can enact as partners.

Obstacles and Opportunities:

With each of these activities, you will want to use a hierarchy of increased naivety to encourage the child to maintain her participation in the game. For example, once she has learned to hand the balloon to you, do not immediately blow it up. Shrug your shoulders with a quizzical look and wait to see if she pushes it to your lips or signals you to "blow it."

Marbles, paper airplanes or balloons can sometimes be a distraction. The child may become distracted by the objects and protest their return. Increasing the pace of the exercise, so that the child doesn't have time to focus on the object may eliminate this problem.

Beanbag Medley II

ACTIVITY HIGHLIGHTS
° Rapid attention shifting

° Sustained excitement

° Active participation

Summary:

Once again we return to out beanbag chairs, this time to reinforce rapid referencing and attention shifting. Here we present four fast paced activities that almost all children will love to play again and again. The only caveat is to be careful if you play these with any child who has problems with aggression.

Participants:

Coach and child.

Getting Ready:

All you need is about 8 beanbag chairs and a dozen very soft balls that can be thrown without causing damage or hurting anyone. You will need to clear out a room of all furniture before you play "Beanbag Dodge" and "Beanbag War."

Coaching Instructions:

There are four activities in this exercise:

■ **ACTIVITY 1   BEANBAG ISLANDS:**

Spread out the beanbags leaving spaces of varying sizes in between them. The activity is to go from island to island to reach a destination of safety, which may entail climbing a bit onto a table or platform. Make the game more exciting by talking fearfully about the sharks in the water that will eat us if we do not stay on the beanbags. Explain to the child that the sharks are invisible, but that you have special glasses that allow you to see the sharks coming. Begin the game, then after a few minutes, suddenly lose your voice. Dramatically indicate that you cannot talk by pointing to your throat and gasping, etc. Now the child can only tell when the sharks are coming by looking at the scared expression on your face. Start at any beanbag and make sure that you and the child always stay together, even if it means holding hands the entire time.

■ **ACTIVITY 2   BEANBAG FORT:**

There are two ways to play this game. The first version entails each of you selecting one beanbag that acts like a moveable shield. In the second version, you both construct larger "Beanbag Forts." Either way, when ready, you begin "bombarding" each other with harmless balls. Periodically peek out from your fort and try and move your pile of beanbags closer and closer to the child, without saying a word or uttering a sound. When you peek out, do so with a really "sneaky" expression on your face.

■ **ACTIVITY 3   BEANBAG DODGE:**

This is our beanbag chair equivalent of "Dodge ball." Use masking tape to designate a center line which neither of you can cross. Begin by trying to hit the child with beanbags (remember to throw softly). The child has to "dodge" and avoid being hit. He cannot throw any of his own. You can play this with as many beanbags as you would like. The key is to use many "feints" where you pretend to throw the beanbag but do not. Try to catch the child off guard. Only your face will give away whether you are going to throw the beanbag or not. Make sure the child knows he has to keep moving and dodging if he doesn't want to get hit.

■ **ACTIVITY 4   FALLING TOGETHER:**

Coach and child stand directly in front of the pile of beanbags, facing each other but with their sides to the beanbags. You should kneel and adjust your height to be more even with a young child. Hold hands, unless this is unpleasant for the child. Count to three together and fall together onto the beanbags. The cadence of the counting should be completely controlled by you. Once you have landed, take a few seconds for shared laughter and, depending on the child, tickling or a similar action. With older children a "high five" after landing together is an option.

Variations:

If the child can keep his excitement from overflowing you can get rid of any taped lines and play a "free-for-all" version of "Beanbag Dodge" we call "Beanbag War." By now we believe that you can begin to generate your own beanbag chair activities.

Obstacles/Opportunities:

Do not do any of these activities to win or score points. This is just fun and not a competition. If the child insists upon making them competitive, stop the activity immediately.

LEVEL I, STAGE I, ACTIVITY 19

Challenge Course

ACTIVITY HIGHLIGHTS

° Creating focused attention
° Referencing adults for safety and security
° Associating excitement and mastery with adults
° Improving body awareness
° Sensory integration
° Improving balance skills

Summary:

As we noted earlier, Arnold and Eileen Miller were the first to notice that children with autism became much more focused and oriented to their immediate environment when placed on elevated structures. We find that structured, movement on challenging, elevated courses is a great way to develop vigilance and rapid attention shifting. This is an excellent activity to implement in both a home and school setting. The version of elevated activities we use is suited to younger and older children in any school or home setting. Some of our students have a poor sense of their own bodies in space. They also have little sense of competence in their ability to manage motor challenges. In this activity, we erect a "challenge course" tailored to the motor skills of our students. The course is adjustable so we can accommodate students of widely different motor abilities and competencies. Our Novice students practice on the course for at least 30 minutes daily.

Participants:

The number of children depends upon the number of "spotter" Coaches you have available and the degree to which you can trust children to not take risks on the course. Within a short while after beginning this activity, we are able to conduct our Challenge course with one Coach spotting for up to four student Novices. We often use older students as spotters.

Getting Ready:

You will need to construct a basic challenge course, using logs or thick boards that have planed surfaces. You will need a means of increasing elevation of boards while keeping them safely anchored to the ground. Check out the "Activities" section of our website, *www.connectionscenter.com,* for relevant links to sites that provide plans to construct your own challenge course.

Coaching Instructions:

This activity requires Coaches to carefully consider the elevation, width and positioning of the "course" that they will design. The goal is to create a structure that is challenging but not terrifying or dangerous to the child. It has to create sufficient anxiety so that the child will desire and orient to the Coach who serves as the "spotter" but not so much fear that the child will not enjoy the experience. You can start as low as you need to and gradually work your way up so that it becomes more challenging. Make sure you do not actually touch the child, but always be in easy reach to steady and hold the child if needed. The Coach should place himself on the ground, directly in front of the child and just out of "grabbing" range.

Variations:

Another variation is a series of trails such as those developed by Dr. Neal Sarahan. Neal has taken a small two-acre forested area on the school property and developed a maze of over two miles of trails through the forest. Students go into the forest and have to reference adults' non-verbal expressions at various points in the course, in order to figure out which trail to take to get out of the "maze."

Obstacles/Opportunities:

The challenge course is a great way to improve motor skills and sensory integration ability. But it is amazing to watch the heightened social awareness that emerges after a period of challenging activity, where the child has had to rely on visually referencing his "spotter" for security. As children make progress, we allow them to aid in designing the course, adding variations and eventually new elements. We even have them aid in the construction of new elements to the course.

Sample Challenge Course Variations

(All materials are assumed to be in an elevated position)

° One board.
° Two boards placed end to end with a gap of varying length between them.
° Two boards placed side by side. The child places one foot on each board.
° A series of boards that turn in different directions with varying-length gaps between them.
° A series of boards placed at different elevations.
° A two-board walk, with boards placed at different elevations.
° Adding a simple "ladder walk" at one point in the course.
° A varied course, with single boards, double boards, gaps, different elevations, ladder walks, barriers, "cheese boards" and other objects that create more novelty and challenge.

STAGE 2: REFERENCE

Goals and Objectives

As the title implies, the activities of Stage 2 are geared to increase a child's use of other people as his primary reference point for interacting with the world. In Stage 1 we worked on building-up referencing for enjoyment and excitement. Now, we develop new reasons to spend so much time and effort observing our social field. Excitement is a necessary but not sufficient reason to reference the social world on a constant basis. Other people have to be important, even when they are not entertaining you. In Stage 2, children learn that you have the ability to decrease their distress and anxiety and increase their understanding of the world. If they watch your face and your body, you can lead them to exciting discoveries about their world as well as helping them avoid dangers.

Activity Summary

In this stage, children learn that if they are not monitoring what people around them are doing, they cannot predict or anticipate what is going to happen to them. Many Stage 2 activities try to provide the Novice with awareness that he has to keep track of you, even as you move around rapidly. Another crucial reason to visually stay in touch with your face is that it provides important information about the safety of the environment and the acceptability of actions, including potential consequences for taking or persisting in some action.

One of the critical skills we work on in Stage 2 is rapid attention shifting. Rapid shifting is often necessary in situations where we are involved in some task or activity, but still wish to monitor what is happening around us in our social world. When children learn to rapidly shift attention from objects to persons, they are more likely to continue referencing in their more complex, everyday lives.

By the close of Stage 2, children have taken a much more active role in the communication process. Rather than passively glancing at your face for information, they learn to "actively" reference, by inquiring more about their environments. Children also become aware that they are information senders. At the close of this stage they learn that their own faces are reference points for others and a powerful source of communication effectiveness.

Critical Tips

- Learn to distinguish between referencing facial expressions and making eye contact.

- Limit verbal communication to develop facial referencing.

- Make sure your face is a powerful reference point. Exaggerate your facial expressions!

- Provide constant reasons for the Novice to reference your face.

- Be careful to observe the amount of unconscious prompting you engage in.

- Spend sufficient time and energy for the Novice to master rapid gaze shifting, including shifting from a non-social activity to referencing your face.

- Be careful not to engage in any activities that are competitive ot goal driven while you are teaching social referencing.

Sneaky Partner

ACTIVITY HIGHLIGHTS

° Carefully monitoring the whereabouts of social partners

° Develop greater social awareness and vigilance to actions in the immediate environment

Summary:

We often work with children who become so focused on one activity or object that they tune the rest of the world out. Trying to "break in" and disturb this closed system can be quite an ordeal. This activity introduces us to the concept of "Vigilance." This is a skill that requires breaking attention into two parts, a "foreground," where most attention is devoted to a main activity and a "background," where some attention is reserved to regularly monitor potential changes in the environment. In this activity, the foreground task is building a small mountain out of beanbag chairs. A Coach and a child choose beanbag chairs and carefully carry them over to the opposite end of the room and proceed to stack them carefully in a pile. Like the prior "Beanbag Mountain" activity, when the pile is complete, the child, if willing (and small enough), can climb the pile to the top. But there is a twist! If the child does not continue to watch his partner, he, or another Coach will grab a beanbag and slip away with it.

Participants:

You can do this activity with two or three people. One variation uses the Coach as a partner and thief, helping to carry the beanbags. In the other variation, one Coach is the partner and a second Coach plays the role of the "beanbag thief." We will describe both versions.

Getting Ready:

If you are doing this activity with three people including yourself, you must decide whether you will work with two children or an Assistant Coach. The Assistant Coach can be a more proficient child, or an adult.

Coaching Instructions for Two Person Version:

Instruct the child, visually and verbally as needed, to grasp one side of each beanbag, while you grasp the other side. Begin walking together, while holding the beanbag, towards one corner of the room and make a stack of beanbags.

After several "safe" trips introduce the following variation. Each time the child stops watching you, pull away from the child's grasp and run away to some other part of the room. The only way to stop you is to "freeze" you with his gaze, walk over to you and take you back to the path, where you proceed to the stack of beanbags and build a tower. Each time you place a beanbag down on the pile, the two of you pat it down into place and then together walk back to the beanbags remaining to be stacked. If the child walks away from you while returning, rush back to the "mountain" and "steal" the beanbag that was just placed there. When the tower is a suitable height (depending on the age of the child) help the Novice to climb to the top, if he would like and then gently bring him back down again.

Coaching Instructions for Three Person Version:

Teach the children to do the basic activity, "Beanbag Mountain." This activity begins with the beanbag chairs piled on one side of the room. The objective is for the partners to select a beanbag, pick it up together, walk together across the room and then place the beanbag in a pile in the opposite corner of the room. . Once partners can do the activity, tell them that you are the "beanbag thief." If the child can't catch you with his eyes, you will sneak up on him and steal the beanbag away. If the child does catch you, his eyes have the ability to freeze you in place, for a count of ten.

Variations:

A variation that serves the same purpose is to play a game of catch with a soft ball, in which you throw the ball high in the air. Hold a second ball in your other hand while you throw the first ball in the air. After about five times, throw the first ball high and when the child's eyes go to follow the ball, throw the second Soft ball right at the child. Give the child the same chance to do this to you. This really heightens the excitement of a simple catch.

Obstacles/Opportunities:

Children with self-regulation problems might require you to slow down the activity if they become too excited.

LEVEL I, STAGE 2, ACTIVITY 21

Sneaky Pete

ACTIVITY HIGHLIGHTS

° Monitoring the social environment during an engaging activity

° Rapid shifting of attention

° Increased vigilance

Summary:

Now we progress to a more sophisticated version of "Vigilance." As we stated in the last exercise, our children often become so focused on an activity of interest that they tune out everyone and everything else. This makes any attempt to interrupt them or transition a potential nightmare. "Sneaky Pete" works on the ability to maintain divided attention, even when you are involved in something very engaging. We hope that the "game-like" nature of the activity makes attention shifting a positive experience that can be practiced repeatedly.

Participants:

Coach and child.

Getting Ready:

Find an activity that the child will become moderately involved in. As our goal is success, we don't want to begin by choosing the child's favorite activity. Avoid anything he is absolutely obsessed with, or something that is completely novel.

Coaching Instructions:

The activity has three steps:

☐ STEP 1

Warn the child that you will be playing a game, where you are a "Sneaky Pete" and your job is to try and sneak up on him. As in the prior activity, the child has the power to freeze you with his eyes and make you go back to the starting position. But, if he doesn't catch you before you reach him, you will do a "sneaky trick" – some slightly annoying action, like tickling, or taking one piece of the material that he is working on. Make sure the action is only mildly annoying and not likely to elicit a tantrum or meltdown!

☐ STEP 2

Now have the child sit on a carpet square and place the chosen activity materials in front of the square, positioned so that he has his back to you while working. Wait until you believe he is fully focused on the activity. Then gradually begin sneaking up on him. Depending upon the ability of the child, you can be as sneaky as you need to be, even "camouflaging" yourself behind furniture and "moving" beanbag chairs. If the child is particularly insensitive to your approach be more noisy and obvious in your approach. If you need to, you can even use some "unexpected action" like a noise, a fake fall, or phrase, to orient the child that you are approaching. You can even use an ever-increasing drumbeat, that stays soft and steady when you are standing still, but gets louder and faster as you approach.

☐ STEP 3
If the child is willing, you should reverse roles.

Variations:

If you want to increase the excitement and don't mind getting a bit wet, you can provide both yourself and the child with small water pistols. Instead of freezing you with his eyes, he gets to squirt you and of course, if you make it all the way you get to squirt him. Make sure the child knows he is not allowed to leave the carpet square where he is sitting. This is not a game of chase.

Obstacles/Opportunities:

Make sure that you do not choose "sneaky" activity that the child enjoys. Otherwise you might find yourself playing a different version of the game, where the child deliberately averts his gaze, so you can successfully sneak up on him. This is an interesting variation. But make sure it is the one you want!

LEVEL I, STAGE 2, ACTIVITY 22

Disappearing Coach

ACTIVITY HIGHLIGHTS
° Referencing adults for safety and security
° Increased vigilance

Summary:

Children may experience anxiety and frustration because they have not learned to keep track of the whereabouts of important adults. The world is a confusing place yet they lack a natural wariness of unfamiliar places, leading to an inability to judge safety. These children have the expectation that their parents will always be there, thus taking no responsibility for visually checking in or moving carefully alongside adults. These children are the "wanderers" and it is not unusual for them to run off in a busy parking lot or mall. This exercise is designed to increase a child's understanding that he must visually attend to his parent's whereabouts, or else!

Participants:

Parent and child.

Getting Ready:

You will need a large pile of beanbag chairs scattered throughout a room. The activity is best done in a very dim room, where you will be able to "disappear" quickly from a child who does not watch carefully.

Coaching Instructions:

This activity has five steps:

☐ STEP 1

Introduce the activity by sitting at a small bare table with the child. Ask the child, "Do you want to fly?" referring to the "Swing and Fly" exercise in Stage 1.

☐ STEP 2

Take the child's hand and move toward a pile of beanbag chairs. Approximately five feet from the beanbags suddenly run away and hide within close proximity of the child.

☐ STEP 3

The child may not immediately notice your disappearance but will quickly realize that there will be no "flying" without you. Usually the child will begin to retrace steps to find you. If, after about 30 seconds, he cannot find you, whisper his name. If he still does not find you, wave a small beam of light in the air using a flashlight.

☐ STEP 4

Once you are found, hug the child with exaggerated excitement and again say, "Time to fly?" Now, complete your journey to the beanbags.

☐ STEP 5

Continue to hide more frequently as the child becomes more competent and wary of your disappearance.

Variations:

An amusing variation, attributed to the father of one our patients, requires a full-size trampoline and music. Parent and child bounce together on the trampoline. As you bounce, face each other and bounce higher and higher in time to the music. If the child loses his visual connection with you, "disappear" under the trampoline until found.

An additional variation requires a wheelbarrow or supermarket shopping cart. The child should sit facing you at eye level. Begin this activity by running in an exciting zigzag pattern and laughing with the child as you do so. When the child's gaze shifts from your face, crouch under the shopping cart or wheelbarrow. Return to the activity only after the child has repaired the disconnection, usually through sound or physical touch. Continue this activity, enjoying shared laughter with the child and continuing to hide when referencing is lost.

Obstacles/Opportunities:

Highly verbal, controlling children may resist the introduction of delays such as these. Tantrums can make learning difficult and if these become prominent, most likely this activity has been taught prematurely. Go back and review Stage 1 objectives before attempting this one again. The opportunities for using this activity to work on a child's ability to access facial information are endless. Never hide from a child outside their visual range or in areas where he might bolt into an unsafe situation.

LEVEL I, STAGE 2, ACTIVITY 23

Save Me

ACTIVITY HIGHLIGHTS

° Social referencing for safety and security

Summary:

We have all enjoyed the emotional contagion generated from a campfire story. The controlled scariness creates an unparalleled level of excitement and enhances emotional bonding. One of our favorite games replicates this excitement. "Save Me"(from the monster) provides excitement generated from anticipating the appearance of the monster. The enjoyment of the activity is enhanced by the sense of competence children feel when they are successful in scaring off the monster. The point of the activity is lost however, if time is not taken to teach the child to visually shift gaze between the mountain and the Coach at three crucial junctures: prior to calling the monster, while the mountain shakes and when the monster emerges.

Participants:

Two Coaches and child.

Getting Ready:

This activity requires eight beanbag chairs, two rectangular pieces of carpet and a set of exciting but unthreatening masks. The beanbag chairs are piled high to form a "mountain" barrier. This mountain hides the "monster" and the masks. On the opposite side of the mountain the child and Coach sit on carpet squares facing the mountain.

Coaching Instructions:

There are five steps in this exercise:

☐ STEP 1

The "monster" begins the drama by crouching behind the beanbags and placing a mask on his face. He begins to make ominous growling noises. The Coach, seated next to the child exclaims, "It's the monster. Oh no. What are we going to do?" They may hold each other tightly, increasing the tension and shifting their gaze from each other's face to the mountain of beanbags.

☐ STEP 2

From behind the mountain, the monster shouts, "What is your name little boy (girl)?" When the child answers, the monster replies, "(Name). I am going to get you and eat you." The monster begins to shake the mountain while making horrible noises.

☐ STEP 3

Suddenly, without warning, the monster, wearing a mask, comes out from behind the mountain he tries to grab the child and drag him back behind the beanbags to his mountain, which is the only place he can eat the child. The monster should narrate this as he is pursuing the child, "I must get you and take you to my mountain. I can only eat you in the mountain. I am so hungry! Stop and let me eat you!"

☐ STEP 4

The Coach and child work together to defeat the monster. The monster grabs the child, takes him out of the Coach's grasp and begins to take him away. The Coach yells, "I will save you from the monster." He grabs the child back and says, "Monster, monster go back to your mountain." These special words defeat the monster and he is forced to return to his mountain. As he returns he says to the pair "Now, I must go away. I cannot return until you say, "Monster, monster, come down from the mountain."

☐ STEP 5

The Coach and child return to their carpet square. The monster is back behind the mountain. The Coach asks the child if he wants to say the words to summon the monster – "Monster, monster come down from the mountain." Eventually Coach and child will say the words and the game will begin again.

Variations:

The Coach and child can also become "monsters" in the mountain and gang up on their opponent. In order to work as a "monster team" the child will need to accept the mask chosen for him and use non-verbal cues from his Coach in order to know when to shake the mountain and attack.

The monster may also become more unpredictable. For example, the game has built in a predictable sequence of shaking the mountain prior to the appearance of the monster. On occasion the monster should simply jump out without shaking the mountain. To prevent the activity from becoming too predictable and mundane, the monster should also appear from unpredictable places: sometimes over the top of the mountain, from either side or from another location entirely

Obstacles/Opportunities:

Fear of masks should be carefully analyzed. While it is important to find unpredictable "masks" to cover the face, we believe Coaches should always stay away from the gory ones, even when such things do not easily frighten the child. Another obstacle that occasionally presents difficulty is the desire of the child to grab the masks and take over the game. Careful introduction and staging of the game from the beginning will usually prevent this.

LEVEL I, STAGE 2, ACTIVITY 24

Non-Verbal Towers

ACTIVITY HIGHLIGHTS
° Sensitivity to non-verbal communication
° Introduction to social referencing

Summary:

What distinguishes referencing from eye contact is that referencing is all about looking at your social partner's face to gain important information about what he is feeling, perceiving or desiring. In this introduction to non-verbal communication we teach the value of referencing our faces not through instruction but through direct experience. We do not explain our actions in advance, but rather communicate a clear invitation for the child to read our faces and extract necessary information.

Participants:

Coach and child.

Getting Ready:

All you need is a pile of building blocks. The child must be ready to sit across from you at a table without running away.

Coaching Instructions:

This activity has three steps:

☐ STEP 1

Place three blocks in a row on your side of the table. Now place your hands behind your back in an exaggerated fashion, so that the child can see that you will not have use of your hands.

☐ STEP 2

Now use sound effects, head movements, nods, head shakes and facial expressions, but without using any words, to communicate to the child that you want him to take one of the three blocks. See if you can communicate that you want him to place the block in front of him. Only point if you absolutely have to. When he has placed the block in front of him, repeat the process with another block. Now see if you can communicate for the child to place the second block on top of the first. Try the same thing with a third block.

☐ STEP 3

Take out five blocks and repeat the procedure to create a five-block tower in front of the child. Make sure that the child is taking the block that you are specifically indicating.

Variations:

Try and reverse this activity if the child is willing to do so. Forbid the child from saying any words, but allow him to use pointing in addition to sounds and facial expressions.

Obstacles/Opportunities:

If the child is oblivious to your sound effects, head movement and points, you may initially require a second Coach who will turn the child's head in the right direction so that he will notice your communication. If this occurs it is an indication that you need to focus more on Stage 1 activities.

LEVEL I, STAGE 2, ACTIVITY 25

Follow my Eyes to the Prize

ACTIVITY HIGHLIGHTS
° Following the eye gaze of social partners
° Using non-verbal cues for problem solving

Summary:

People often talk about the importance of eye contact. We believe that merely teaching someone to stare at other people's eyes leads to a social "dead-end." Our emphasis is to teach children all of the various payoffs they accrue from watching the eyes and faces and bodies of social partners. This activity provides one key reason for watching another's eyes – they can often lead you to some very interesting things!

Participants:

Coach and child. An Assistant Coach is needed if the child cannot be trusted to leave the room, wait right outside and return when requested.

Getting Ready:

You will need six beanbag chairs, two carpet squares and a number of small objects that might be interesting to the child. Scatter beanbags throughout the room.

Coaching Instructions:

The activity has three steps:

☐ STEP 1

Explain to the child that his job is to find a hidden object. Show him the object prior to his leaving the room. He will be leaving the room and when he returns, he is to enter and sit on the carpet square next to you. Explain that that he only has one chance to look for the object. The clue to the object's location can be found only on your face. While the Novice is out of the room, place an object under a beanbag.

☐ STEP 2

The child now returns to the room and is seated in a side-by-side position next to you. Tell the child not to begin searching until after you indicate it is time to get up. Make sure he is referencing your face. In a highly exaggerated manner, first look at the child, smile broadly and then intensely look at the beanbag where the object is hidden. Now signal the child to begin searching. If the child is unable to follow your gaze and begins to search in another location, immediately stop him and return him to the carpet square. This time point to the correct beanbag and then signal the child to begin searching. Keep working on this exercise until he can easily follow your gaze to the indicated object.

☐ STEP 3

Once the child is able to find the prize easily, roles are reversed so that the child should hide the object while you are out of the room, wait for you to return, and be seated and gazing toward the hiding place indicating where you should look for it.

Variations:

When you are both ready, you can modify this activity to become "Follow my Face to the Prize." In this variation, your degree of smiling and frowning provides information to the child about how close or far he is to the object. The broader your smile, the "warmer" the child is to the prize. The broader the frown, the "colder" he is becoming. We also include "Follow the Sound of my Voice." Without any words, use your voice volume and tone to indicate if the child is "hot" or "cold" while he is searching.

Obstacles and Opportunities:

If the child does not visually reference, you will need to spend time teaching him to understand the meaning of pointing and to follow your pointing to an object. Remember to begin by pointing to objects that are very close and gradually increasing the distance.

LEVEL I, STAGE 2, ACTIVITY 26

Trading Places

ACTIVITY HIGHLIGHTS

° Rapid observation of facial expressions
° Inhibiting actions based on non-verbal information

Summary:

We continue with the theme of referencing non-verbal information but now we engage in a much more fluid activity. We want children to learn to check the facial expressions of social partners rapidly. "Trading Places" is a fast moving activity that can be a great deal of fun if you maintain a heightened level of excitement.

Participants:

Coach and child.

Getting Ready:

You need two beanbag chairs, positioned several feet apart.

Coaching Instructions:

Begin by sitting on beanbag chairs, facing each other. Teach the child that when you both nod, it is a signal to change places and run to each other's beanbag chair. If either of you shakes his head in a "no" expression, you cannot trade places. Your response should be unpredictable but not delayed to the point that the activity is no longer fun. Exaggerated expressions should signal a trade of places.

Once the child understands the game add an additional person, either an Assistant Coach, or another child, depending upon the needs of the first child. Now the game will become interesting. For anyone to move, all three participants must nod their heads "yes" at the same time.

Variations

If the child is really proficient at this game, you can play a version where first participants first hide behind beanbag chairs and then trade places. The Coach and child each crouch down behind a pile of several beanbags. They peek their heads up and trade places only when each has non-verbally agreed to do so.

Obstacles/Opportunities:

Problems with attention, including distractibility and impulsivity, can detract and interfere with this game. If this is the case use two Coaches and assign one to sit next to the child and help with the wait. While attention can be an obstacle, this activity provides an opportunity to learn the heightened excitement that stems from waiting and referencing.

Mother May I

2

ACTIVITY HIGHLIGHTS
° Visually referencing before engaging in activities
° Using non-verbal responses for decision making

Summary:

This childhood classic precedes television and computer games and was a staple of peer interactions years ago. Once learned, it can include siblings or classmates as well. Those who remember "Mother May I" recall that at least two participants lined up side by side at a starting line with a goal of reaching an end line first. A third player assumes the role of "mother" and directs the players to take different types of steps towards the goal. There are giant steps, baby steps and more creative types including scissor steps, snake steps and bird steps. Movement toward the goal relies on remembereing to first ask " Mother, may I take a _____ step?" and awaiting an answer. Failure to do so results in having to return to the start line. With our modifications, which substitute visual referencing for verbal responses, this game teaches the child to accurately read facial expressions and make choices depending on the expression of the "Mother" following her request.

Participants:

Coach and child.

Getting Ready:

Two carpet squares should be placed eight to ten feet apart. For non-verbal children, the following pictures should be available: giant, baby, scissors, snake and bird. Make sure that non-verbal children know how to use the cards to indicate what type of step they wish to make. You can eliminate cards for children who are confused by any particular step.

Coaching Instructions:

This activity has four steps:

☐ STEP 1

The child learns the physical actions related to each term or picture. Giant steps consist of large noisy steps. Baby steps are made of tiptoes. Scissor steps move in a zigzag motion. Snake steps are a belly crawl. Bird steps combine tiptoes and flapping hands.

☐ STEP 2

The child stands on his carpet square facing the Coach. Teach the child the regular version of the game.

☐ STEP 3

When the child is proficient enough, tell him that you are now making a change. Only your face will tell him if the request has been approved. Your smile means that you can take the requested step. Your frown indicates that another step must be requested. If the child proceeds to move following a frown, he or she must take a giant step backwards.

☐ STEP 4

If you believe the child is ready, reverse roles and see if the child can be the "Mother."

Variations:

Once the child learns this activity he may want to participate in it with siblings. If competition undermines the fun of the game, participants may all move together. For example, the leader might say, "Everyone take three snake steps." The children should visually reference you as a group and wait for your facial response. Once mastered, children will not only wait for you to signal, but learn to signal each other before moving the requisite steps.

Obstacles/Opportunities:

Gross motor difficulties may make this activity difficult for some children. Accuracy of movement, however, is not necessary. The game is to be played for fun and so the steps should be revised and fluidity of movement related to the success of the exercise. This activity easily includes other family members.

LEVEL I, STAGE 2, ACTIVITY 28

You Lose

ACTIVITY HIGHLIGHTS

° Visually referencing before engaging in activities
° Using nonverbal responses for decision making
° Visually referencing for evaluation
° Introducing humor and shared laughter into unexpected outcomes

Summary:

"You Lose" emphasizes to the child that the fun of an interaction is in our shared experience and not in winning. Teaching the child to enjoy a game that is not exactly what it seems makes this game more exciting. It is usually important to use auditory distraction to make your whereabouts unknown. For example, pocket change can be rattled in one place before you move to another.

Participants:

Coach and child.

Getting Ready:

For this activity, the child should sit in the middle of a ring of beanbag chairs. Beanbag chairs should be piled higher than the child's head so that you cannot be seen. Dim the lights to make it even more interesting.

Coaching Instructions:

This activity has four simple steps:

☐ STEP 1

Tell the child to cover his eyes, count to ten and listen carefully in order to determine where you are hiding. He cannot peek out over the pile of beanbags and must use only his hearing to determine your location.

☐ STEP 2

As the child counts, circle the beanbags, being as sneaky as possible and finally hide behind one before he reaches ten.

☐ STEP 3

When he reaches "ten," he must remain seated and point to the location where he thinks you have hidden.

☐ STEP 4

Suddenly, jump up from a different location and shout, "You lose!" Laugh together and then start the next round. After several trials it is your turn to get in the middle and the child's turn to hide.

Variations:

Try playing a simple game where the sole purpose is to lose as quickly as you can. Turning losing into winning is an excellent way to defuse a "must win" attitude.

Obstacles/Opportunities:

The intense need to win can make this game frustrating if not introduced correctly. Exaggerated excitement related to the mistaken location, usually undermines this unproductive tendency. Also, it is important to keep your words light-hearted and funny so that the child understands that the important information is on your face and not in your words.

LEVEL I, STAGE 2, ACTIVITY 29

Silent Card Game

ACTIVITY HIGHLIGHTS
° Developing non-verbal expression
° Teaching cooperative teamwork

Summary:

This is our first "teamwork" activity. It is also the most difficult exercise presented so far and the one with the most potential for frustration. Children must practice reading and sending non-verbal signals to help their team win the game.

Participants:

Two Coaches and two children.

Getting Ready:

You will need a deck of "animal cards" which contain animals whose noises and appearance are easy to mimic. Make sure that the child first learns to play the normal version of the game "Go Fish" prior to beginning this activity. For those who do not know the game, Go Fish begins with each partner being dealt several cards which are not revealed to the other player. Players attempt to obtain a set of three of the same type of card. When they have three of a kind, they can lay that set down. The first player to lay all of his cards down wins. Players obtain new cards by asking the other player if they have a specific type of card ("Do you have any Zebras?") The other player must hand over the card if he has it. However, if he does not have it he says, "Go Fish." The other player must begin picking cards from the deck and keeping them until he picks the card he requesred.

Coaching Instructions:

Show the child the deck of animal cards. Teach him to play the regular version of Go Fish. When he has a degree of proficiency, teach him to play our version called "Teamwork Go Fish." The goal is to get three of a kind so that you can "play" the threesome and get them out of your hand. In this version, you and the child are playing as a two-person team and not against one another. There are two roles. Initially you take the role of "Player" and the child takes the role of "Holder." The child must guess which card you want by reading your non-verbal gestures, noises and facial expressions. The "Player" has to make the sets so that they can be played. The "Holder" holds the deck of cards and must provide the right card to the "Player." The "Player" can see the "Holder's" cards, but the "Holder" should not be allowed to see the unfinished sets that the "Player" has in his hand. You can use gestures, animal noises and miming to ask for a card (but

2

no pointing) and the child can only use non-verbal communication to respond (the child can point to a card). If the child gives you the wrong card he must "Go Fish" and pick cards from the deck until you non-verbally indicate to the child that he has picked the one you were asking for. Make sure that the child gets to pracice both the "Player" and "Holder" roles.

Variations:

After children become proficient, you can play the more advanced version where neither the "Player" nor the "Holder" can see the other's cards.

Obstacles/Opportunities:

You will not be able to do this activity with children who cannot tolerate the frustration caused by your mistakes, even when you try your hardest. You may want to return to this activity after the child works on frustration.

LEVEL I, STAGE 2, ACTIVITY 30

Stay Tuned to this Station

ACTIVITY HIGHLIGHTS
° Attending to background information
° Rapid attention shifting
° Monitor changing environmental demands
° Visual vigilance

Summary:

The skills of rapidly shifting attention to a source of communication and monitoring the demands of the environment are crucial to developing social competence. This activity, like the ones before and after should be performed over extended periods of time. While there is no reason that you cannot employ this method in a home setting, we specifically designed it for use in schools. We wanted to develop a method to teach students to continually monitor their environments, even while engaged in work or enjoyable activities.

Participants:

This method requires one Coach. It can be conducted in any classroom or home setting.

Getting Ready:

Warning: This activity clearly requires a bit of technical skill. Skip it if you are a technophobe! Here is what you will need:

1. You will need a TV or video monitor large enough for all students to observe clearly, without getting out of their seats. Remember to place the monitor where Novices must shift their gaze to view the information being presented.

2. You need to have a computer hook-up to the monitor. Most laptops already come configured to connect to a larger monitor.

3. You will need to know how to construct simple "slides" that you can select to display on the monitor. While theoretically you can use a word processing program to do this, we highly recommend using a presentation program such as Microsoft PowerPoint. PowerPoint allows you to prepare programmed shows, so that you can automatically present a series of slides at intervals and presentation lengths of your choosing, without having to constantly click your mouse or select screens.

4. You will need to mix up your presentation of slides so that students do not learn that their slide appears at any specific interval or sequence. We recommend that you do this daily, as it only requires a few seconds.

5. Each student will need a worksheet to record or select which code he has observed on the screen. Students can check off a symbol, or write in the code. If the student is not yet reading he will need a recording form or a sheet with copies of different symbols, so that he can select the symbol that is flashed on the screen.

6. Finally, Novices will need to be working on competing tasks such as school assignments, while the slide show is "running." It is best if Novices have already learned to work independently from a simple activity schedule.

Coaching Instructions:

There are a total of seven steps:

☐ STEP 1

If you are using PowerPoint, place a simple audio signal of your choosing to sound for one second each time a slide is presented on the screen. Next, determine the proper interval to display a slide. Start with an interval that is long enough to ensure a high degree of success. Finally, decide upon the frequency with which slides will be presented. You want to make sure that slides are not appearing so often as to make concentrating on any other activity impossible.

☐ STEP 2

Once you determine the proper signal and interval, you will need to construct simple "basic" slides for each student. Each slide can have a specific color, border and image to help the Novice rapidly discriminate if the message is for them. PowerPoint includes a number of slide "themes." You can simply select a unique theme for each student. Depending upon the Novice's reading ability, their slides should contain his name, the student's photo, or a similar symbol. You should create four screens for each student, with a different code word or picture (code symbol) on each screen.

☐ STEP 3

Now you will "shape" students to shift attention to the monitor following the audio signal. Instruct students that each time their hear the tone, it means that there is a message for one of them. If they understand, you can explain that the monitor will serve as their group "e-mail" from you. They should look at the monitor, to see if the message is for them. If the message is for them, it will contain a special code. If they copy down the code correctly, or check off the symbol, they earn points they can use for rewards. But, if they want the points, they also have to complete all of their assigned work. They cannot spend their time looking at the monitor. Make sure that students know that nothing will be displayed on the monitor if any student is staring at it. Also, make sure that your message interval is not so rapid as to encourage constant observation.

☐ STEP 4

As students become more proficient, reward them for tracking the correct order of codes in the sequence in which they appear. You can also increase intervals between screen presentations and decrease the length of each presentation.

☐ STEP 5

When students are routinely referencing the monitor after hearing the signal, you are ready to display important information. Begin interspersing codes with instructions and directives to specific students. Explain that they can obtain a reward if they can read and follow the instructions on the screen. Gradually fade out the code screens and substitute instruction screens. Begin with very simple instructions, such as "sharpen your pencil" or "do the problem on page 5." As the student is successful, the instruction screens can tell students to make social overtures to a specific student, check in with the Coach's face to ensure she is happy with the student's performance and to engage in a number of other social actions.

☐ STEP 6

When students are proficient at using the instruction screens, it is time to gradually fade out the auditory "cue" signal and teach students to shift attention on their own, to periodically monitor messages. Begin providing some slides with an accompanying sound and others with no sound. Provide "bonus" points for Novices who attend to the non-cued messages, while still completing their assignments. Gradually fade out the sounds, as students take more responsibility for referencing the screen themselves.

☐ STEP 7

Begin to add screens that provide praise, so that you can gradually fade out external reinforcements.

Variations:

You can use this method for an infinite number of instructions and messages to students. If you would like to wean students away from the monitor, start substituting video images with signs on your desk. Students have to periodically stop what they are doing and reference the sign to obtain a reward and later to obtain important information. You can initially use the auditory signal to alert students that it is time to attend. Remember to gradually fade out the signal, so students do not remain prompt dependent.

Obstacles/Opportunities:

As we stated earlier, this is not an activity for technophobes. This is a great opportunity for students and parents to teach the student to stop being "prompt dependent." Because it is a method that you can employ all day long, it is highly effective in teaching the habit of rapid attention shifting and eventually independent monitoring of the social environment.

STAGE 3: REGULATE

Goals and Objectives

With attention and referencing established, children are now ready to learn the "nuts and bolts" of becoming good Apprentices. Stages 3 and 4 cover the essential elements that prepare the child to eventually become a relationship partner. The goal of Stage 3 is establishing a Master–Apprentice relationship, where the child is carefully referencing his or her Coach for instruction and guidance. Now the child will be referencing you to learn how to become a more competent person in his actions with the social and object worlds.

Activity Summary

Initial activities focus on the elements of establishing a Novice-Master relationship for learning. The child functions as an assistant, accepting the limited role provided by you to aid him in whatever activity he is engaged in. Gradually he is given his own parallel activity and works on matching his actions with yours. Next, you move into a "Guiding" function, where the child is required to actively reference you and determine what he should be doing next. Along with guiding proper actions, children learn to accept your guidance to determine the proper speed and quality for their work efforts. Stage 3 ends with exercises focusing on making transitions and understanding basic emotional expressions. Both are essential skills for becoming an Apprentice.

Critical Tips

- Carefully transition the Novice from an assistant to a parallel role.

- Do not allow the child to insert his own variations yet.

- Remember to teach the concept of "good enough" but not perfect work.

- Attention shifting will become less difficult but still requires practice.

- Practice "Self Talk" out loud every time you are with the Novice.

- Teach transitions slowly and carefully.

LEVEL I, STAGE 3, ACTIVITY 31

Assistant

ACTIVITY HIGHLIGHTS
- Following a designated activity role
- Functioning in an assistant position
- Accepting instructions

Summary:

Any Apprentice worth his salt starts out as an assistant to a Master, doing whatever is required of him. These are often simple tasks. Gradually the Apprentice is given the opportunity to do the more important work, but under close supervision and only if he can duplicate the actions of the Master. Finally, the Apprentice may be taught to function independently. In this activity, the Novice serves as an assistant, providing the materials needed for the project, while the Coach functions as both "builder" and "architect."

Participants:

Coach and child.

Getting Ready:

For most children you will need a set of regular wooden building blocks. Some seven- and eight-year-olds might require the additional challenge of a wooden "Blocks and Marbles" set. Instructions for the "Blocks and Marbles" activity are found in the "Variations" section.

Coaching Instructions:

Explain to the child that you will be building a house with blocks. His job is to supply you with the parts you need. Your job is to build the house. If he does well, you will teach him to build his own house. Lay out the different blocks needed to build the house. Make it clear that you are not in a teaching role. Rather you are working together to build a specific design for the house that you have chosen. The child is in charge of the "parts department." Each time you need a block, you will request the specific block from the child, who will hand it to you. As you work, be sure to narrate your actions out loud. Narrate how you are making decisions, why you need the parts you request, when you are working slowly and carefully and when you are less precise. When you reach a good stopping point, declare the house finished and take a photograph of it. Your house will be built in a highly structured sequence. We will use this same sequence for building in future activities. Try not to vary it unless you must simplify it for a younger child. Practice this activity as many times as needed until the child recognizes each step. Again, make sure to clearly and slowly narrate each action you are taking.

☐ STEP 1

Four rectangular blocks are placed together to form a 2 x 2 square. These make up the floor.

☐ STEP 2

Four identical rectangular blocks and two square blocks, half the size of the rectangles, are placed on top of the "floor" blocks along their perimeter. These blocks are laid on their narrow sides and used to make the first floor walls of the house. The two square blocks are placed on either end of one side of the structure, leaving room between them for a pretend front doorway.

☐ STEP 3

Three additional rectangular blocks are placed directly on top of their mates and used to form the second floor. A fourth rectangular block is placed on top of the smaller first floor square blocks. Now the door should be framed out./

☐ STEP 4

Four rectangular blocks are placed across the top of the "walls" to make a flat roof. The windows should now be framed.

☐ STEP 5

If you like you can add a chimney.

Variations:

There are many different activities where children can practice functioning as assistants. These can include real-life home repair, gardening or any other projects of this nature.

Blocks and Marbles Variation:

Explain to the child that you will be building a marble maze. His job is to supply you with the parts you need. Your job is to build the maze. If he does well, you will teach him to build his own maze. Lay out the different blocks needed to build the maze. Make sure that you provide simple names for the different types of blocks – "small ramp," "medium-size ramp," "large tower block," etc. Make it clear that you are not in a teaching role. Rather you are working together to build a specific design that you have chosen. The child is in charge of the "parts department." Each time you need a block, you will request the specific block to the Novice, who will hand it to you. Periodically allow the child to "test" the maze by rolling marbles down it, to make sure that it works. As you work, be sure to narrate your actions out loud. Narrate how you are making decisions, why you need the parts you request, when you work slowly and carefully and when you are less precise. After you have reached a good stopping point, declare the maze finished and take a photograph of it.

Obstacles/Opportunities:

We hope this activity teaches children to enjoy participating as a team member working toward a common goal.

LEVEL I, STAGE 3, ACTIVITY 32

Bill Ding

ACTIVITY HIGHLIGHTS

° Carefully observing to match your actions with a social partner

Summary:

There are games that have met their demise, crushed into oblivion by the competitive high energy, fast paced, video and computer games. Bill Ding is, unfortunately, one of those that has been lost, but it can still be ordered over the Internet. This is an extremely clever building game. It consists of one white stationary clown and four duos of clown-like yellow, red, blue and green men with notches that provide the means for constructing interlocking sculptures. Each clown has notches on his feet, arms, shoulders head and legs so that he can hang upside down, right side up or sideways onto each of the other clowns.

Participants:

Coach and child.

Getting Ready:

Coach and child sit side by side at a small table. Materials are in a small box under the table next to the Coach.

Coaching Instructions:

The activity has five steps:

☐ STEP 1

Begin by demonstrating the various ways the clown-like figures can be attached to each other. Narration accompanies each demonstration. For example, "Look, he's hanging by his feet. I'll make this one do the same."

☐ STEP 2

Place the white stationary Bill Ding in place. Now, choose a yellow clown and place him on the white Bill Ding.

☐ STEP 3

Hand the other yellow clowns to the child and indicate that he should imitate you.

☐ STEP 4

Following the completion of the sculpture you and the child on a predetermined count, such as eight, try to blow the sculpture over.

☐ STEP 5

The collapsing of the Bill Ding figures signals a moment of shared laughter before beginning again.

Variations:

You can now use Bill Ding along with "Building a House" as activities in this stage to teach being an assistant, matching, pacing and guiding. Once the child is familiar with the variety of ways the clowns can be reconfigured to make a sculpture, you may create new sculptures. To begin, place two matching clowns on the stationary figure. The child will add two matching clowns to the sculpture. Turn taking continues until the sculpture is complete at which time you should count and blow it over.

Obstacles and Opportunities:

Impulsivity can interfere with shared enjoyment during the crash of the Bill Ding figures. If a child tries to knock the clowns over with his hands prior to jointly blowing them over, return to the beginning of the game and let him practice "watching" so that the game will continue appropriately.

LEVEL I, STAGE 3, ACTIVITY 33

Matching

ACTIVITY HIGHLIGHTS
° Engaging in careful observation for learning
° Carefully matching adult's actions
° Observing "Self Talk" of adults

Summary:

Now that the child has demonstrated he can be a good assistant, it is time to move on to learning how to match the Master's actions. Now, the child and Master will work side by side. The child must continually reference the actions of the Master and attempt to duplicate them. Initially he will learn to duplicate the sequence and selection of blocks.

Participants:

Coach and child.

Getting Ready:

For this activity you will require enough blocks to construct two identical houses as per the instructions in the "Assistant" exercise. It is also helpful to have two Bill Ding sets. Once again you might need two Blocks and Marbles sets for older children.

Coaching Instructions:

This activity has three simple steps:

☐ STEP 1

Explain to the child that he has now graduated from Assistant to Novice Builder. This means that he will be allowed to work with his own materials. However, he must carefully watch your actions and do just as you do. He must select the same blocks as you do and place them in exactly the same places. Each time you take an action, he must wait to make sure he knows what you are doing, before he tries to do it himself. He is not allowed to make any changes in the structure. Make sure that you talk out loud to yourself, slowly and clearly while you work. Narrate every action that you take, even if it appears minor, like straightening one of the blocks, and make sure that the child duplicates the action. Make sure you narrate the reasons for every action, but be careful not to narrate so specifically that the child has no need to look at your actions.

☐ STEP 2

Now work on building a house, exactly as you did it in the "Assistant" activity. Now you and the child are side by side, each with his own set of blocks. If the child it not waiting to duplicate your actions, stop immediately and dismantle what he has done differently. If the child has memorized the sequence and does not need to reference you to duplicate your efforts, begin systematically adding variations and changes to make sure he has to keep looking.

☐ STEP 3

Alternate house building with constructing the Bill Ding figures.

Variations:

You can try this same activity while baking a cake, or following a recipe.

Obstacles/Opportunities:

Impulsive children will have difficulty with this task. They will state that they know what you are going to do, even before you are finished doing it. Remember to stop their action and require that they wait until you have taken your action, prior to attempting to duplicate it. Other children will believe that they can improve on the structure and want to do it their own way. Do not accept any variations at this stage.

Guiding

ACTIVITY HIGHLIGHTS
° Accepting guidance
° Rapidly shifting attention
° Working independently

Summary:

Now the child is ready to learn to work more independently and you can move into a "coaching/guiding" position. For the Novice, the challenge is to allow you to remain in a primary role, even while they are fully engaged with the project.

Participants:

Coach and child.

Getting Ready:

Completion of the prior three activities is essential. You will need one Blocks Set and one Bill Ding set if you can get it. You will also require a small LEGO construction set, appropriate to the child's age.

Coaching Instructions:

This activity has five steps:

☐ STEP 1

Sit behind the child and serve a guiding role. Initially instruct the child on how specifically you want the house to be constructed. Use the instructions from the "Assistant" activity. Do not vary them unless the child has memorized them and can follow the sequence without you. In that case, use a totally different sequence to build the house. In this initial step, you guide the child's actions in each step of the construction, however, do not handle the materials directly.

☐ STEP 2

When the child is working to your specifications, it is time to teach him to work independently on a small set of written/pictorial instructions and then stop for more instructions. If you like, you can use a small LEGO kit for this step.

☐ STEP 3

Guide the child to exert a proper level of care. Instruct the child to work at the pace that you indicate is correct

☐ STEP 4

Establish the completion point for the project and indicate to the child when the project is completed to your satisfaction.

☐ STEP 5

The frequency of stopping points and evaluating points is gradually decreased, as the Novice demonstrates that he can work more independently.

Variations:

Like the other two activities, it is important that guiding be done with a variety of activities.

Obstacles/Opportunities:

The child may have difficulty shifting attention when he is primarily interacting with materials and you are out of direct visual sight. If this is the case, return to a side-by-side position, next to the child.

LEVEL I, STAGE 3, ACTIVITY 35

Transition

ACTIVITY HIGHLIGHTS
° Accepting changes in routine
° Accepting insertion of new elements into a schedule of activities
° Transitioning from one activity to another
° Stopping activities and transitioning, even when they are not completed

Summary:

This activity begins to prepare the child for the constant changes and transitions that occur in all relationship encounters. In this exercise we focus on four basic types of transitions: Following an activity schedule where children move seamlessly from one activity to another, inserting and omitting elements of an activity, inserting and omitting activities in a schedule and finally, stopping one activity in mid-stream and moving on to another without coming back to complete the first.

Participants:

Coach and child.

Getting Ready:

Before beginning this activity, provide children with some experience in understanding and following simple daily activity schedules. Choose schedules that are suited to their developmental level. The TEACCH program of the University of North Carolina, directed by Dr. Gary Mesibov, presents excellent guidelines for constructing and teaching children to use various kinds of activity schedules (*www.teacch.com*). You should prepare two activity schedules that are appropriate for the child. Make sure the activities are affixed to the schedule with Velcro, so you can remove and move them around when needed.

Coaching Instructions:

This activity has six steps:

☐ STEP 1

Children learn to use an activity schedule that you have prepared. The schedule should simply outline their shared activities for a period of time. Choose a time interval that is easily manageable for the child but that is long enough to contain several different activities. Make sure the activities are not ones that easily distract the child. There is no need to include a time factor in the schedule. A simple sequence of activities, indicating where the child should go when "finished" with a prior activity, is sufficient.

☐ STEP 2

Create a second schedule that contains completely different activities. Now you are going to teach the child to use each of the schedules on alternate days (for younger children you may use the two schedules as alternate periods of the same day). Explain to the child that now there is an "A" schedule and a "B" schedule. You will alternate using each. Begin alternating the two schedules on a regular basis. Make sure the child can easily note which schedule is being used. Make sure to clearly define what "finished" is for each of the activities in a manner that is understandable to the child.

☐ STEP 3

Affix five alternating "A" and "B" schedules to the wall in a left-to-right fashion. Place a special symbol right over the schedule to indicate which one you are using that day. After one or two weeks, bring the child to the schedules and change the order of schedules so that there are two "A" days followed by two "B" days and so on. After the child has success with this, make more changes in schedule alternation.

☐ STEP 4

After the Novice can transition fluidly from "A" to "B" and has finished at least one activity to your specifications, place the two schedules side-by-side. Stand in front of them with the child and, while he is watching, choose an activity from the "A" schedule that has been completed. Remove the activity and place it on a "finished" chart on the wall. Now go to the child's "future" schedule, remove one activity and place it in the empty space on the "A" schedule. Do the same thing at a later time with the "B" schedule.

☐ STEP 5

When the child is ready, choose an item from the "A" schedule that is not yet finished and remove it. Go to the "future" schedule and remove one activity.

Insert the activity in its place. Now go to the "B" schedule and remove one activity that has been finished. Put the finished activity on the "finished" chart. Replace it with the unfinished "A" schedule activity you just removed.

☐ STEP 6

Now make sure that the identical activity is placed on both schedules. Next to the activity name, provide a short description (or picture) of how the activity should be "finished." Make sure that the description in the "A" version of the activity is completely different than in the "B" version. The "A" activity is to be considered finished at a later stage of completion than its "B" version. For example the "A" version of a puzzle will define finished as putting all the pieces together. The "B" version will specify in advance that the Novice is finished when he places five pieces correctly in the puzzle. Now make the "A" version finish at the same point as the "B" version. Keep varying this.

Variations:

You can help the child adjust to unforeseen schedule changes and postponements using the same method. Draw a monthly "events" calendar on a large whiteboard. Place all the events that are important to the child on the calendar. Any time an activity has to be delayed or postponed demonstrate this to the child on the whiteboard by circling the activity with a marker on the date it was originally to take place, writing in the activity at the new date and time, and drawing a line to signify the movement of the activity from one date to another. Finally, erase the original activity and the connecting lines when the Novice demonstrates he understands the transition. You can also do this with last-minute daily activity time changes.

Obstacles/Opportunities:

The variation presented above is a great way of helping children who become fixated on events having to occur exactly when they expected them. While this will not satisfy everyone, many "melt-downs" occur because the child cannot readily grasp that the expected event has not disappeared, it has simply moved to a new location in time.

Incomplete Completion

ACTIVITY HIGHLIGHTS

° Learning to define activity completion through social referencing

° Learning that being "finished" is a relative and not absolute term

Summary:

Many of our children define the completion of an activity by their own standards. Others are completely "bound" by the elements of the activity and cannot move away from it, until it is precisely completed in the exact same manner each time. The goal of this activity is to help children learn to define the standards, for being either temporarily or permanently finished with an activity, by the standards of their Coach. Referencing others to determine "completion," and eventually deriving a consensual definition of completion that meets our mutual needs and desires, becomes a critical step in forming flexible relationships of all kinds.

Participants:

Coach and child.

Getting Ready:

Children who have difficulty leaving activities that are not completed to their rigid standards, should first practice and master the "transition" activity prior to attempting this exercise.

Coaching Instructions:

There are five steps in this exercise:

☐ STEP 1

How much is enough: In this activity children practice "filling" cups with water. Mark a "finish" point very near the top of three cups. Now request that the child fill the cups with water, making sure that he references the finish line on the cup. Now bring out three more cups whose finish lines are at the halfway point. Instruct the child to fill these cups, once again using the finish line for a reference point of when to stop. Finally, bring out three more cups with the finish line drawn about one third of the way up and repeat the exercise. Bring out a final set of cups with no finish lines and request the child to fill them up.

☐ STEP 2

How tall is tall enough: Instruct the child that you are going to build some towers for jumping off. They have to be tall enough. First have the child build a tower with small blocks that is less than one foot high. Show the child how high he needs to build it. When he reaches the designated point tell him that this is tall enough. Put a very small toy person on top of the tower. Now use bigger blocks and make a tower twice as big and place a larger toy person on top. Finally use the biggest blocks you have and make a tower even larger with a larger toy person on top.

☐ STEP 3

A house with no roof: Now tell the child that you will be building a house out of blocks. What is special about this house is that it will have no roof. Proceed to build the house with blocks. Include a floor and walls and declare it finished.

☐ STEP 4

Incomplete puzzle: Tell the child that you are going to work together on a jigsaw puzzle. You will be in charge of the stopping point. Warn the child that some of the pieces are missing. Try this with varying "missing" pieces. Next, tell the child that you will do some more jigsaw puzzles, where no pieces are missing, however, they are going to be "finished" before all the pieces are in place. Tell the child on each trial what the stopping point will be.

☐ STEP 5

Incomplete completions without preparation: Now warn the child that he will no longer be receiving preparatory warnings about what constitutes "finished" before he begins. In the initial trials you will provide briefer and briefer warnings such as "finished in two more puzzle pieces." After the child adjusts to this you will practice communicating that you are "finished" without providing any warning.

Variations:

We can think of an infinite number of ways that you can reinforce the subjective nature of "good enough" as well as the concept that sometimes "finished" is a relationship term and not an absolute term. Practice a "one sock" day on a particular Sunday morning when you don't have anywhere to go and everyone in the family puts on just one sock. We know you will come up with many of your own creations.

Obstacles/Opportunities:

We do not have to emphasize that some children will balk if we move too quickly in this exercise. But the good news is that even the most rigid of children will gradually "loosen up" if we work slowly and gradually through all of the steps outlined above.

LEVEL I, STAGE 3, ACTIVITY 37

Expression

3

ACTIVITY HIGHLIGHTS

° Learning to express basic emotions

° Awareness and proper use of voice volume tone and speed

Summary:

In order for a child to share in the emotions of another, he must first have a sense of his own emotional state. For many of the children we see, emotions appear undifferentiated. By this we mean that different emotional states may not feel that different to the child.

Participants:

Coach and child.

Getting Ready:

We like to begin with the following emotions: proud, happy, frustrated, curious, sad, and angry. You will need books and posters that clearly demonstrate these emotional expressions. You will also require tracing paper and a pencil or a magic marker, one hand mirror and another mirror, large enough to reflect two people. Finally, you will need a cassette recorder. The Coach and child sit at a 90° angle at an appropriate-sized table. The hand mirror, magic marker and tracing paper should be under the table and the larger mirror within close proximity to the table.

Coaching Instructions:

There are two main activities in this exercise:

■ **ACTIVITY I   MATCH MY SIMPLE FACIAL EXPRESSIONS:**

☐ STEP 1

The coach should draw the child's attention to the emotion represented in the book or poster and name it.

☐ STEP 2

Now, focus the child's attention on the tracing paper and explain the facial expression as you draw it. For example: "I can tell this boy is angry because this is the way his mouth looks. His eyebrows arch this way." Under the picture, write the name of the emotion.

☐ STEP 3

Ask the child to make his face look just like the face in the picture. Focus his attention on the various aspects of the facial expression. Once he has attempted to make his face exhibit the same emotion as the one you have drawn, give him the hand mirror and tell him to try again. Typically, for expressions that are not happy, we have to help Novices make their faces less cheerful, by saying "No, that looks too happy."

☐ STEP 4

Now close the book and tell a short vignette related to the emotion you are dealing with. "When I was (choose the child's age) I got very angry one time when my dog bit a hole into the tire of my bicycle. This is the way I looked." You should make the face and ask the child if it looks angry.

☐ STEP 5

Now, both of you should face the mirror side by side and practice making the face in the mirror.

■ **ACTIVITY 2   MATCHING MY VOICE:**

Record your voice and immediately afterwards, tape the child attempting to match it. There are three elements to matching:

☐ STEP 1

Voice volume: practice a loud and a soft voice.

☐ STEP 2

Inflection: in this simple version, work on raising tone and lowering tone at the end of a short sentence.

☐ STEP 3

Speed of talking: again, in this simple version, work on a fast and slow speed.

Variations:

Use videotapes of other people modeling the same expressions. Use tape-recorded vignettes of other people to work on expression recognition.

Obstacles and Opportunities:

Some children may lack motor planning necessary for facial imitation. They will require more help from the Coach. This may include developing the kinesthetic "feel" of facial muscles as they model different expressions. We have not found anyone who has been unable to master imitating the basic emotional states of others.

Goals and Objectives

The final stage of Level I exposes children to the basic elements of coordinated actions. This is often the first time that the child may have experienced the excitement of taking actions alongside a social partner, with both operating as a single, synchronized unit.

Activity Summary

Activities in Stage 4 cover the entire gamut of synchronized activity. Early exercises focus on simple coordinated movements, including sequential and simultaneous actions. Exercises progress to more complex aspects of coordinating movement such as coordinating your physical position and orientation. We take a brief detour in an important exercise where the child is exposed to the concept of "Connections and Disconnections" and learns to begin perceiving whether things are connected or disconnected. A final exercise practices staying coordinated within the medium of rhyming words.

Critical Tips

- Remember to celebrate your small successes.

- Resist the temptation to allow the Novice to add his own variations to activities.

- Add excitement by introducing "world records" to some of the repetitive activities in this stage.

- You may work with more than one child at a time in this stage. However, no matter how many children you have, you should still remain the center of attention for each child and work with them in turn, rather than trying go get them to interact with one another.

LEVEL I, STAGE 4, ACTIVITY 38

Beanbag Mountain

ACTIVITY HIGHLIGHTS
° Accepting coaching to guide actions
° Demonstrating pride in actions
° Observing to match a partner's pace when working side by side.

Summary:

If you have been following along with the program, you will notice that this is the third time we have returned to the activity of building a "Beanbag Mountain." We love to get extra mileage out of the same activity. For children in the Autism Spectrum it is just one less variable that they have to deal with. Throughout these exercises you will see activities repeated with variations that enable children to learn new skills. In this version of "Beanbag Mountain" children become partners in building the structure. In addition we include the role of picking cards to determine which color beanbag chair we will choose.

Participants:

Coach and child.

Getting Ready:

This activity requires eight to ten large beanbag chairs of different colors scattered randomly around a room. Two carpet squares for you and the child should be placed approximately three feet apart so that you are able to sit facing each other. An index card corresponding to the color of each beanbag should be made prior to the onset of this activity. Index cards are placed between the two carpet squares.

Coaching Instructions:

This activity has five steps:

☐ STEP 1

Tell the child that together you will build a mountain so high that he will be the tallest boy in the world. Select a card, identifying the first beanbag you will use to begin building their mountain together. Show the card to the child making sure that he shifts his gaze between you, the card and the beanbag chair that has been selected.

☐ STEP 2

Place the card on the floor and ask, "Are you ready?" Once the child has responded positively, walk together to the appropriate beanbag, pick up opposite sides and carry it to a corner of the room. As you are carrying, groan and moan about how heavy it is, "Help me! Oh, this is so heavy."

☐ STEP 3

Return to your carpet squares and draw a card to identify the next beanbag chair you will use. Continue groaning and pretending to have difficulty moving the beanbags to the construction site. Remember to carefully pat down and stabilize each beanbag after you place it on the pile. You and the child should stop frequently to examine the mountain and make sure it is being built sturdily.

☐ STEP 4

As the mountain grows, the struggle to make it higher without falling over becomes magnified. You should amplify the excitement with statements like, "This is the biggest mountain ever. Push it. Careful, it might fall on us!" It is also important to make sure that their gaze is at least intermittently on facial expression and does not become focused on either the beanbag or the mountain that is under construction.

☐ STEP 5

As in prior versions, once the mountain is built, the child can climb to the top and carefully slide down, with your active assistance.

Variations:

If siblings are available, they can help build the mountain and then slide down it on the same beanbag as the child.

Obstacles and Opportunities:

This presents a wonderful opportunity for the Novice to gain a sense of his ability to learn to conquer fears and master an activity that may be hard for a child with motor difficulties.

LEVEL I, STAGE 4, ACTIVITY 39

Breaking the Chain

ACTIVITY HIGHLIGHTS

° Learning to carefully regulate actions for coordination

Summary:

This game sensitizes children to the subtleties of coordinating movement and touch with their partners. The cues to change roles are subtle and can require intense concentration. Children learn to enact their roles by referencing your non-verbal facial expressions.

Participants:

Coach and child.

Getting Ready:

Choose a strong toy truck. Secure a two-foot long colorful ribbon to both ends of the truck. Initially you will tie both ribbons to the truck. Then you will remove them and tape them to the truck. Finally, you will replace the ribbons with taped tissue paper. This activity will take place face to face within the same room, from behind beanbags within the same room and at a 90° angle from room to hallway.

Coaching Instructions:

This activity has six steps:

☐ STEP 1

Sit across from the child about three feet away. Hold the back of the truck with one hand and the ribbon in your other hand. Let go of the truck and roll it to the child. Show the child how to receive and hold onto the front end of the truck. When he grabs it yell out, "Coming back" and pull the truck back with the ribbon. Make sure he learns to let go when you shout "Coming back."

☐ STEP 2

Play this game for a short while. Then, on one trial let go of the ribbon and call out, "Oh no, we broke the chain!" Have the child push the truck back to you. Now try again. This time say, "Let's see if we can do five in a row without breaking the chain." After success at five passes, try for ten passes in a row, but on the eighth pass, let go of the ribbon and again "break the chain." Now see if you can be successful for all ten trials.

☐ STEP 3

Now you will teach the child how to push and pull the truck using only the ribbon. This entails letting the ribbon slide through your hands while your partner is pulling on it and then using both hands to pull it back, hand over hand.

☐ STEP 4

When ready, both you and the child will take your ribbons and "pass" the truck back and forth without ever letting go of your ribbons. Make sure that both you and the child use the signal, "Coming back!" before beginning to pull on the ribbon. To add even more excitement you can both hide behind beanbag chairs and pass back and forth while hiding from each other.

☐ STEP 5

When you are successful the child is ready for the next challenge. Untie the ribbons and affix them to the back of the truck, but this time use scotch tape to affix them to the truck. Tell the Novice it is going to get harder and you both have to be much more careful not to "break the chain."

☐ STEP 6

The final step is to replace the ribbon with tissue paper. Show the Novice how easily the paper breaks and emphasize that now we have to be very careful if we do not want to "break the chain."

Variations:

This game is even more fun as an outside activity; for example, moving objects up and down on a slide, on a jungle gym, or seesaw. For older Novices they can use ropes and pulleys to make the activity more complex and interesting.

Obstacles/Opportunities:

Younger children may not know how to receive the toy truck, turn it around and send it back to you. You will need a second Coach in this phase, seated right behind the child and guiding his actions, until he learns how to enact his role independently. With some children this may take several weeks. Some children will not be able to get through all six steps at this time. Make sure to have a good celebration each time you are successful.

LEVEL I, STAGE 4, ACTIVITY 40

Vegetable Delivery

ACTIVITY HIGHLIGHTS

° Introduction to synchronized role-taking

Summary:

In this activity, children get to participate in a more complex role enactment under the guidance of their Coach. While the roles are simple, they may take a good bit of practice for younger children who are not used to activities with this many steps. It may even be difficult for older children who have never coordinated a pretend role with a partner before.

Participants:

Coach and child.

Getting Ready:

You will need one large toy pickup truck, a set of plastic vegetables and fruits, and some wooden blocks. You can add two play telephones if you think the child will not be too distracted.

Coaching Instructions:

There are two simple steps in this exercise:

☐ STEP 1

Explain to the child that there are two jobs, a farmer who grows vegetables and the store owner. To begin the activity, he will be the farmer and you will be the store owner. Build a road together from blocks that stretches from the farm to the market. Now set up some simple structures to indicate the farmhouse and the vegetable patch. Lay several of the plastic vegetables in the patch. Place the truck on the road next to the vegetable patch. Finally, build a simple "store" at the other end of the road.

☐ STEP 2

Get on the telephone; call the child and request that he sends you a particular vegetable. The child should put the vegetable in the truck and roll it to you. Place it inside the store, turn the truck around and roll it back to him. When it is time to send you the next order, the child must turn the truck around so it is facing you, prior to sending it off again. Make sure that you switch roles and the child becomes proficient in both.

Variations:

The vegetable patch can turn into any kind of farm and in fact it can become any kind of production facility, including a factory. You can even let the child be an automobile producer and you can play the role of a dealer if you have enough cars and a trailer large enough to transport them.

Obstacles/Opportunities:

Younger children will need practice in various aspects of the mechanics of this exercise. They may never have turned a truck around to send it back to a partner. Remember to break the exercise into a series of even simpler steps and proceed gradually. If the child insists on setting a price for the vegetables you can go along with this, unless it begins to dominate the game.

LEVEL I, STAGE 4, ACTIVITY 41

Store

ACTIVITY HIGHLIGHTS
° Chaining together activities to create more complex versions
° Enacting a role in a multi-stage activity
° Practice buying and selling in a store

Summary:

Now that our merchandise has been transported from farm to market, we are ready to open the store for business. This activity maintains the role of the store-keeper, but, now we introduce a customer to the store and, temporarily, eliminate the farmer. Children are now able to practice making transactions from the perspectives of consumer and seller.

Participants:

Coach and child. Once the store is in operation, it can be visited by whoever is willing to take the role of customer without adding variation or complexity.

Getting Ready:

Children should have a basic understanding of what happens in a store. The Coach and child should be seated across from each other, separated by the "store." Make easy to read prices for each of the vegetables. The customer should have enough play money to make his purchases. A play cash register makes the activity more exciting.

Coaching Instructions:

Make sure that the child is eventually able to play all three of the roles of farmer, storekeeper and customer. This activity has three steps:

☐ STEP 1

The child will begin by playing the role of storekeeper and you will be the customer. The customer tells the storekeeper which vegetable he wants, "Mr. Storekeeper. I want a tomato please." The storekeeper tells the price. The customer takes out his money and pays the storekeeper. The storekeeper takes the money, places it in the cash register and then wraps up the vegetable for the customer. The storekeeper says, "Thank you." The customer says, "Have a good day," and takes the package.

☐ STEP 2

In this step the customer asks for a vegetable that is not available at the store. The storekeeper informs the customer that he doesn't have the vegetable or fruit today and suggests that the customer buy something he does have. He tries to sell another vegetable. The customer buys the new vegetable and finishes the transaction as before.

☐ STEP 3

Now, combine the farm to market activity with the store activity and enact the entire sequence together. Initially, you will play the farmer and then will switch to the role of customer, while the Novice stays in the role of storekeeper. Eventually you can allow the Novice to be the one changing roles.

Variations:

Why not make the store more real by setting up a lemonade stand? Making things and setting up a store is a great activity in a classroom, or school setting, as well.

Obstacles/Opportunities:

To enjoy this game, children must not really care about the price of things, or about accumulating money. Make sure that the pace of the activity is such that children do not fixate on the numbers. You should stay in charge of every aspect of the activity, including the price of products.

LEVEL I, STAGE 4, ACTIVITY 42

Stop and Go

ACTIVITY HIGHLIGHTS
° Learning to begin activities together
° Learning to stop activities and end together
° Coordinating a mutual endpoint

Summary:

In other cultures, it is expected that people who are in a relationship with one another will walk side by side and converse as they do so. By contrast, people in the USA tend to walk in front or behind each other, with little regard for their partner's physical proximity. Consequently, it is not unusual for families to ignore or simply not notice that they are physically unrelated until a child runs off in a parking lot or simply disappears from a parent's visual range. A typically developing child will panic when this happens; a child in the Autism Spectrum may not. Most children are familiar with the words "stop" and "go" but rely on others to anticipate their needs and get in synch with them. Through the use of this activity, children learn to appreciate the joy of physically coordinating themselves with others.

Participants:

Coach and child.

Getting Ready:

Begin this activity in a hallway that has a clear beginning and ending point.

Coaching Instruction:

This activity has three steps:

☐ STEP 1

Begin at one end of the hallway, standing side-by-side and holding hands with the child. Begin the activity by saying, "Go." Walk side by side until you say, "Stop." This is the signal that you will stand quietly together. When stopping, you should wait approximately 30 seconds for the child to visually reference you. If he does not do so, move into the child's visual range and place his hands next to your eyes.

☐ STEP 2

Once referencing and movement are mastered, discontinue speaking. The child is now expected to move and stop alongside you without verbal cues.

☐ STEP 3

The next step is to drop hands and continue to walk side by side. If a child has problems staying in synch when he is not holding your hand, teach him to lightly hold onto your skirt or pants. This intermediate step is usually sufficient to help a child master the skill.

Variations:

Once walking alongside another person is mastered, running, skipping and hopping are all possible. Especially fun are spontaneous changes between these different forms of movement. Children who are physically uncoordinated often cannot walk and visually reference at the same time. We teach them a sequential ritual. You and the child walk side by side for three steps while looking ahead. On the fourth step teach the child to visually reference you.

Obstacles and Opportunities:

Many children in the Autism Spectrum typically have little sense of timing. They often do not know how fast or slow they should walk. They become targets as they walk through hallways because their pace is so out of synch with that of their peers. In this case practice makes perfect and there is no substitute for it.

Start and Stop

ACTIVITY HIGHLIGHTS
- Coordinating "start" and "stop" actions
- Visual referencing for synchronized movement

Summary:

We now progress from walking together to teaching the child to coordinate a variety of "start" and "stop" actions with a partner. In this exercise children learn to visually reference their partners, rather than relying on verbal cues, to synchronize their actions.

Getting Ready:

Choose the activities you will use. Practice with at least three different simple motor activities. We recommend the following: falling together onto beanbag chairs, pushing an object (such as a toy car) off of a table at the same time, banging drums together.

Coaching Instructions:

The exercise has six steps:

☐ STEP 1

Make sure that the child has learned how to reference your counting "one, two, three" and uses the "three" as a starting cue.

☐ STEP 2

Eliminate verbal counting. Continue to be the "counter" but now only mouth the numbers in a highly exaggerated manner with no sound.

☐ STEP 3

Next, substitute head nods for counting. Nod your head in a similarly exaggerated manner and begin on the third nod.

☐ STEP 4

Now we introduce an element of variation into the routine. Return to counting out loud, but after you count to "two" pause for two seconds before saying "three." Make sure to smile very broadly while you are pausing, to communicate the fun element in this variation. When the child has learned to reference your pause, repeat this variation for silent counting and then for head nods. Now add more variations, one at a time. Practice "one, two, three, Go" using the same progression of complexity. Try "one, two, three, four."

☐ STEP 5

Now we move to starting and stopping in a fluid manner. We first practice this skill with drums. Make sure that the child knows how to bang the drum and make a sound. Now explain to him that you will be the leader and tell him when to start and stop. There is no need to count to three. Initially use lots of amplification in word and gesture to communicate starting and stopping. As in the previous steps eliminate the verbal element when ready. With the drums there is no need to mouth start and stop. Instead use your hand or drumstick in an exaggerated motion. Of course, the sound of the drum is an added cue.

☐ STEP 6

Now we practice "Start and Stop" with movement. You can play a game of "tag" where you chase each other around a central object. The child learns that you can "freeze" both players by saying or signaling stop. Each stays frozen until the "go" signal is given.

Variations:

Another fun activity is for each partner to start at opposite ends of the room and, at the count of three quickly trade places. At this stage we are not yet concerned with partners remaining exactly side by side, only that they are starting and stopping in a coordinated manner led by the Coach. We use another exciting variation with elementary aged children. A small class sits around a table. The leader signals "start" and bangs on the table and the students all bang along. Then the leader lifts his hands and signals "down" and the whole class crawls under the table and does a group hug. Then the leader signals "up" and the class quickly goes back in their seats and awaits the leader's signal to "go" before banging again.

Obstacles/Opportunities:

Remember to celebrate all of your successes, even the small ones! Also remember to stay firmly in control. The child is not yet allowed to add his own variations.

LEVEL I, STAGE 4, ACTIVITY 44

Role Actions

ACTIVITY HIGHLIGHTS
° Coordinating role actions
° Connecting two different roles for a common goal
° Role reversals

Summary:

Role activities require a type of fluid turn taking and coordinated movement similar to the prior exercise. The difference is that now each partner has a different "job" or role. The two roles have to fit together like a lock and key in order for the activity to succeed. We describe two simple role activities in this exercise: Builder–Giver and Cups and Marbles.

Participants:

Coach and child.

Getting Ready:

You will need a long table, a number of small plastic cups and several dozen marbles.

Coaching Instructions for Builder–Giver:

Explain to the child that you are going to be building together using blocks, but you each have a different job. The child's first job is "giver." He selects a block and hands it to you. You are the "builder." You receive the block from the "giver" and place it on the structure as you see fit. The builder is not allowed to select a block. The giver is not allowed to participate in the actual construction. Practice this until proficient and then reverse roles.

Coaching Instructions for Cups and Marbles:

In this simple activity, one person places a number of plastic cups on a long table, while the other drops one marble in each cup. The "cup placer" stands directly in front of the "marble dropper." As quickly as possible, he places a cup on the table and then moves to the side, in position to place the next cup and providing space for the "dropper" to approach and drop in one marble. He cannot place an additional cup until the "dropper" completes his action. After you become proficient, see if you can increase your speed and set a "world record."

Variations:

Remember to replicate these activities with peer dyads.

Obstacles/Opportunities:

This is a great opportunity for children to practice their awareness of body position in relation to another person. If they are the "cup placer" they have to move onto the next position, leaving sufficient room for the "dropper." If a child has severe visual organizational difficulties the "placing" task may be quite difficult. Try placing grids on the table to indicate where each cup should be placed.

Parallel Pretend Play

ACTIVITY HIGHLIGHTS
° Shared pretend play
° Coordinating parallel roles

Summary:

Observing beginning pretend play with typical children, we are struck by the limited variety and redundancy of their play. Two simple parallel activities follow. They require lots of frequent gaze shifting and timing actions to occur together.

Participants:

Coach and child.

Getting Ready:

For the first activity you will need two dolls, two bottles, two sets of clothing, two sets of toothbrushes, two blankets and two diapers. For the second activity you will need one set of blocks and two dinosaurs. Materials for each activity should be stored in individual boxes.

Coaching Instructions for Activity One:

Face the child and open the box containing materials for play with dolls. Take out a doll for yourself and then give one to the child saying, "This is my baby. Here is a baby for you." Give the child time to look at his baby. Then ask if the child wants to keep his baby or trade babies. Show the child the various toys in the box, laying them out in pairs. "Here are two bottles," etc. Wait for the child to shift his gaze to you. Once he has done so, pick up a bottle and say, "Let's feed our babies, mine is hungry." Now shift gaze between babies and each other as you pretend with each of the items available to you. Other activities with the babies should not be overlooked, such as comforting the baby with kisses and putting Band-Aids on the baby, while pretending it has a "boo boo."

Coaching Instructions for Activity Two:

Remove two blocks from the box. Place yours on the carpet and indicate for the child to place hers alongside. Continue removing the blocks two at a time and build two parallel roads simultaneously. Once the road is built, remove two dinosaurs from the box. Keep one and hand the child the other. Again, the child is given time to explore the dinosaur and trade if she so desires.

Place your dinosaurs on the road. Suggest to the child that you walk together, then run and skip. The dinosaurs may also walk backwards or sideways, always keeping in synch with each other. If you like, you and child can chant, "We're walking, walking, walking" in time to the rhythm of the dinosaurs.

Variations:

This game is easily adapted for older children by choosing objects that she may find more appealing. For example, if a child is interested in Star Wars, two characters might move alongside each other on a road headed to a space station. Or, two Tai Fighters might fly in synchrony around the room.

Obstacles/Opportunities:

If, in the midst of the activity, a child begins to quote facts about dinosaurs, explain that this is not a "fact" game it is a "being together" game and that you will start over so that you can be together. If you and the child are walking your dinosaurs and the child suddenly leaves the road, runs to the beanbag and says they are taking a nap, you have two possible options. The first is to simply follow the script suggested above. The second is to ask the child if he would like for the dinosaurs to take a nap. Upon agreeing that this is what he wants, you may agree that at the end of the walk there will be a nap before they turn around and run back down the road. This activity provides yet another occasion for the child to experience play with objects that may be typical for his age. When mastered, he will have added another activity in his repertoire to enjoy playing with another child.

LEVEL I, STAGE 4, ACTIVITY 46

Cars and Ramps

ACTIVITY HIGHLIGHTS
° Turn taking and sequential role actions
° Visual gaze shifting

Summary:

Once a child has learned to physically move or refrain from moving, in response to your facial cues, it is now possible to introduce toys into simple coordination actvities. "Cars and Ramps" was chosen for two reasons. It is an exciting activity that utilizes the love many children have for transportation toys. Left to their own devices, however, play is often repetitive, lacking social richness. Through this activity, the child learns to use simple toys within the context of a reciprocal relationship.

Participants:

Coach and child.

Getting Ready:

In order to play this game, you will need an appropriately sized table and chair, ten matchbox cars and one mailing tube with a large enough circumference to accommodate two matchbox cars at the same time. Coach and child face each other at the table. The mailing tube leans from table to floor between you. Ten matchbox cars and two harmony balls, small metallic balls that emit a pleasnt sound when rolled or shaken, are under the table outside the child's visual range.

Coaching Instructions:

This activity has five simple steps:

☐ STEP 1

Reach under the table and prior to displaying the first matchbox car say, "Vroom, vroom, beep, beep" and then send the matchbox car to the child.

☐ STEP 2

Point to the mailing tube but cover the opening with your hand so that the child is unable to place the car inside. Receiving this double message will confuse the child and cause him to shift his gaze to you. Make a sad face and shake your head "No."

☐ STEP 3

After a moment, change your sad face into a smile, nod "Yes," wait for the child to nod in return. Remove your hand from the opening to the tube and allow the child to send the car down the tube.

☐ STEP 4

Once a few trials have gone well, you can say, "Vroom, vroom" and wait for the child to say, "Beep, beep" before sending the car across the table to him. If the child does not do so, hesitate, wait ten seconds and say, "Vroom, vroom" again. Give the child approximately 30 seconds to respond. If the child does not fill in the missing "Beep, beep" you say it and continue using the unfinished verbalization every three times until the child begins to fill it in independently.

☐ STEP 5

Now shake or nod your head unpredictably. Once all ten cars have been placed in the tube, shake the harmony ball, roll it to the child and say, "We're finished." This step should not be overlooked because children often find it difficult to leave this game and this provides a clear, predictable signal that the game is over.

Variations:

The first variation requires that you and the child sit on opposite sides of a table each holding a matchbox car. You both nod for agreement and move your cars slowly towards the center of the table where the tube is leaning. Once the cars reach the edge of the tube, you must both nod "Yes" while looking at each other before placing them in the tube together.

It is also fun to place the cars in the tube backwards. This will require that the child follow your lead. Other articles may be placed in the tube. For example, the child might sit at the end of the tube with a puzzle frame. You can nod to the child who signals back that she is ready to receive the puzzle piece. You can send the pieces down the tube one at a time until the puzzle is complete.

Obstacles/Opportunities:

Some children simply love cars too much to play this activity as designed and may become overly focused on the cars. If the pace is quickened so that the child has no time to focus on an individual car, it is possible to overcome this distraction.

Crashing Cars

ACTIVITY HIGHLIGHTS
° Learning to coordinate release actions with a partner
° Observe and modify actions to increase coordination with a social partner.

Summary:

The next step in coordinating actions is to learn timing. Crashing cars is an activity that all children seem to enjoy. It is a simple way to move to the next level of complexity in coordinating actions.

Participants:

Coach and child.

Getting Ready:

You will need two sturdy cars, approximately six inches long, with good alignment, two carpet squares and plain, red, yellow, blue and green masking tape. Take the plain masking tape and make a straight line that is eight feet long. Use the red masking tape to make a foot long square in the center of the line. Use the yellow tape to make two yellow lines perpendicular to the long line, each two feet on either side of the square. Make two blue lines two feet farther back. Finally two green lines are placed at the ends of the eight-foot line. Give the child a choice of cars.

Coaching Instructions:

This exercise has three steps:

☐ STEP 1

You and the child kneel side by side, with your cars on the "start" line. In this step children learn to release their car with you at the same time. Teach the child to count out loud with you and to check in visually after each number, "One (look), two (look), three (look)." Initially both partners have to nod their heads and say, "GO!" prior to releasing their cars.

☐ STEP 2

Synchronize distance and speed of cars: Once simultaneous release has been mastered, we work on coordinating the distance our cars will travel. Tell the child that the goal is now to keep our cars together and try to get them to stop near each other. To do so, we have to release them with the same amount of force. Make sure not to modify your actions to correspond to the child's. It is the child who must learn to make the behavioral adjustments necessary for his car to roll in a more closely coordinated manner. This will rarely be possible without a good deal of repetition and practice. It is a good opportunity for children to practice observing and modifying their actions to correspond to yours.

☐ STEP 3

Now move to opposite sides of the middle square. Choose a start line that you believe is challenging but not overwhelming, count to three together, release your cars together and try to crash inside the middle square. If the crash is successful yell, "We did it!" Your main role is to act as a guide to regulate the child's actions and increase the number of successful crashes, using phrases such as: "Let's try to go a little slower this time. Let's see if this works." Once you are successful in crashing your cars while sitting in close proximity, move farther back to the blue line and eventually to the green line.

Variations:

Try variations of the activity once you are successful in your crashes. Vary trials of crashing with the cars passing one another. Try to crash the cars while they are facing backwards.

Obstacles/Opportunities:

Some children are obsessed with cars and may over-focus on unimportant aspects: the number of a racecar or the wheels moving back and forth. Because we choose really cool cars, children may also be drawn to them and want to play alone with them.

LEVEL I, STAGE 4, ACTIVITY 48

Two Ball Roll

ACTIVITY HIGHLIGHTS
° Coordinate simultaneous release
° Careful referencing of partner's actions
° Sense of competence and mastery

Summary:

When we first developed this activity, it seemed too difficult for young children. However, during one assessment we observed a father teach his motor-challenged, legally blind young daughter to do this. It took time but he was a patient, master teacher and she a good apprentice. His success made us realize that many of our children's limitations are impacted by our inability to understand the specific steps necessary for mastery of a skill. Having said this, approach this game not at the end but at the beginning. Some children may be able to stand, or sit down, and have a good two-ball roll or toss. Most will enter at an earlier point in the sequence. Because the activity is so difficult, accomplishment signals a boost in self-esteem and a sense of team accomplishment.

Participants:

Coach and child.

Getting Ready:

You will need two balls and two carpet squares, or two taped lines. Carpet squares are set at a distance appropriate for a simple game of catch.

Coaching Instructions:

There are two steps in this activity:

☐ STEP 1

Begin by making sure the distance between carpet squares is appropriate. The ability to send the ball back and forth, ten times is adequate. You may either stand or sit on carpet squares for this activity. For very young children, or highly impaired children, the squares should be fairly close and the balls should be rolled back and forth, before being tossed.

☐ STEP 2

Because children have already learned the concept of trading, this idea is used to explain the activities. Therefore say, "I am going to count to three and we will trade balls." Together with the child, count "One, two, three, roll." After each count the child should shift her gaze from the ball to you. Say, "One" then hesitate until the child looks at you. Continue counting and hesitating until there is a gaze shift. At "three" wait for the gaze shift and then say, "Roll!" or "Throw!" There should be excitement on your face and in your voice as you roll the balls simultaneously toward each other. Continue in this manner until there is consistent mastery.

Variations:

Change of objects can keep interest in this activity alive. We have used mallets made of tinker toys with two wood discs on a table top with great success. Harmony balls, lend a melodious counterpoint to the activity.

Obstacles/Opportunities:

For a reason that is not especially clear, some children occasionally find great enjoyment from behaviors that work against success. Make sure that these are not reinforced. Also, be careful not to allow the child to introduce variations in this stage. We will work on introducing novelty in the next level. In the same vein, be careful not to introduce novelty yourself. After a while we can create a wonderful sense of mastery by successfully beating "world records" in two-ball-toss.

LEVEL I, STAGE 4, ACTIVITY 49

Ropes

ACTIVITY HIGHLIGHTS

- ° Coordinating stop and go actions
- ° Coordinating hard and gentle actions with a partner
- ° Developing self-regulation

Summary:

We have been exploring several activities that address the steps of coordinated actions. These activities require the evaluation of your partner's actions in relation to your own and a much more fluid relationship between both partner's actions to achieve success. The first activity, "Stop and Go" involved more of a sequential "first-me-then-you" coordination of actions. Following this, Novices were required to increase the fluidity of their actions as we moved away from a sequential "turn-taking" type of action to more of a simultaneous motion. In this activity, we review the prior concepts and add a new one. We practice hard and gentle actions. The rope provides clear and immediate feedback.

Participants:

Coach and child.

Getting Ready:

You will need a strong rope with plastic handles on each end that can be firmly grasped and do not easily slip. Ideally, you should purchase a rope with handles that can be adjusted to different lengths of the rope, so that you can practice being farther and farther apart. Make sure that, if needed, the child has cushions to land on or a "spotter" to check his fall.

Coaching Instructions:

This exercise has four steps:

☐ STEP 1

Both partners remain standing on carpet squares, facing each other. We begin with a simple turn-taking movement activity: You pull and then I pull. Take the rope with two handles and teach the child how to firmly grasp his handle and gently pull without leaving his assigned spot. At this stage you are only practicing a smooth back and forth movement where you each pull and allow yourself to be pulled in a gentle motion. You should function as the "caller" and say, "Pull" when it is either partner's turn. The activity should rapidly become a fluid back and forth exercise.

☐ STEP 2

Now practice both "hard' and "gentle" pulls.

☐ STEP 3

Pull hard at the same time and experience how you remain in balance.

☐ STEP 4

Pull gently at the same time and continue to maintain balance.

Variations:

With younger children you can do the identical activity by grasping forearms. As the child becomes more proficient, vary the activity by adding "Stop and Start" elements as well as pauses into the rhythm. You can use a piece of exercise equipment known as a "rubber band" with two handles that provides a bit more elasticity. If you like, you can tell the child to pull hard while you pull gently and illustrate the effects of a mis-match. Just make sure you do it safely.

Obstacles/Opportunities:

This is a good activity for children who seem unaware of their own strength and might act on objects, pets or people too roughly. Remember to repeat this activity with peer partners in Stage 8, when you form peer dyads.

LEVEL I, STAGE 4, ACTIVITY 50

Drums

ACTIVITY HIGHLIGHTS
° Coordinating loud and soft actions with a partner
° Coordinating a combination of elements

Summary:

This exercise introduces the next element of action coordination, that of synchronizing loud and soft sounds with a partner. It also teaches children to synchronize a combination of coordination elements practiced together. By the way, we love to use drums in this activity.

Participants:

Coach and child.

Getting Ready:

Children should be proficient in prior Stage 3 activities.

Coaching Instructions:

The activity has five steps:

☐ STEP 1

Provide a drum for yourself and the child and make sure he can use it without too much effort. Teach the child to bang in two speeds – fast and slow.

☐ STEP 2

Combine elements so that the child can practice "Stop/Go" along with "Fast/Slow" in a fluid manner.

☐ STEP 3   LOUD/SOFT:

Begin with a simple straightforward progression. Hit the drum loudly one time, wait for the child to repeat. Now hit the drum softly one time and provide an opportunity for the child to repeat you again.

☐ STEP 4

When you are sure the child can distinguish between loud and soft, move from sequential to parallel actions. Start drumming together with the child and announce shifts from loud to soft, both with words and with your own drumming. The child will learn to shift rapidly with you and play at the same rate you are playing. As proficiency increases, add more shifts from loud to soft but omit verbal announcements.

☐ STEP 5   COMBINING ELEMENTS:

Once this pattern has been established, begin simple rhythms of stop/go, fast/slow and loud/soft. Here are sample patterns to work on:

> Start/Stop and Loud/Soft
>
> Start/Stop and Fast/Slow
>
> Start/Stop, Fast/Slow, Loud/Soft

Variations:

Return to the rope activity and add "fast/slow" variations to the back-and-forth movement. You may want to practice this activity with speech as the "instrument." While you are shifting from "loud" to "soft" you can provide appropriate contextual cues like, "Talk loud, I am far away," or "Talk soft, we are in church."

Obstacles/Opportunities:

Resist the temptation to allow children to add their own variations to this exercise. It is tempting to turn this into an improvisational session, but if the child is truly at this stage, he will not be ready for the behavioral regulation necessary for improvisation. There will be plenty of time to enjoy and work on improvisation during future activities.

Patterns

ACTIVITY HIGHLIGHTS

° Learning to coordinate patterns

Summary:

Now we move to a new type of coordination; matching simple patterns. Most children love using music keyboards and we find many uses for them throughout the program. In this first appearance we limit our actions to playing with one finger and only on the black keys. This increases the chance that the music we create together will be melodic and pleasing.

Participants:

Coach and child.

Getting Ready:

Ideally, you can use a piano or a music keyboard with various stops. Sit side-by-side facing the keyboard with the child sitting to your right. Cover the settings on the keyboard for now.

Coaching Instructions:

This activity has three simple steps:

☐ STEP 1

Tell the child that you will make music together. You will use only the pointer finger on each hand and play only the black keys. Take enough time to model and guide the child so that you are sure he understands the limits of the activity.

☐ STEP 2

Now, play a very slow, simple, repetitive rhythm. Vary using the pointer finger of each hand. Play a black key with the left hand, the right hand and then the left. Each note should be held for the same amount of time. When you are finished, nod at the child and instruct him to nod back when he is ready to play on the upper black keys. The child has to match the pattern that you have just played on the lower keys.

☐ STEP 3

Now play a slightly faster and longer pattern. The child should join in when you invite him to do so with a nod. Once again, the child joins in by replicating the pattern you have established. The piece is "finished" when you nod again.

Variations:

You can use drums or any other instrument. You can also work on movement and visual patterns using markers and papers.

Obstacles and opportunities:

When we first began experimenting with piano duets, some children who were rarely impulsive or distractible became so on this instrument. They delighted in playing full hand crashing noises and the louder the banging the more enjoyable the instrument became. If introduced carefully, this should not be a problem.

LEVEL I, STAGE 4, ACTIVITY 52

Position

ACTIVITY HIGHLIGHTS
° Body awareness
° Physical relationships

Summary:

In this exercise our goal is to teach children to be aware of the position of their body in relation to social partners. We focus on close/far apart, facing towards/away and standing side by side/face to face/lined-up as our different positions.

Participants:

Coach and child initially and then two children.

Getting Ready:

Make sure that the child understands the words "close" and "far away." If you are not sure whether he understands, you work first on the other two body positions which do not require words.

Coaching Instructions:

This exercise has three steps:

☐ STEP 1 FACING TOWARDS/ AWAY

The essential element of "towards/away" is whether you can see your partner or not (assuming there is no obstacle between you). Make sure to first teach the child the meaning of "towards" and "away from" using signs turned away or towards the child. When you believe he understands the concept, begin the following simple activity: hold out a sign with an instruction the child must read, in order to carry out a required action (for example the sign can say: Walk over to the door and open it. If the child cannot yet read, the sign can be a picture symbol). The child is not allowed to move to read the sign. Initially the Coach faces towards the child, so he can see the sign. After several trials, hold out the sign but face away from the child so that he cannot see it. If the child tells you he cannot see the sign, agree and don't do anything. If the child requests that you turn, do so, but do not turn into the child's line of sight. If the child indicates that you should turn "towards" him, then do so in a manner which makes it easy for the child to read the sign.

☐ STEP 2   SIDE BY SIDE, FACE TO FACE, LINED UP

In this activity we create an experience of the adaptations we have to make, based upon the different ways we line up with each other. In this case, children have to pass a ball back and forth three different ways. First, children line up face to face and pass the ball back and forth. Then children line up side by side and successfully pass the ball back and forth without moving or turning any part of their body. Finally, children line up and pass the ball back and forth through their legs.

☐ STEP 3   CLOSE/FAR

This is the first "subjective" body position, in that whether you are near or far is dependent on the action you are trying to take. If I am walking to a store that is two miles away it will feel far. If I am driving two miles on the freeway it seems near. In this activity "close" and "far" are defined by whether we can hear each other or not. Repeat Step 1, where you presented the child with important information. This time present the information orally instead of through cards. First, get close enough so that the child can easily hear your instructions. After several trials move far enough away so that the child cannot hear you. Do not change the volume of your speech. If the child says he cannot hear you, move even farther away. Only move closer if you are specifically requested to do so. Then move back to your original close position.

Variations:

You can practice other body positions where one person is in a related but not identical position to another. Back to back is a logical addition. You can also work on "above and below" and continue the ball passing game with one partner standing and the other lying down.

Obstacles/Opportunities:

As you might have guessed, these are wonderful opportunities for working on language in a meaningful, contextual manner. You will find many such opportunities in our activities, which are frequently used in language and occupational therapy remediation programs as well as "social" development.

LEVEL I, STAGE 4, ACTIVITY 53

Connections

ACTIVITY HIGHLIGHTS

° Learning to distinguish connections from disconnections

° Working collaboratively to complete a simple project.

Summary:

Relationships are fundamentally about connections and disconnections. The crucial variable is being aware of when you are in either state. In this exercise we provide five different activities and various modalities to introduce the child to the concept of being connected or disconnected.

Participants:

Coach and child.

Getting Ready:

You will need two hula-hoops, some objects that can be traded, a toy train and tracks, a music keyboard, a large table and four beanbag chairs. The child should be familiar with our "Trade Me" game from Stage 1.

Coaching Instructions:

This exercise has five steps:

☐ STEP 1 CONNECTING CIRCLES

In this first step we create two personal boundary areas, one for each of you. Place two hula-hoops on the ground. They should be near but not touching each other. Sit within one and ask the child to sit inside the other. Explain that you must both stay within your hula-hoop. Now put several objects inside each hula-hoop area. Explain that each of you has some things to trade with inside your space. But you can only trade when the hula-hoops are "connected" (touching each other). When the hoops are touching you can trade, but without words. Connect the hula-hoops and hold out objects for trading. Conduct a few trades and then move the hula-hoops apart. Indicate non-verbally that the trading "exchange" is closed. Then connect the hula-hoops and begin trading again. Connect and disconnect the hula-hoops in a fluid manner.

☐ STEP 2 CONNECTING TRAIN TRACKS

In this activity, you each build part of a railroad track and then join the tracks together. First, use masking tape to indicate the area on the floor or an area on a large enough table, within which you will place your tracks. Indicate a starting place for each of you and a "meeting place" where the two sets of tracks will meet up. You can lay out the tracks using any shape you wish. Provide yourself and the child with a sufficient number of track pieces to make the activity interesting but not overwhelming. Seat the child by your side but several feet away from you.

Tell him that you will guide the building project. Each of you takes turns placing one track in the designated taped area. Keep laying track until you meet up with each other at the designated "meeting place." Celebrate your "connection" by running the train – if powered – and taking a photo of the finished product. Of course you can decorate your train track with whatever objects you desire.

☐ STEP 3   CONNECTING SOUNDS

Return to the music keyboard. Have the child pick just one note. You pick another matching note. Play each note separately with varying degrees of delay. Finally, play the notes together as a "two note" connected piece. Make sure you emphasize that the notes are now connected. Now, alternate playing "disconnected" and "connected" notes.

☐ STEP 4   CONNECTING WORDS

This activity, invented by a family in California we are privileged to know, involves taking a word or two-word phrase and temporarily disconnecting and then reconnecting it. Begin by choosing a word or phrase that can easily be divided in half, like "School Bus." Put each half of the word or phrase on a separate card. Put a small "base" under each card so they can be moved like game pieces. Give one card, for example, "school" to the child and take the other card, "bus," for yourself. Sit on one side of a table that is of a size that allows the child to reach all the way to the middle and have the child sit across from you. Place a taped line across the table between you and the child. Place ten taped cross strips along the line to mark five stopping places that each of you will use. The final two cross strips should be in the middle of the table touching one another. Now, teach the child that you will give a signal for him to say his word. After he says his word and you say your word, you both move your cards to the next stopping place. The activity proceeds with the child moving to a line, saying "school" and you moving your card to the next line and saying "bus." Each time you move to a closer stopping line, decrease the time between saying, "school" and "bus" in order to intensify the excitement and increase the degree of connection. As you are getting closer repeatedly say, "We're getting more connected!" At the final stopping place the two words should finally be reconnected as "School Bus" which should be said with as much excitement and celebration as possible.

☐ STEP 5   CONNECTING TWO ACTIVITIES INTO ONE

In this final activity, you practice connecting two smaller activities into one larger activity. Place four beanbag chairs on one side of the room. Tape a line across the room from the beanbags to a starting line. Now place a "stopping point" about one foot in front of the beanbags. Stand on the "stopping point" and practice falling together onto the beanbag chairs. Make sure the child knows that the name of the activity is "Falling Together." Put the activity name, or a visual symbol to represent the activity, on a whiteboard or a sign. Now, teach him to walk together with you to the stopping place just short of the beanbags, then turn with you and return together to the starting place. Once again make sure he knows you are "Walking Together" and that there is some visual representation of the activity. Finally connect the two activities into one. Begin at the starting line, count together, walk quickly to the stopping place together and then fall onto the beanbags together. This activity should be clearly called "Walking and Falling Together." The two prior signs should be combined into one. This is cause for another "connection celebration!"

Variations:

Try running and falling together if you are successful. If the child looks away from you when falling, teach him to fall with his face and body facing you. Make sure to use an exaggerated facial expression and, if desirable a bit of "rough-and-tumble" when you land. If you are successful with your two-note piece, try to connect notes in larger groups to make a short piece. Another activity is "connected pictures" in which you each draw a picture that will be connected and then tape them together, like a house and garage, or each draw a half of a tree or person. It can be really funny if each draws the top half of a boy and girl, or one draws the top of a girl and the other the bottom of a boy.

Obstacles/Opportunities:

See if you can find opportunities during the day to point out connections and disconnections of all sorts. Our world is full of them!

LEVEL I, STAGE 4, ACTIVITY 54

Rhyming words

ACTIVITY HIGHLIGHTS

° Learning to be playful with words
° Being creative with word combinations

Summary:

This is a great activity for children who have learned to use language in a rote or overly rigid manner. Typical children are used to playing with words – creating every manner of nonsense combination as a normal activity. In this exercise we begin with rhyming words and progress to non-sensical combinations.

Participants:

Coach and child.

Getting Ready:

The child will have to be comfortable using words and sounds in a playful manner. The child must also be able to read the simple words we provide below. Make a set of rhyming word cards and make sure to divide them into two sets. A sample set is provided below.

Coaching Instructions:

Each of you gets one set of rhyming words or you can lay out one set, so you can both work from the same set. Explain that you are going to play a game of rhyming words. Make sure the child understands that the point of this exercise is to put together words that sound good, but that do not mean anything. They just need to be fun. You demonstrate until you are sure the child understands. Each of you takes turns laying down a wooden block and then putting one of the cards on top. Initially, the child goes first and you follow with the appropriate rhyming word. When you think the child has the hang of it, you can go first and let him follow. Make sure to put the two words together with amplified facial expressions and intonations. After you have laid out your rhyming words, start playing with different combinations that may not rhyme but may be very funny.

Variations:

See if you can create your own words and combine them in ways that make you laugh. We cannot emphasize enough the importance of developing a playful, creative approach to language development. It is a certain means for the child to feel competent with language and avoid a stilted, scripted style of talking.

Obstacles/Opportunities:

Some children will object to connecting words that are not "supposed" to be together. If this occurs, make sure to emphasize that you are deliberately trying to connect words that do not mean anything. You can take turns and play two versions – one in which you put words together that are meaningful and the other where the words are nonsense.

Rhyming Word Sets:

Funny	Fat	Wall	Hit
Bunny	Hat	Ball	Bit
Sunny	Cat	Tall	Sit
Money	Bat	Call	Pit
Honey	Sat	Fall	Fit
Runny	Mat	Hall	Kit

LEVEL II: APPRENTICE

Introduction

Summary

The move to the Apprentice Level signifies that children are ready to become "Co-Regulators." The major goal of Level II is to teach children to take responsibility for maintaining the coordination of their actions with social partners. By the final stage, children are required to do half the work of keeping their interactions regulated, without resorting to rules or scripts to do so. By accomplishing this, they demonstrate they are ready to introduce variation and novelty and become "Co-Creators" as well, which is the major focus of Level III. In Level II physical actions are still emphasized. Movement is the way we learn to coordinate actions with social partners. A game that epitomizes Level II is "Hide and Seek." By the way, a very interesting element of this game is that when a typical child is "found" she produces the biggest smile of the entire game, even though from an instrumental point of view she has lost the game.

Participants

Level II sees the introduction of peer partners into our activities. Peers are carefully matched to be approximately equal in the stages they have mastered. It is important that each peer knows that his partner will not do the work for him. We often begin with partner combinations in Stage 7.

Settings

We still carefully restrict the settings in which we practice activities. However, typically by this stage, while we still have to carefully limit objects, we are not as concerned by every aspect of visual distraction.

Getting Ready

We cannot over-emphasize the importance of making sure that all Level I skills are in place before moving on to Level II.

Language

In Level II, language is used to teach enactment, to communicate need for regulatory actions (slow down), to enhance joint effort – we did it – and to communicate encouragement of the partner. Language also begins to be used for purposes of regulation and repair. We may verbally check to make sure our partner is ready. We might express confusion. We can also verbally take repair actions like saying, "I'm sorry," when a ball is thrown too high or too hard.

Language used for Encouragement, Regulation and Repair

- Encouragement
- We can do it
- You can do it
- Regulation and Repair
- Are you ready?
- I'm ready
- Start
- Stop
- Faster?
- Slower?
- Slow down
- Harder
- Softer
- Wait
- Come on
- Your turn
- I'm not ready
- Do it again
- Try again
- Change time!

- Watch out!
- I got it
- I can't hear you
- Did you get it?
- Do you understand?
- I'm confused
- What?
- What did you say?
- Now?
- Do you like it?
- Where are you?
- Here I am!
- Uh oh!
- Oh no
- We missed
- Try again
- Say it again
- Sorry!

Coaching Points:

- A key concept in this level is that change occurs in small, manageable degrees.

- Allow the child to gradually introduce more variation into joint activities.

- Continue to carefully monitor your use of language.

- Similarly, carefully monitor your pacing during activities. Always sacrifice speed for coordination.

- In Stage 6, try to create dyads that combine two, well-matched children.

- When you add any type of complexity, always revert back to earlier mastered activities

- Be on the look out for a child's need to win taking prominence over sharing joy and excitement.

STAGE 5: VARIATION

Goals and Objectives

The children we work with often see change as a black-and-white, on-and-off phenomenon. They do not understand that most of the time we spend in relationships consists of determining whether to walk a little faster or touch a bit gentler. In Stage 5, we expose children to the fact that in the relationship world, change is constant and occurs in very small degrees, rather than in on/off segments.

Activity Summary

The Apprentice first has to become consciously aware of his actions, so we begin with a very simple illustration of degrees of a simple change. Next, we move onto learning to coordinate small changes in a number of different areas. Children learn to crash cars with varying degrees of speed. They practice "number crashes" where two numbers close in on each other and eventually become one larger number. Later exercises explore the enjoyment of gradual change while rolling balls, beating drums and walking alongside one another. In the latter part of the stage we begin to explore change as a subjective experience. We investigate the perception that we are too close or too far from one another. We learn that emotions like happiness come in degrees and that they are determined by our own unique experiences and reactions to events. Finally, we examine the changes in ourselves over time as we explore the concept of "improvement." In Stage 5 we continue to use very simple exercises. We are engaged in breaking complex things apart and working on just one element of coordination at a time.

Critical Tips

- Be careful to watch for Apprentices who are too focused on "winning" or perfection.

- Try not to emphasize speed of completion as an important factor.

- You can always use visual communication if language is limited.

- Stay in control of the activities.

- Make sure to practice walking side by side on an everyday basis, with the Apprentice taking more and more responsibility for keeping himself at your side.

Degrees of change

ACTIVITY HIGHLIGHTS
° Introduction to small changes in action
° Learning to use relative thinking

Summary:

This exercise is a nice, simple introduction to making small shifts in action (degrees of change) in order to coordinate with a partner. There was a comic strip we used to enjoy called "Hi and Lo." A nice play on nicknames, it described the small shifts in relationships inherent in our daily lives.

Participants:

Coach and child.

Getting Ready:

You will need two styrofoam "poles" which can usually be found in the pool section of a local store, eight beanbag chairs and other objects that are needed for elevation, along with one small stepladder. The beanbags are stacked like stair steps, with four graded levels of elevation, in two parallel rows. Place them close enough so that the ends of the poles can rest at each level. They should be far enough apart so that the child can easily move between the rows. The stepladder is placed at the very end.

Coaching Instructions:

You and the child face each other on the floor in front of the first level of beanbags. Hold the same styrofoam pole on the ground. When you say, "Higher," together lift the pole to the first level of the beanbags. The next level is approached in the same manner. The final level not only signals the "highest" but the most exciting. Now you should shout, "Higher?" Suggesting that it might be an impossible task. Help the child climb the stepladder, and place the pole at the top. The two of you can savor the moment before you say, "Lower." Now, the child carefully descends the stepladder and together you place the pole on the next lowest stack of beanbags. Then say, "Lower" again and continue down in a fluid motion. Finally, vary higher and lower movements in an unpredictable fashion to make the game more exciting.

Variations:

Place a styrofoam pole on each of the four levels. Play Limbo music and do the Limbo, beginning at the highest level. You and the child can become a Limbo team, holding hands and moving together under each pole, trying not to jar them. See if you can move them lower and lower. Make sure you carefully record "How low can you go!" See if over time you can lower the bar.

Obstacles/Opportunities:

Be careful not to let a child take control of the activity, even if he proves quick to master it. In Stage 5 you are still firmly in control!

LEVEL II, STAGE 5, ACTIVITY 56

Car Crash Variations

ACTIVITY HIGHLIGHTS
° Practicing degrees of speed changes
° Rapidly adapting to activity variations

Summary:

Now we work on adapting to more complex degrees of change. The next exercise features our exciting car crash. Children learn to regulate several factors. First, they must alternate between "crashing" and "passing" their cars. Next, they will vary the force of their release to make the crashes gradually harder and then gradually softer.

Crashing and Passing:

Demonstrate to the child how to deliberately "pass" your cars to each other without crashing them. Alternate trials of "crashing" and "passing." Fluidly change from crashing to passing in an unpredictable manner.

Harder and Softer:

You and the child face each other on carpet squares and recall how much fun crashing cars was earlier. Explain that you will now crash cars in more exciting ways. First teach the child to roll his car gradually faster and then gradually slower, then say, "Let's crash them faster now." Once successful, tell the child to crash, "Even faster." To teach slow crashes you can emphasize the changes by lowering and dragging out your voice, for example, "Eeevennn slooooweerrr."

Variations:

Crash trucks and even boats in a bathtub. Practice backward crashes and passes. Think up your own crashing variations.

Obstacles/Opportunities:

Remember to keep control of the count and release. Despite what may, on the surface, appear to be a violent activity, we have not seen a single negative generalization from this exercise over the 12 years we have been doing it. Children of all ages seem to be thrilled to crash things in a playful, pretend manner.

LEVEL II, STAGE 5, ACTIVITY 57

Number Crash

ACTIVITY HIGHLIGHTS
° Managing several different variations
° Monitoring communication
° Great activity for children who love numbers

Summary:

While similar to the car crash exercise, this activity coordinates the rhythm of movement, building on a child's increased understanding of the shades of gray so common in relationship interactions. Whispering is an important addition introduced in this activity. In order to be successful, the child will have to check whispered information to make sure he has heard correctly.

Participants:

Coach and child.

Getting Ready:

You will need two sets of large wooden numbers from zero to ten, approximately six inches high and two large gardening gloves that can hold the numbers inside them.

Coaching Instructions:

The activity has four steps:

☐ STEP 1

Sit opposite each other at a table, each with your own pile of numbers in front of you. Select a number from your pile. The child selects a number from his pile. For the purposes of this example assume you pick a "four" and the child picks a "seven." Do not show each other the numbers you select.

☐ STEP 2

Place your number inside a glove without the child seeing it. Then place the glove on the tabletop right next to you. The child does the same, using his number. Now, you say, "Four" and the child should say, "Seven." Next, move your gloves a bit closer to each other, with each of you saying your number. You should both shift your gaze to each other each time you "declare" your numbers and move closer. When the two gloves finally come together, there is a "number crash." The person who has begun will assume the "tens" place, while the other partner takes the "ones" place. In this example, when the two gloves finally crash, both of you would shout "forty seven!"

☐ STEP 3

After the activity is clearly understood, play another round where you speak so softly you cannot be heard. If the child does not notice this, you should simply not move your number and wait for the child to look. Then mouth your number again and wait for the child to ask, "What did you say?" Prompting may be necessary, but usually children figure out that the game is not going to proceed if they do not inquire about what you have said.

☐ STEP 4

Another facet of this game is to increase and decrease the numerical value. For example, using the previous number you can say that you will make a higher or lower number. Because you control the tens place, this is easily done. You may also decide to keep your number the same and tell the child to make it higher or lower this time. Gradations of higher and lower are now possible as you work together as a team.

Variations

It is possible to use color cards from a paint store in a manner similar to the way you used numbers above. By the time most children are in kindergarten, they have experienced color mixing to some extent. This activity assumes a fairly thorough understanding of this. Choosing a color card, say, "Red," the child, "Yellow." As you crash you can jointly say, "Orange." Both misunderstanding and value can be addressed through this as well. For example, you might say your color so softly that the child has to ask what you said. You can also suggest, "Let's make the orange lighter." You would each then choose a lighter variation of the previous chosen color. For children with no color mixing experience, introduce this concept concretely. Mix colors. Begin with eyedroppers and food coloring or color from an Easter Egg decoration set. You should drop one drop of red, the child a drop of yellow. Mix the colors and shout, "Orange" together.

Obstacles/Opportunities:

If children have mathematical learning difficulties, the initial exercise may be more difficult. Cautiously use numbers that are familiar to the child or teach them prior to the crash. This activity can be used in a variety of ways at school to increase interaction between children in classroom settings. For example, two plus four equals six. One child has the two, their partner has the four. They move them closer and closer, and when they collide they say, "Six."

LEVEL II, STAGE 5, ACTIVITY 58

Ball rolling variations

ACTIVITY HIGHLIGHTS
° Rapid attention shifting
° Rapid adaptation to activity variations
° Coordinating speed of release

Summary:

We continue with the theme of "degrees of movement" variations by returning to the "Two ball roll" activity learned previously. This exercise is quite similar to our previous car crashing activity. However, it requires fairly rapid gaze shifting, as players have to shift between making sure their ball's are aimed correctly, and getting ready to catch their partner's ball, all in the blink of an eye.

Participants:

Coach and child.

Getting Ready:

You will need two balls, sized to accommodate the child's motor needs and masking tape. A one-foot center square is bordered on opposite sides by lined intervals that are four, six and eight feet apart. This will indicate four possible starting points for the activity if the small central square area is included.

Coaching Instructions:

This activity has six steps:

☐ STEP 1

Choose a sitting position at a distance where the child will find success. Using one ball, see how quickly you are able to roll the ball back and forth without stopping. Adjust the distance as necessary.

☐ STEP 2

Now change balls. Try rolling with smaller and larger balls. See if you can both agree on the size that is the most fun.

☐ STEP 3

Next, try alternating standing and sitting, as you keep the ball rolling between you.

☐ STEP 4

Now practice rolling the ball at an increasingly faster pace. Then, gradually slow it down.

☐ STEP 5

Introduce a second ball. Repeat steps 2, 3 and 4, only this time each of you should release balls simultaneously.

155

☐ STEP 6

When this is mastered, add the variations of alternating "crashing" balls and "passing" balls, as in the prior activity with cars.

Variations:

If the child has the motor proficiency, you can vary rolling with throwing and catching and kicking.

Obstacles/Opportunities:

A child may become overwhelmed by the pace of this activity if not carefully monitored. This can result in controlling behavior or a refusal to play. Most children will respond well to a break in the activity, followed by decreased expectations and slower pace. This does not mean that the child will never tolerate a faster pace, rather that his needs were not adequately anticipated. This becomes an opportunity for children to respect your role in allowing them to achieve a degree of competence that they would be unable to attain by themselves.

LEVEL II, STAGE 5, ACTIVITY 59

Drum Changes

ACTIVITY HIGHLIGHTS

° Using drums to create rhythms that gradually change
° Developing an awareness of coordinating small changes in several variables

Summary:

In this stage we give our Apprentices the experience of maintaining the coordination of their actions while they adapt to subtle shifts. This activity uses drums to provide auditory feedback.

Participants:

Coach and child.

Getting Ready:

You will need two drums.

Coaching Instructions:

This exercise has three steps:

☐ STEP 1   DRUM FASTER AND SLOWER

Practice gradually faster and slower drumbeats. Start with a steady slow beat that the child matches. Increase your speed in gradual increments, pre-announcing each change carefully, "A little faster!" When you approach a rapid speed, begin to decrease speed in equally gradual increments, again pre-announcing each change, "A little slower!"

☐ STEP 2   DRUM LOUDER AND SOFTER

Now repeat the same procedure, but this time vary the loudness until you reach a very high volume and then gradually decrease the volume until you can barely hear your beat.

☐ STEP 3   COMBINING THE TWO

Now we will combine faster/slower with louder/softer. First practice "fast and loud." Then move to "slow and soft." Finally work on "fast and soft" and "slow and loud."

Variations:

A very important exercise is to teach the Apprentice to use his subjective senses to determine preferable degrees of change. As you play the drums, see if you can agree on the speed that is the most fun and the volume that sounds best. In a similar vein, try and agree on the optimum sounds for waking up in the morning and going to sleep at night. See if you can relate volume, speed and intensity of sounds, to different rudimentary emotions such as happiness, anger or sadness. Is there a "happy" drumbeat? How about an "angry" drumbeat?

Obstacles/Opportunities:

If the child shows proficiency with this exercise, it may be an opportunity to try the more complex "Rhythm Changes" activity in the volume for older children, using a keyboard.

LEVEL II, STAGE 5, ACTIVITY 60

Walking Changes

ACTIVITY HIGHLIGHTS
° Learning to walk side by side with another person
° Keeping pace with your partner's movements
° Enjoying gradual coordinated movement changes

Summary:

One of the most important things to teach children in this stage is simply to stay with other people when they are walking. It is very rare for someone at this level of development to be aware when he is not keeping pace with another person.

Participants:

Coach and child.

Getting Ready:

Tape a start line, finish line and two parallel "walking" lines on any floor or outside area.

Coaching Instructions:

This exercise has three steps:

☐ STEP 1   WALKING FASTER AND SLOWER

Count and begin walking together. Make sure that the child is carefully referencing you and regulating his movement to remain at your side. Initially, do not vary your pace, but make sure that the child is matching your pace and not vice versa.

☐ STEP 2   SPEEDING UP

Now instruct the child that you will be starting off slowly and then gradually walking faster on each trial. Begin with one round trip (from start to finish and then back to start) at a moderately slow speed. On the next trip gradually increase your speed while clearly narrating your actions. Keep working at this until the child can remain side by side with you at any reasonable speed. Practice without start and stop lines and in many different settings.

☐ STEP 3   VARYING SPEED

Now you will vary your pace within particular round trips. Tell the child that you are going to start out slow, then speed up a bit on the "return trip" (coming back to the start line). Continue to increase pace at each round trip. Once again, clearly narrate each change that you make. When the child has mastered this, tell him that now you are going to increase your speed more frequently. Make sure to carefully announce when you are going faster, as you increase your speed every few seconds. When you get to the fastest reasonable step, begin decreasing speed gradually. See how fluidly you can perform this without stopping between round trips.

Variations:

If the child is able and willing to do some simple types of coordinated dancing, you can pick a piece of music that gets gradually faster and faster (such as the theme from *Zorba the Greek*) and dance to it together. Another fun variation is to walk together in time with a metronome.

Obstacles/Opportunities:

This exercise is a great start, but, it will only have long-term meaning if you apply it to everyday life. You can practice walking together any time you are at a shopping mall or just going for a walk. In all situations, make sure the child is following your pace. It is quite easy to subconsciously fall into step based on the child's pace instead.

LEVEL II, STAGE 5, ACTIVITY 61

Too Close or Too Far

ACTIVITY HIGHLIGHTS
° Learning to be aware of body position relative to others
° Using subjective impressions to determine optimal body position

Summary:

Children in the Autism Spectrum often have a very poor sense of the position of their body in relation to their social partners. We have constructed a number of exercises to address this. In Stage 5, body awareness activities center on learning to be aware of small degrees of change in distance and orientation with social partners. There are many body position variables that can be addressed. Here we have selected one critical variable – physical distance – moving closer and farther apart from one another.

Participants:

Coach and child.

Getting Ready:

Closer/Farther Apart is best done in a large area, such as an outdoor patio or even better a driveway. Try and pick a flooring surface that is level and one where you can mark off spots that do not have to be erased for long periods of time. Children should have mastered the body position and movement objectives in all prior stages.

Coaching Instructions:

We describe two activities:

☐ STEP 1   CLOSER/FARTHER APART

Play a game of "One-" or "Two-Ball Roll." Chose a center point and various "rolling" points and mark them with tape. Move so that you are very far apart at the farthest points, which should make the game impossible to successfully complete. Start the game. Frequently pause the game and say, "I think we should move closer" and then both of you should move to the next closest "rolling" line, before starting again. Now get very close. Make sure you are really too close and the game is no longer fun. Tell the child, "We are too close. The game is not fun anymore. Let's start moving back." Start the game again, while periodically pausing to move progressively farther apart, continuing to throw or roll the ball back and forth. As you move, try and determine the point where you are too far away to roll or throw a ball and be successful. Try and place two taped lines on the ground to indicate the "too far for throwing" point. Then gradually move in until you find the spot where you are almost on top of each other. Then try to move closer to each other once again while throwing and try to judge when you are too close to have any fun playing the game. Mark those two spots off as well. Now start to move backwards again. The goal this time is to try and find the spot where the game is most fun; where there is still some challenge, but also a good chance for success. Mark these lines off as well. As you practice playing catch, make sure the Apprentice notices as these lines begin to change. If possible, do not remove the old lines just date them. If you have a more physically coordinated Apprentice you can compare the "just right" point for "One-Ball Toss" with the optimal distance for "Two-Ball Toss," just to reinforce one more time the relative nature of physical distance.

☐ STEP 2   WHISPERS AND SHOUTS

Now we will do a similar activity with our voices. Both of you should stand very close together, touching if possible, and practice whispering short appropriate phrases to one another. Make sure that you both can understand each other. Now gradually back away from each other, one step at a time until you reach a point where one or both of you cannot understand the whispering. Keep checking that you both understand each other. When you reach the point of "no whispering" mark it off as a line. Now slowly approach one another and try to determine the point of "best whispering." Repeat the same activity with "shouting" and then with "normal talking voices."

Variations:

Try to create your own activities that address the variables of "ahead of" and "behind" or facing more towards and more away from your partner. As we have said previously, judging when we are too far ahead or too far behind is a completely subjective event. If we are trying to toss a ball back and forth while running together, falling just a bit behind or ahead can be the cause of immediate failure. The issue of relativity is what is so confusing about teaching appropriate physical space and distancing. It all depends on your goals. As you move through degrees of movement changes, continue to provide feedback on what you are now too close for, too far apart for, etc. A more advanced activity is to reference the degree of comfort as a measure of determining what changes are needed in coordinating movement.

Obstacles/Opportunities:

This exercise is yet another that will have no lasting impact unless it is translated into everyday life. We can all see how we can continue to work on relative body positions outside of any specific practice time. We want children to be constantly considering the optimal distance in relation to others for every conceivable type of activity.

LEVEL II, STAGE 5, ACTIVITY 62

Degrees of Happy

ACTIVITY HIGHLIGHTS
° Understanding degrees of emotional expression
° Learning that different events can trigger degrees of emotion
° Appreciating that your social partner's emotion changes are important

Summary:

In this activity, children begin to appreciate emotional expressions as occurring in relative degrees, as opposed to "On/Off" events. This is a crucial step in learning to reference subtle changes in our social partners emotional states. In this exercise, we focus on degrees of happiness. However, it is equally important to repeat the activity with degrees of anger, sadness and fear. We associate degrees of expression change with different events in the child's life that we believe might trigger that reaction. However, at this stage, we are not yet concerned that the child understands the meaning of each subtle change in expression. We are more concerned that he learns that it is important to observe these subtle changes in self and others, and perceive them as important information.

Participants:

Coach and child.

Getting Ready:

The child should have completed prior expression exercises.

Coaching Instructions:

☐ STEP 1

Choose two different events that for the child are related to two different degrees of happiness which you will call "happy" and "very happy." For example, having a dish of ice-cream might result in a "happy" feeling, while getting to go to your favorite amusement park might engender a "very happy" reaction.

☐ STEP 2

After you have connected one event with each level of happiness, it is time to practice making a different facial expression for each level of happiness. Have the child practice making two types of happy faces in front of a mirror corresponding to "happy" and "very happy." When you feel that you can clearly distinguish the different expressions of happiness, take a photo of each one.

☐ STEP 3

Now, show the child each of the photos and teach him to correctly associate it with the event that would cause that specific degree of happiness. An example would be seeing a photo of one of his faces and then saying, "That is my chocolate ice cream face."

☐ STEP 4

Next reverse the game by revealing the event first. Ask, "Which is your chocolate ice cream face?" Have the Apprentice pick out the appropriate facial photograph and then demonstrate the expression that would correspond to the degree of happiness evoked by the event.

☐ STEP 5

Now, discuss your different degrees of happiness to specific events in your life. Make sure that these are not the identical events that would trigger the child's same reactions.

☐ STEP 6

Now, the Apprentice should learn to associate your different facial expressions with your personal events. The child should learn to see one of your faces and tell you which level of happiness you are portraying for example "A going on vacation smile."

Variations:

Find lots of different events and activities that correspond to the two different degrees of happiness and repeat the procedure with these different events. After the child has mastered degrees of happiness, move on to degrees of anger, sadness and fear using the same method. If you think she can be successful, see if she can perceive differences in four degrees of an emotion.

Obstacles/Opportunities:

Some of our sensory delayed children have very poor awareness of their own facial expressions. They don't seem to receive the muscle feedback to help them make subtle distinctions. They may require additional feedback and practice to master this activity, but we know it can be done.

LEVEL II, STAGE 5, ACTIVITY 63

The Sound of Excitement

ACTIVITY HIGHLIGHTS
- Using changes in voice tone to express different degrees of excitement
- Learning voice equivalents of simple emotions
- Becoming sensitive to your social partner's voice for emotional information

Summary:

In prior activities we have worked on two other essential elements of non-verbal communication, body distance and facial expression. Now we address the third critical element of voice. As in the prior exercise we will be linking degrees of voice change to a specific emotion, in this case, excitement.

Participants:

Coach and child.

Getting Ready:

Children should have completed prior non-verbal communication exercises.

Coaching Instructions:

This exercise parallels the last one on facial expressions.

☐ STEP 1

Choose two events or activities that are clearly related to two different degrees of excitement for him, for example, "excited" and "really excited."

☐ STEP 2

After you have associated the events with the two degrees of excitement proceed to associate a different vocal expression with each. Have children listen to audio-tapes of different people conveying the levels of excitement.

☐ STEP 3

Next, have the child practice recording each of the two levels. Provide lots of audio feedback via the cassette recorder and make sure that the child can distinguish one from another. When you have decided on the best voices, record them.

☐ STEP 4

Present the child with one of the two voices and ask him to correctly associate it with the event that would cause that specific degree of excitement. An example would be, "That is a going to Disney World really excited voice." Next reverse the game by providing the event and having the child produce the voice that would correspond to the degree of excitement evoked by it. "This is what a going to Disney World voice would sound like."

☐ STEP 5

Now relate your own degrees of excitement to specific events or activities in your life. Make sure that these are not the identical events that would trigger the child's reactions. Create a tape of your own voices. Now, have the child associate your degrees of excitement with your personal events/activities. Finally, the child should learn to hear each one of your excited voices and tell you which level of excitement you are portraying, for example, "A going on vacation, really excited voice."

Variations:

Find many different events and activities that correspond to the different degrees of excitement and repeat the procedure with each. After the child has mastered degrees of excitement, move on to degrees of anger, sadness and fear using the same method. If you believe she can be successful, see if she can perceive changes in four degrees of an emotion.

Obstacles/Opportunities:

As in the prior exercise, you will come across some children who have a difficult time distinguishing voice qualities and thus enacting two separate excited voices. But given practice we have found that every child can complete this important exercise.

Getting Better

ACTIVITY HIGHLIGHTS

° Learning to perceive degrees of improvement

° Experiencing the excitement of improving as a team or unit

Summary:

Like some of our prior objectives, learning to understand improvement is not a social skill per se. However, being able to perceive degrees of improvement is critical in remaining motivated to work on any skill that does not provide an immediate payoff. As relationship skills get more complex, children must be provided with temporary "markers" to show them that they are making progress, even though they are not yet receiving the benefit of their increasing skill. One thing you should know about us is that we love to fabricate "world records" as a motivation for many of our activities.

Participants:

Coach and child.

Getting Ready:

If you are doing car crashes you will need your cars. You will also need a tape measure. Choose a specific activity that you and the child can jointly work at to improve in gradual steps. Make sure it is an activity that lends itself to easy recording of progress. For example, in the prior exercise, we demonstrated how to demarcate lines indicating the optimal distance for a game of car crashing or rolling the ball back and forth. For example, you can define the goal as seeing how many crashes you can make in a row. In a variation, we ask that you determine how far apart you can get and still have ten successful rolls, or five crashes in a row. In this example, you can actually measure the distance apart to illustrate your improvement.

Coaching Instructions for Car Crashing:

The activity has two steps:

☐ STEP 1

Tell the child that you are going to "get better" at the chosen activities. You will practice together and see how much better you get. Divide up your crashing activity into five-minute practice intervals. Count the number of successful crashes during your practice period and keep a performance chart on the wall, with an entry made each time you practice. Later you can count the most successful crashes in a row during any period.

☐ STEP 2

Now try to get farther away. Start three feet apart (measured by your tape measure) and try to make five crashes in a row. Then progress backwards one foot, every time you make five in a row. Keep a chart of your continued progress with an entry for each date. Remember to celebrate your success. To make it more exciting, you can designate "achievement labels" for different distances. For instance, when you reach six feet you can say you have made it to the "intermediate level," seven feet can be the "advanced level." Eight feet can be the "professional level" and so on.

Variations:

The sad truth is that life is not always about getting better. Sometimes there are temporary setbacks on the road to success. Along with celebrating our small triumphs, we try and find ways to mutually "mourn" our temporary defeats. There is nothing like keeping a meaningful record of past successes to provide perspective at the time of a setback. Make sure to keep your "getting better" charts handy and use them as a reference point each time the child encounters a setback.

Obstacles/Opportunities:

Try not to use any criteria based on speed, as this seems to increase stress and the potential for meltdowns. Be wary of children who become too focused on winning or achieving a specific result. They may not be ready for this exercise.

STAGE 6: TRANSFORMATION

Goals and Objectives

Until this stage we have focused on only one half of what we refer to as the "relationship balance." Apprentices have practiced acting as "Co-Regulators," learning to keep their actions coordinated with their partners. Now we begin to address the other half of the balance – learning to enjoy novelty and unpredictability – the creative part of relationships. This will set the stage for Level III, where the child learns to function as a "Co-Creator." In the variation stage, Apprentices learned to enjoy degrees of change such as moving faster and slower even when introduced in an unpredictable manner. In the transformation stage, new elements emerge, patterns are altered, and one activity may be transformed into an entirely new one, albeit in a gradual manner. "Follow the Leader" is an activity that epitomizes the transformation stage. The leader can turn walking into skipping, balancing on a beam, etc. at a moments notice and similarly the "followers" match his change at a moment's notice.

Activity Highlights

Activities in this stage revolve around gradual transformations. These occur not all at once, but in an observable step-by-step sequence so that the Apprentice is not mystified or overwhelmed. It is like doing time-series photography so that an action that actually occurs in a split second can be slowed down and studied. We begin the stage by learning how one activity can gradually be transformed into another one in a surprising, yet enjoyable manner. We go on to explore transformations in functions of objects – the way we use them and rules. In the middle phase of Stage VI we enter "Opposite World," a place where things are always the opposite of the way they were before. Then we explore the role of unexpected changes in producing hilarious humor. We take a side trip into the world of "morphing emotions," an exercise designed to demonstrate how our emotional worlds can change dramatically from one moment to the next. Then we return to humor to design wacky role-plays, where characters rapidly change role actions. In this activity, mommys climb into their cribs for a nap, while babies grab their briefcases and head off to the office. We close the stage with an exploration of the aesthetic world of transformation, with an activity where children experience how music can be used to portray transformations in the natural world.

Critical Tips

- Add variations in a slow gradual process so that each change is understandable to the Apprentice.

- Make sure to give transformed activities and structures new names, so the Apprentice can remember them as different from the original.

- By the close of this stage, Apprentices should be hungry for novelty and see variations as major sources of fun and excitement!

- You should also observe a significant increase in flexibility and tolerance for change.

- Make sure that humor develops apart from reliance on scripts.

LEVEL II, STAGE 6, ACTIVITY 65

Activity Transformations

ACTIVITY HIGHLIGHTS

° Enjoying unexpected novelty and change

° Understanding how one activity can transform into another

Summary:

In the last stage, we taught children to adapt to degrees of change in a single variable like faster/slower and harder/gentler. This exercise is the first in exposing children to a new type of variation in which there is a gradual transformation of one activity into another. As in many of our exercises, we present a sample activity that will hopefully give you ideas for many more.

Participants:

Coach and child.

Getting Ready:

For the base activity that we have chosen, you will need 48 cards or pieces of different colored paper cut into different shapes. Twelve cards will each be in the shape of triangles, squares and circles. You also need 12 cards cut out as two rectangles with a "bridge" between them at the top (in the general shape of a torso – two legs and a small abdominal area). You should also make them in three colors, again evenly distributed between the four shapes.

Coaching Instructions:

Begin by teaching the base activity, which will soon be transformed. Divide the cards into two piles, one for you and one for the child. Begin a simple matching game, where the child has to work out which of his cards he should play to match the one that you turn over. After you turn over a card and place it on the table, the child turns over one and places it directly underneath yours. If the child is incorrect, have him take the card back and try another until he makes a match. Now you should do the first activity which is about matching shapes. Lay out three triangles, side by side. Any color triangle is a correct match. Then lay out three yellow shapes. Any yellow shape will be a match. Next, lay out three triangles again. This time only a circle will be a match. Now directly underneath the child's circle, lay out any color square. The only correct match will be a "torso." When you have completed the three rows, if the child hasn't already noticed, point to what you have made and say, "Look what we made! A person! Let's make more!" Lay down three new rows of triangles and see if the child has caught on. Hopefully, the activity has now moved from one of correct matching, to building human figures with triangle hats, circle faces, square mid-sections and rectangular torsos. Now take markers and together draw on the facial features and other embellishments you wish to provide for your figures.

Variations:

Build towers out of wooden blocks and then get out a ball and practice knocking them down. Make popcorn together and practice with one of you holding a basket and the other tossing the popcorn into it. We hope that the examples above provide many ideas for how you can present transformations, where by one activity turns gradually into another one.

Obstacles/Opportunities:

You may have to "tweak" this activity to get it to work, depending upon the age and understanding of the child. You can use any number of cards, colors and presentations.

LEVEL II, STAGE 6, ACTIVITY 66

Function Transformations

ACTIVITY HIGHLIGHTS
° Flexible, divergent thinking
° Rapid adaptation

Summary:

Functional transformations are quite similar to activity transformations. The difference is that now the activity remains the same, while the means we use to perform the activity are suddenly transformed in unexpected and enjoyable ways.

Participants:

Coach and child.

Getting Ready:

You will need baskets, paper clips, balls, chairs, blocks, a table, two hats a box of biscuit crackers and play people.

Coaching Instructions:

There are three main formats presented below:

Unexpected Substitutions:

Start out with both of you wearing hats and playing a game of throwing a ball into a basket. The child should start out as the thrower and you should be the catcher. Now put down the basket, take off your hat and tell the child that you are continuing the game, but now you will be using a hat as the basket. Switch roles with the child and have him use his hat as a basket to catch the balls in. Continue playing the game and switch from tossing balls to tossing small stuffed animals into the hat.

Unexpected Reversals:

Begin having a pretend dinner by sitting on chairs and placing your food on a table. Suddenly tell the Apprentice it is time to switch. Now sit on the table and place your food on your chairs.

Strange Endings:

Build a house together with blocks and make sure you run out of blocks right before its time to build the roof. Take out a box of crackers and make the roof by attaching them together with paper clips.

Variations:

You can end the last activity by having two pretend "monsters" (you and the Apprentice) come and devour the roof. We also like to use model Godzillas or King Kongs. If you do, make sure to place some play people inside the house so you and the Apprentice can make some screaming sound effects. You can also repeat the activity and now build the entire house from crackers if you can.

Obstacles/Opportunities:

This is another great opportunity to teach flexible thinking and rapid set shifting. These are just a few examples of literally scores of activities that we practice in this stage to gradually increase the children's understanding and love of unexpected improvisations. By the end of this stage the children we work with are hungry for new unexpected actions and especially excited by opportunities to participate in their creation and enactment.

Rule Changes

ACTIVITY HIGHLIGHTS
° Flexible adaptation
° Adapting to rapid rule changes
° Enjoying a degree of unpredictability

Summary:

In this activity, we completely alter the rules of familiar games to make them very different: We begin with a simple game like Candy Land. One by one you will introduce changes in the rules that "morph" the game into something entirely different.

Participants:

Coach and child.

Getting Ready:

You will need to carefully choose a game to play. Check the sample transformations to see what other materials you may need.

Coaching Instructions:

For this example we will use the game of Candy Land, but any game or activity with rules will do just as well. Inform the child that you are going to play the game, but you are going to play it a special way. You are going to practice making lots of rule changes. Prior to any change you will announce, "Rule change" and check with the child to make sure he is ready by saying, "Here comes the change. Are you ready?" Between rule changes, keep the excitement and attention focused on the next rule change and make sure the child does not get too focused on the game itself. Begin playing the game with the standard set of rules. Make your first rule change after you both have taken one turn. Stop, announce, "Rule change" and say, "Now we will pick two cards instead of one." Practice this for several turns prior to the next change and then continue to make regular changes. We provide some sample changes below.

Variations:

As well as the sample changes, feel free to provide your own. Remember that you can use any game you would like. When you are finished adding a number of changes, make sure to provide a new name for the game like "Silly Candy Land." Make sure that the child recognizes that you have created a brand new game that only looks like the old version. Write down the new rules and play it regularly along with the regular version.

Obstacles/Opportunities:

Remember not to choose any game which the child is likely to become particularly obsessed with. With highly competitive children it might be better to teach them a new game first and before they get involved in it, begin playing this version. This will make an excellent activity in Stage 8 when we introduce our peer dyads. It will also be repeated in Stage 10 when partners will "co-create" game variations and in Stage 11 when Challengers "improvise" variations in their game "On-the-Fly."

Sample Changes for Candy Land

° Use a stuffed dog as one of the players. Play "Dog Candy Land" where you have to bark to communicate instead of talking.

° Pick two cards and choose the best one.

° Every time you pick a green card (pick your color) you have to move backwards.

LEVEL II, STAGE 6, ACTIVITY 68

Opposite World

ACTIVITY HIGHLIGHTS

° Enjoyment of activities that turn into their opposites
° Appreciation for unexpected transformations

Summary:

Another type of transformation occurs when one thing surprisingly turns into its opposite. We all love these types of surprises and hope that our children come to enjoy them as well. In this exercise, we turn a game of catch into a game of "drop the ball," we say goodbye when greeting instead of "hello," and generally enjoy the silliness of creating opposites. One other important change in this exercise is that now we introduce our transformation at a much more fluid pace and without warning. By this point our children should be ready for this type of fast-paced change.

Participants:

Coach and child.

Getting Ready:

By this stage, children should be comfortable with sudden changes that are aimed at generating mutual laughter. You will need a ball, a white board and markers, a jigsaw puzzle, a board game and some props for a simple domestic role-play.

Coaching Instructions:

You can begin the series of activities by explaining "Opposite World" to the child. When you enter Opposite World, whatever you are doing at that time suddenly turns into its opposite. At this stage, only the Coach has the power to turn on Opposite World. We are presenting four steps of what can be an unlimited number of "opposite" activities:

☐ STEP 1 SUCCESS OPPOSITES

Begin a simple game of catch. See how many times the two of you can catch the ball without dropping it. Now tell the child that you are entering Opposite World. The new game is to see how many times you can "just miss" the ball without catching it. Demonstrate how to "just miss" which requires partners to almost catch the ball but not quite. See if you can demonstrate two or three different ways to "just miss" and then start the game. Try to invent new ways of "just missing" and record them for future demonstration.

☐ STEP 2 GOAL OPPOSITES

Go over to a white board and begin an activity of taking turns drawing an elaborate figure together. Once you have drawn all over the white board, make an "Opposite World" announcement and tell the child that the new game is taking turns erasing pieces of the drawing. Do a similar activity with a jigsaw puzzle.

☐ STEP 3 RULE OPPOSITES

Begin playing a game like Candy Land. At some point in the game make an "Opposite World" announcement and inform the child that now the goal of the game is to go backwards to the starting point as quickly as possible. Go backwards to the color card that you draw. Play this way for a while and then shout "Opposite World" again. Now return to moving forwards.

☐ STEP 4 ROLE-PLAY OPPOSITES

Practice a simple role-play where you wake up in the morning, eat breakfast, go to school and/or work, come home, eat dinner and go to bed. You can have parallel roles and pretend to be two brothers or sisters, or complementary roles where you are a parent and child. Make an "Opposite World" announcement and teach the Apprentice how to do the role-play backwards. Wake up at night, take off your pajamas, put on your clothes, eat your dinner, go to work, come home, eat breakfast, put on your pajamas and go to bed. Now do the role-play in the original order again.

Variations

As in the prior activity we are sure you can come up with unlimited variations.

Obstacles/Opportunities:

As you might imagine this is excellent training for our children who have difficulty in flexible thinking and set shifting. After a short time, most of the enjoyment should be derived from the unpredictability. The child never knows when the Coach will shout, "Opposite World!" and the fun will begin.

LEVEL II, STAGE 6, ACTIVITY 69

Unexpected Jokes

ACTIVITY HIGHLIGHTS
° Learning the true function of humor
° Finding alternative to "scripted" jokes
° Developing improvised humor

6

Summary:

Those of you who have read Steve's first book probably remember a bittersweet vignette I shared about a child who had worked hard to learn "Knock Knock" jokes only to encounter a younger child who did not know the format and, though very amused, provided the "wrong" response, which provoked rage from my client. We work hard to help children learn that the main function of jokes and humor is shared laughter, rather than getting the joke to be performed correctly. In this activity we reinforce this notion by teaching children to alter jokes so that they deviate way off their scripts in unexpected ways.

Participants:

Coach and child.

Getting Ready:

Completion of prior humor and absurdity activities is essential for the child to appreciate the sudden shifts. Once you use up our joke examples you will need to create your own.

Coaching Instructions:

Tell the child that you are going to teach him how to be really funny. First teach the "funny" version of a joke. The "really funny" version works best when you tell it right after the "funny" version. Teach the "really funny" version right after the child learns the "funny" version and teach him to tell the two versions in rapid sequence. Make sure the child practices these jokes with family members and familiar people. Please make sure that everyone laughs much harder for the "really funny" versions of our jokes! We will present four formats for transforming jokes. We will expect you and the child to develop many more:

- **Format 1** *Transform one essential element of a joke and make it equally as funny.*
  "Funny" Version

  > Knock Knock
  >
  > > *Who's there?*
  >
  > Banana
  >
  > > *Banana Who?*
  >
  > Knock Knock
  >
  > > *Who's there?*
  >
  > Banana
  >
  > > *Banana Who?*
  >
  > Knock Knock
  >
  > > *Who's there?*
  >
  > Orange
  >
  > > *Orange Who?*
  >
  > Orange you glad I didn't say banana

  "Really Funny" Version

  > Knock Knock
  >
  > > *Who's there?*
  >
  > Coconut
  >
  > > *Coconut who?*
  >
  > Knock Knock
  >
  > > *Who's there?*
  >
  > Coconut
  >
  > > *Coconut who?*
  >
  > Knock Knock
  >
  > > *Who's there?*
  >
  > Duck
  >
  > > *Duck Who?*
  >
  > Duck! There's a coconut falling on your head!

- **Format 2:** *We criss-cross the main subjects of the joke.*
  "Funny" Version

  > Why did the chicken cross the road?
  > > *To get to the other side.*

  "Really funny" Version

  > Why did the road cross the chicken?

Because it was crossing into Kentucky.

- **Format 3:** We turn one joke into another joke.

"Funny" version

Why did the chicken cross the road?

To get to the other side.

"Really funny" Version

Why did the turkey cross the road?

To get to the other side

Why did the turkey cross the ocean?

To get away from Thanksgiving

Variations:

Have children practice making their own silly endings to these predictable beginning lines. Do not worry if they have any meaning, as long as they make you laugh.

Obstacles/Opportunities:

This activity, like many others we present, sets the stage for framing social encounters as improvisational and creative. This is an invaluable set for our children to maintain in order to behave in a manner that is inviting to their peers. Remember that you will have to practice this with many joke variations and not just the examples presented above. Also remember that young children appreciate enthusiasm and shared laughter from their peers much more than logic and "getting it right."

LEVEL II, STAGE 6, ACTIVITY 70

Morphing Emotions

ACTIVITY HIGHLIGHTS

° Introduction to rapid changes in emotions

° Exposure to how quickly situations change

Summary:

Sometimes in life we may rapidly go from feeling one emotion to its exact opposite. We may believe that something has happened and find out that, in fact, it was the exact opposite of what we thought had happened. This activity provides an introduction to unexpected emotional transformations. It also exposes Apprentices to the concept that context can change rapidly and that we should not always expect a situation to play out the way we think it will.

Participants:

Coach and child.

Getting Ready:

Include some props to make the role-plays more exciting and realistic. It is helpful if you can change hats to indicate role shifts.

Coaching Instructions:

We will present four simple scenes to illustrate this exercise. Tell the child that you are going to learn role-plays that you can perform for parents and other children. You and the child should match your emotional expressions to the characters in the story, pretending to be happy and sad together as the story unfolds.

☐ HAPPINESS TURNS TO SADNESS:

Teach a simple role-play where the child is at home and answers the door. The Coach, pretending to be the mailman, knocks on the door and the child opens it. The mailman says, "Congratulations, you have just won one million dollars. Here is your check. Have a great day." The child should receive the check and pretend to be quite happy and excited. Now there is another knock on the door. The Apprentice opens the door and it is the tax man, who says, "Hello. I am the tax man. I heard that you just received one million dollars. Is that correct? Well, you will have to pay taxes on that." The Tax Man pretends to add up numbers on a calculator and then says, "Well the total taxes you owe come to a one million dollars. Please pay me now or I will have to take you to jail." The Apprentice hands over the check to the tax man. Now the Apprentice is very sad.

☐ UNEXPECTED EMOTION 1:

The child knocks the door dressed as the mailman. The Coach answers the door. The mailman says, "Congratulations, you just won a million dollars." The Coach begins to cry in sadness. The mailman asks, "What's wrong? Didn't you hear me? You just won a million dollars!" The Coach still crying says, " I heard you, but I need two million dollars to pay my bills. How terrible that I only won one million!" Make sure to reverse roles.

☐ UNEXPECTED EMOTION 2:

In the final play, the child pretends to be a robber. He breaks into the Coach's house and steals a TV set. Then he yells, "Ha-ha, I just stole your TV" and proceeds to run away with the TV. The Coach hears this and acts very worried and scared. Later there is a knock on the door and the child, this time pretending to be a policeman is there. When the policeman sees the Coach, the Coach is laughing and smiling. The policeman says, "Hello, I am a policeman. Why are you so happy? Don't you know your TV was stolen?" The Coach laughs and says, "I have two TVs. One TV is broken and it was so big I could not lift it to throw it out. The robber stole the broken one. If you catch him, thank him for helping me get rid of it!"

Variations:

You can vary the last play by having the robber feel great about getting away with the TV, then going home to turn it on and finding out that it is broken.

Obstacles/Opportunities:

You will have to practice these scripts before performing them, for the child to become fluid in his role. Remember to break them up into parts before combining them. You will also have to adjust the scripts based upon the age and level of understanding of the child.

6

LEVEL II, STAGE 6, ACTIVITY 71

Role Reversals

ACTIVITY HIGHLIGHTS
° Recognizing that roles are not always scripted
° Learning to not make stereotyped assumptions
° Enjoying seeing people behave "out of character"

Summary:

In this activity we explore a different type of role reversal than that practiced in prior stages. Rather than switching roles, it is the characters in the play whose role actions are transformed in hopefully ridiculous and enjoyable ways.

Participants:

Coach and child.

Getting Ready:

Provide sufficient props so that the children enjoy the plays. Props for each play are fairly self-evident.

Coaching Instructions:

We will present three different reversed character scenes. Please create many of your own.

☐ MOMMY AND DADDY

Coach and child take on the roles of mommy and daddy. They also pretend to have a baby. The play starts with mommy, daddy and baby at the breakfast table, eating their breakfast and talking about what they are going to do today. There is a very "business-like" briefcase on the table. The "daddy" announces it is time to go to work. Now pretend to have the baby pick up the briefcase and go off to work. Mommy goes to her crib for a nap and daddy puts on an apron and washes the dishes.

☐ POLICEMAN AND ROBBER

The Coach starts the play as a policeman and the child starts as a robber. Make sure that each dresses in some way that easily identifies the characters. Both the policeman and the robber are in a bank. The policeman takes off his police uniform and underneath there is a robber outfit. He pulls out his gun and says, "Everybody freeze. This is a bank robbery. I fooled you. I am really a robber, not a policeman. Give me all the money." Now the robber takes off his robber outfit and underneath he has a police badge. He pulls out his gun and says, "Drop your gun robber. I am really a policeman pretending to be a robber. You are going to jail!"

☐ DR. TUSK'S CLINIC

Make a big sign that says "Animal Clinic. Dr. Tusk in residence." Build a "clinic" out of blocks and tape the sign to the front of it. Make sure the clinic has two different rooms. Provide the child with a large plastic elephant. Provide the Coach with a large plastic human figure that might appear to be a doctor. The play starts with both characters inside the clinic. Each is in a different room. The elephant walks into the human's room. There is a pretend exam table in the room and a play stethoscope lying on the table. They greet each other. The human sits on the exam table and says, "Dr. Tusk I am not feeling well. I hope you can help me." The elephant then examines the human with the stethoscope and says, "Well, Well! I think you have the elephant flu. I am sure I can help you."

Variations:

A similar play to the one we presented first is a mother–child reversal that all children love to enact. The characters are a mother or father and child. The play opens late at night, with the child watching TV downstairs in the living room. The parent is upstairs. Suddenly, the parent quietly comes downstairs on tiptoes. The child looks around, notices the parent, scowls and says, "I told you to stay in bed!" The parent looks "caught," says, "Sorry" and runs back up to bed. Now see how many of these reversals you can create!

Obstacles/Opportunities:

These plays, along with the jokes of the prior activity really work if they can performed many times for appreciative audiences. The applause and laughter of family members and peers makes all the hard rehearsal worthwhile.

Transforming Rhythms

ACTIVITY HIGHLIGHTS
° Aesthetic judgment
° Making subjective impressions

Summary:

In the final exercise of Stage 6, we make a leap into a new area we can call Aesthetic Transformations. As our activities have progressed we have moved from very concrete structural changes to altered rules, roles and humorous elements. Now we transform our subjective reactions based upon changes in musical rhythm, volume and speed.

Participants:

Coach and child.

Getting Ready:

You will need two drums for this exercise.

Coaching Instructions:

This exercise has four steps:

☐ STEP 1

Begin by teaching the Apprentice to recognize how different types of music can evoke either a peaceful, relaxed feeling or a stormy, scared or angry feeling. Only proceed when you are sure that he can easily make the distinction.

☐ STEP 2

Teach the child to beat the drum in a soft, peaceful manner. Teach him to play a simple rhythm with you that, when played softly, evokes a calm feeling. When you have mastered this tape record it.

☐ STEP 3

Next you will practice the stormy part of your piece. This time you will begin softer but progressively get louder and louder in drumming. When you are playing very loudly, see if you can create a real storm-like effect. When you are ready, record this piece as well and name it "Thunderstorm."

☐ STEP 4

The final part of the exercise entails combining the two pieces on the tape recorder. You can also try combining them "live" if you think you are both up to it. When you are successful, play the tape for yourselves and many others with the new title, "Peaceful day turns into thunderstorm."

Variations:

Try using your drums to turn a soft song called "Raindrops" into a loud raucous version of "Thunderstorm."

Obstacles/Opportunities:

Besides being a great vehicle for working on emotions, visual perception and motor skills, this exercise is an introduction to our next stage, Synchronization. In this stage Apprentices learn to regulate their actions and simultaneously coordinate them with ours in order to produce many different types of "duets."

STAGE 7: SYNCHRONIZATION

Goals and Objectives

Now we begin a stage where Apprentices take responsibility for regulating their interaction to make sure they remain coordinated. In Stage 7 we engage in more complex coordinated activities. The Apprentice learns more of the elements needed to be a partner in real-life, complex interactions. "Ring around the Rosie" is a good Stage 7 example. There is a framework but to be successful it requires mutual regulation and coordination. Walking together and holding a pail is another example of a Stage 7 activity. You pick up something and carry it together while staying side by side.

Activity Summary

We begin the stage by working on a simple, yet critical part of synchronizing actions – learning to start and stop together. Children learn several ways of referencing their social partner's state of readiness, as well as communicating their own degree of readiness. This leads us to the new skill area of Self Talk. For children to synchronize their actions in complex activities, they must have a means of rapidly altering their own actions. Self Talk supplies the means for ongoing regulation. Now we are ready for the move into more complex requirements for synchronized movements. For the first time we deliberately practice breakdowns of coordination. Communication and relationships are constantly breaking down. We use systematic, predictable breakdowns that are incorporated as a part of the activity. We want Apprentices to get used to the breakdowns and so we practice them over and over again. We make them into games. This also increases the sense of competence and confidence, and the flexibility of our partners.

At this stage jokes become even more important. We again emphasize that humor is a relative thing, completely dependent upon what we find funny. It does not have to be scripted. It can even be absurd and meaningless. We also provide practice in synchronizing conversational topics, our first foray into the world of reciprocal conversation. Also for the first time, we teach Apprentices to consider the potential future actions of their social partners. If we are playing soccer and you have to pass the ball to me and we are both moving, are you going to kick the ball to where I am now or where you think I am about to be? The idea that you can anticipate what someone else is going to do, or say next, and plan your actions based upon their future actions, not their present ones, is a critical breakthrough. Stage 7 contains activities that for the first time include peer partners working together.

Critical Tips

- Remember to modify the speed and complexity of motor activities based upon the motor skills of the Apprentice.

- Reinforce the pride Apprentices will feel for taking greater responsibility in synchronizing their actions.

- Learning Self Talk and Self Instruction takes a great deal of practice. They need to become automatic habits that the Apprentice uses on an everyday basis.

- Practice the "Tricky Partner" exercise sufficiently to prepare Apprentices for the large increase in rapid adaptation they will experience when partnered with peers.

- Remember to go back to early activities when first introducing Apprentices to one another.

LEVEL II, STAGE 7, ACTIVITY 73

Are You Ready

ACTIVITY HIGHLIGHTS
° Taking responsibility to determine readiness of social partners
° Communicating effectively concerning your readiness
° Taking responsibility for regulating activities
° Managing coordination breakdowns

Summary:

A first step in becoming a true interaction partner is ensuring that both participants are ready, prior to proceeding with an action that affects both of you, such as throwing a ball. In this activity, children learn several ways of referencing their social partner's state of readiness, as well as communicating their own degree of readiness. Finally they learn not to expect that their partners will always be ready just because they are and also how to react to situations of non-readiness.

Participants:

Coach and child.

Getting Ready:

No specific materials are needed for this activity other than a ball.

Coaching Instructions:

This activity has three main steps:

☐ STEP 1

Practice different ways to signal to each other so that you can begin an action together. Choose an activity such as walking or running together and practice counting, "One, Two, Three, Go." Make sure to try going on "three" as well as "Go." Shift to "Ready, Set, Go." Next, try a countdown of "Three, Two, One, Go."

☐ STEP 2

Now proceed on to non-verbally "counting." Use head nods to signal the count without saying any words. Next use a single head nod as a start signal. Switch to an activity where you are sending and receiving, like a game of catch. Use the non-verbal signal of "hands outreached" to signal readiness to receive. Use the non-verbal signal of mimicking a throw to signal that you are ready to deliver the ball. Practice synchronizing the two signals. Have one partner mimic a throw and the other place his hands out to receive. Finally, practice verbally asking, "Are you ready?" and replying with "Yes" or "No."

☐ STEP 3

Now practice the application of these various signals in situations where they may or may not occur smoothly. Practice counting "One, Two, …" and then vary the length of time you pause prior to finishing the count. Practice beginning the count and then step off the starting line in the midst of it. Make sure to practice the appropriate way for the child to request that you return to the start line. Return to the game of catch and respond to the child's signaling to find out whether you are ready, by averting your gaze, then putting your hands behind your back and only then indicating readiness. See if you and the child can take turns practicing these types of coordination breakdowns and others you invent, in a manner that becomes mutually funny and challenging.

Variations:

A logical variation is to practice signaling to stop together. There are various forms of "stopping" signals. Practice signaling, both verbally and non-verbally, that you are tired and need a break. Practice requesting an end to an activity, because you want to do something else.

Obstacles/Opportunities:

This is the first clear requirement for children to begin taking responsibility for the success of the interaction. It is critical that they emerge from this activity, not only with the skills in place, but also with a sense of pride in their new abilities.

LEVEL II, STAGE 7, ACTIVITY 74

Talk to Yourself

ACTIVITY HIGHLIGHTS

° Translating instructions into Self Talk
° Self-Monitoring actions
° Using Self Talk to review, plan and evaluate actions

Summary:

In a number of prior activities, we have asked you to narrate your actions. This is a form of talking to yourself out loud. Your Self Talk has two critical virtues. First, because you are not directly addressing the child, there is no "demand character" to your words, evoking less anxiety and making them much easier to process. Second, you are modeling a type of language referred to as Self Talk, which is essential for planning, reviewing and guiding our actions. This activity formally introduces the child to Self Talk. In the first application, the child learns to use Self Talk to "translate" your instructions into his own words. Translating your words is a critical step in "owning" the communication and moving from being a passive to an active information processor.

Later in the exercise, we move on to a second major function of narration, which is using Self Talk to guide our actions. Now we expose the budding Apprentice to various forms of Self Talk that he will begin to use to regulate his own actions. We begin with teaching him to narrate an action that he has just taken. Then we progress to using Self Talk for anticipating an action that he is about to take. Finally, we progress to Evaluation Self Talk, in which he learns to provide a simple evaluation label to a just completed action.

Participants:

Coach and one or two children.

Getting Ready:

You should have used narration extensively in prior activities.

Coaching Instructions:

There are seven steps in this exercise. In each step you must make sure the child is narrating out loud and using language to indicate he is not talking to you. Also, make sure to avert your eye gaze while he is self talking, so he is not confused between Self Talk and communicative language.

☐ STEP 1   FROM MY WORDS TO YOUR WORDS

Start this exercise by having the child practice translating very simple instructions into Self Talk. "Walk to the door" can be translated as, "I need to walk to the door," or even "I walk to door." Keep practicing simple translations until the child demonstrates proficiency. If he is having difficulty, model out loud how you would translate your own words into Self Talk.

☐ STEP 2   MORE COMPLEX INSTRUCTIONS

Now make the instructions more complicated and work on two-part instructions and directions such as, "First walk to the door and then open it." This can be translated into "I walk to door and open it." Continue to add complexity for as long as the child can be successful. As quickly as possible move to meaningful instructions and directions, so that the child can see some payoff for his translation efforts. Try to make a habit of requiring the child to translate your instructions into his own words, prior to expecting him to carry out any actions.

☐ STEP 3   REVIEW

In this step, the child learns to use Self Talk to narrate an action he has just taken. Make a request for the child to complete some relatively simple activity that is within his capability of remembering and narrating. After he has finished the activity, instruct him to tell himself out loud what he has just done.

☐ STEP 4   MULTI-STEP REVIEW

In this step, Apprentices are taught to stop at regular intervals to review the actions they have just taken. Now we move to a more complex activity that has several different steps. These should be natural places to stop and review. A sample activity could be following a LEGO construction set that has several clearly demarcated steps of construction. After each step, the child stops and narrates to himself what he has just completed. If you can, have the child take a photo of the activity at each of the stages of completion.

☐ STEP 5   PREVIEW

In this phase, the child uses the stopping interval to Self Talk the actions he is about to take. Have the child review what he has just done. But, before proceeding on, ask him to "preview" the next step and tell himself what he is about to do. Make sure the child uses future-oriented language. After he has finished the step he has just previewed, ask him if his preview was accurate.

☐ STEP 6   EVALUATION

Now children learn to stop and make a simple evaluation of the activity like; "That was great," "That was fun," or "I did a good job." After completing all the steps of the activity, ask the child to provide a simple evaluative label for the activity. If he is unable to come up with a label on his own, provide visuals for several and have him choose one or two.

☐ STEP 7   RECORDING

The final step entails preserving a review of actions in a simple manner. Now take the photos and the narrations and place them together in an "activity journal." The photos should be placed in order with the narrative under them. The final stage of completion should contain the evaluative label.

Variations:

It is a great idea to use this method with all you children for everyday things such as cleaning up their room, or helping to prepare a meal. It is highly motivating for them to see their room in various stages of completion and then finally to feel the satisfaction of getting it right.

Obstacles/Opportunities:

This is a great exercise for children who believe they are "listening" to instructions while engaged in some other activity such as TV or video games, but are not really stopping to process the information actively. An added element for our more oppositional children is requiring that they not only put the instructions into their own words but also tell themselves the consequences for not complying with the instructions, for example. "If I don't shut off the computer I lose my privileges for two days."

Children with little or no language will have difficulty verbally reviewing multi-stage activities. This is where the photos come in really handy. These children can sequence the photos and with very little language create an excellent review, preview and evaluation.

LEVEL II, STAGE 7, ACTIVITY 75

Synchronized Rhythms

ACTIVITY HIGHLIGHTS
° Making rapid modifications to remain coordinated
° Adapting to fluid variations

Summary:

In this activity we are integrating the skills learned by the children by collaboratively using the electric keyboard. Apprentice and Coach fluidly change speed, volume and pattern without stopping. Apprentices get a first taste in making rapid modifications to remain coordinated.

Participants:

Coach and child.

Getting Ready:

Apprentices should have completed prior keyboard and rhythm exercises.

Coaching Instructions:

This exercise has two steps.

☐ STEP 1

Play a simple pattern. Teach the child to match your pattern so that you are both playing the pattern simultaneously, as if there were only one drummer. When the child is ready, practice a simple pattern, while playing faster, slower, louder and softer in a synchronized manner. Announce and make the change without a pause.

☐ STEP 2

Play a simple duet. Teach the child to play a simple pattern at a steady speed. You can use a metronome to help keep the tempo if you think it will help. Have the child begin to play his rhythm while you join in with a complementary repetitive pattern. Make sure the child maintains his pattern and does not switch to yours. Vary degrees of loudness together, while you are playing.

Variations:

Try and record your music so the child can enjoy it later and share it with others.

Obstacles/Opportunities:

Remember to modify your speed and complexity based upon the motor skills of the child.

LEVEL II, STAGE 7, ACTIVITY 76

Tricky Partner

ACTIVITY HIGHLIGHTS

° Enjoy the challenge of synchronizing actions with an unpredictable partner

Summary:

Now we are ready to focus on the key element of synchronization; carefully observing and rapidly adapting your own actions based upon your partners sudden changes. In this activity we create a "tricky partner" who may move or act in an unexpected manner.

Participants:

Coach and child.

Getting Ready:

Children should have mastered moving and falling together onto beanbags. They should also be proficient in synchronized walking.

Coaching Instructions:

You will not be announcing in advance what you are going to do. For each trial explain to the child that you are going to be tricky and they have to stay side by side with you no matter what you do. You will vary whether you are going to count and "go" or count and "stay." Also vary whether you will go to the end line and "stop" or go to the end line and "fall." If this succeeds, switch roles and tell the child that it is their turn to be the "tricky" partner and you have to keep up with them. Also suddenly vary your rate of movement in mid-stream. When you have succeeded at "Tricky Movement" proceed on to "Tricky Drum Partner." We have provided two "Tricky Partner" variations for you to try.

Variations:

An important variation which teaches children to be highly sensitive to their coordination is "Getting it Wrong." In this activity we practice deliberately introducing small and large degrees of being un-coordinated. For example, we might practice moving and falling together onto beanbags with instructions that the child should land just before the Coach and not together with him. Similarly we can practice playing the drums and have the child be a bit too loud, or a bit too fast, to synchronize with you.

Obstacles/Opportunities:

These are critical exercises that should not be bypassed just because they appear simple. In the next stage when we introduce children to peer dyads, they will be exposed to a great deal more unexpected variation and will have a partner who will not take as much responsibility to keep actions coordinated. This exercise will provide the practice they need to quickly notice and adapt to loss of coordination.

Tricky Partner Variations:

Running and Falling onto Beanbag Chairs:

° Count to three, pretend to move but stay on the start line.

° Count, "one, two," then move your mouth and body like you are going to say "three" but remain silent.

° Run alongside the Apprentice but stop abruptly, just short of the "falling" line.

Tricky Drum Partner:

° Hold your hand high like you are going to hit the drum hard, but come down softly.

° Direct stopping and starting. After you announce stop and both have ceased playing, begin to say "St…" in a very exaggerated manner and say "Stop more" instead of "Start."

° While drumming, use a very loud voice to say, "Soft" and a soft voice to say "Loud."

LEVEL II, STAGE 7, ACTIVITY 77

Synchronized Roles

ACTIVITY HIGHLIGHTS
° Coordinating synchronized role actions
° Checking for social partner's readiness
° Communication for coordination of actions

Summary:

Those of you who have been following the activities will notice that this is the first time that we list two children as participants. As you will see in the next section, we do not advocate using this as the initial activity to introduce children to one another. We believe it is better to back up a bit and re-introduce already learned activities to the new pair. This exercise also presents a different type of transition. Until now children have been participating in what we call "symmetrical" role activities. This means that they are trying to match the actions of their partners. In this exercise we concentrate on coordinating your actions while involved in complementary activities, where each partner has a different role that must be enacted simultaneously to achieve a joint result. We begin with two simple exercises, a complementary role-play and a simple movement activity.

Participants:

Coach and two children.

Getting Ready:

Six to eight beanbags are located in a corner of the room carefully arranged for safety. They should be far enough away from the wall to ensure that those playing this game do not accidentally tumble into the wall or fall between them onto the floor.

Activity I   Role Play:

Teach the children a simple script for a basic role-play. We like to use several different scenarios. We have provided a sample for you:

☐ VET CLINIC

A pet owner, or the animal himself, comes to a Veterinary clinic with an illness or injury. At this stage you will use props to help support the play. Get some "medical" toys or equipment that will be suitable for the age of the Apprentices. Use a plastic or stuffed animal with an identifiable injury or malady (we tend to have many dinosaurs with injured limbs).

At this stage we are not requiring or requesting that children add variation. Make sure that the Coach is in charge of the script and actions of both characters. We will add mutual improvisation at a later stage. Make sure to have children reverse roles.

Activity 2   Push and Fall

Explain to children that they are going to play a push and fall game. Make sure they understand that this has to be done safely and only with the Coach's supervision as the "spotter." The children should face each other, with one facing the beanbags and the other with his back to the stack of beanbags. Make sure the child designated as the "pusher" uses "checking for readiness" skills before enacting her role. Initially, have the child verbally check for readiness and then have the second child practice responding in both the affirmative and negative. Teach the "pusher" not to push until the "faller" says, "OK. Push." Make sure to teach children to make exaggerated facial expressions and sound effects when they land. Reverse roles with each trial. To make the activity more interesting you can by a long "noodle" made from "Nerf" material. Each of them can hold one end while they are pushing and falling.

Variations:

Make sure to work on many different role-plays. With smaller children "mommy and daddy" plays work well.

Obstacles/Opportunities:

We included "Push and Fall" with some obvious trepidation. It is easy for children to become impulsive when playing this game. A child may simply run up to someone and say, "Push me" and try to push him or her over. The enjoyment in such an instance, is clearly not from the synchronized, interaction and shared laughter but from a self-involved, solo enactment of the game. The rules of this game are extremely important to emphasize. You should pay attention to times when a child has pushed too hard and use them as opportunities to practice repair. For example, you might say, "That was too hard, if you push that hard no one will want to play" or "You didn't ask if he was ready. If you don't ask, he doesn't want to play." The child will often say, "I'm sorry" so that he can continue to play the game. Because these words are frequently instrumental, said so that the game can continue, you will need to build in one more step and ask the child, "Are you going to push hard again?" This is crucial for the child's development. Many children will become angered by this question because they have learned that if they say they are sorry there is a standard response.

LEVEL II, STAGE 7, ACTIVITY 78

Synchronized Humor

ACTIVITY HIGHLIGHTS
° Working as a team to deliver jokes
° Appreciating the enhanced enjoyment of collaborating in joke telling

Summary:

As in previous humor activities, we once again emphasize that the critical element that must be synchronized is the enjoyment of the participants and not the specific "script" of the joke. Jokes are for laughter, not for getting them right. In this activity we begin developing the skill of being part of a "joke team." Participants collaborate to enact a joke or simple routine. The key to this activity is to synchronize your timing with your partner, whether your partner is a listener or part of your joke team.

Participants:

Coach and two children.

Getting Ready:

Apprentices should already be familiar with the concept that humor is whatever makes social partners laugh and that it is not connected to any specific script.

Coaching Instructions:

Apprentices are told that they are going to learn how to be a "joke team." Go through the following three steps:

☐ STEP 1   TELLER AND STRAIGHT MAN

Teach children four or five simple jokes. The pair now practice telling each other jokes, with each fluidly taking turns playing the "teller" and "straight man." Pay special attention to the pair's "timing" and their ability to share a "belly laugh" at the end of the joke. The "teller" has to wait until the "straight man" communicates that he does not know the answer. The "straight man's" job is to communicate with emphasis that he is puzzled and has no idea what the answer is. Make sure that after delivering the punch line, both "teller" and "straight man" share their laughter and joy. After practicing with jokes that have been learned, transition to "made-up" jokes, where the "teller" says a punch line, provided by the Coach, that is a different response from the original one. It does not matter if the new punch line makes any sense, as long as it makes both children laugh. In fact we do not want the joke to be scripted in any manner.

☐ STEP 2   JOKE PARTNERS

This step provides practice in the partners telling jokes as a team. They stand side by side and look towards one another as they deliver their lines. One child tells the first line of a two-line joke and the other tells the second line. There is no "straight man" in this exercise. After the punch line, both partners share laughter. Make sure to practice the jokes as learned and also as made-up variations. In both Step 1 and 2, the Coach should provide the new variation if the children cannot come up with anything.

☐ STEP 3   JOKE ROUTINES

Now partners practice being a "non-stop" joke team. Combine as many simple jokes as you can in a comedy routine, that children will tell together in a synchronized manner. When you feel they have mastered the routine, begin finding people to act as an audience for their performance. After one partner delivers the first line, the second partner must wait for the audience to either guess the answer, or indicate that they do not know, prior to telling the punch line. After they tell each joke they need to both wait for the response of their audience, prior to proceeding to the next joke in the routine. We have provided a few simple jokes below. Please feel free to use many of your own.

Variations:

We like to prepare children for the eventuality that some listeners will not appreciate their humor. Role-play a joke routine where the listener clearly demonstrates that he does not find the jokes funny. Children learn to respond by briefly apologizing, and then asking if the listener would like to hear a different joke.

Obstacles/Opportunities:

It is crucial to quickly provide variations to the original jokes that the children have learned. If a child becomes too involved in getting any joke "right" be sure to quickly eliminate it from the repertoire. You may be surprised that some children may need to practice laughing hilariously. Be sure not to skip this step!

Sample Jokes:

Why was the broom late?

It over swept.

What's red and flies and wobbles all over?

A jelly copter.

How can you double your money?

Look at it in the mirror.

What birds are always unhappy?

Bluebirds.

What did one broom say to the other broom?

"Have you heard the latest dirt?"

What did Tennessee?

He saw what Arkansas.

What did the big watch hand say to the small hand?

"Got a minute?"

What's gray and squirts jam at you

A mouse eating a doughnut.

What do you call two rows of cabbages?

A dual cabbageway.

Why do teddy bear biscuits wear long trousers?

Because they've got crummy legs.

Why did the chicken cross the playground?

To get to the other slide.

Where do you send a frog to get glasses?

To a hoptometrist.

LEVEL II, STAGE 7, ACTIVITY 79

Conversation Frameworks

ACTIVITY HIGHLIGHTS

° Introduction to reciprocal conversation

Summary:

In this exercise, Apprentices learn three simple, structured frameworks for having brief reciprocal conversations. In this early stage, we are primarily interested in children appreciating that conversations require both partners to remain focused on a similar topic. We provide three simple frameworks they can use to do so: "Telling and Telling," "Asking and Telling," and "Telling and Asking."

Participants:

Coach and two children.

Getting Ready:

Children should have completed prior conversation readiness exercises.

Coaching Instructions:

Children face each other during this exercise. They should be the center of each other's attention and not the Coach.

☐ STEP 1   TELLING AND TELLING:

Both partners tell each other something about a common topic area. The Coach provides the topic.

Topic: What you did yesterday.

Apprentice 1: "I went to the zoo yesterday."

Apprentice 2: "I went to the movies."

Topic: Restaurants you like to go to.

Apprentice 1: "I like to eat at Chili's."

Apprentice 2: "I like McDonalds."

Apprentice 1: I also like McDonalds."

Apprentice 2: "I like Applebees."

☐ STEP 2   TELLING AND ASKING:

Now partners practice first making a statement "telling" and then "asking" their partner to respond to the same topic.

Apprentice 1: "I went to the zoo yesterday. What did you do?"

Apprentice 2: "I went to the movies yesterday."

☐ STEP 3   ASKING AND TELLING:

Children express curiosity about each other in a reciprocal manner.

Apprentice 2: "What did you do yesterday?"

Apprentice 1: "I went to the zoo."

Apprentice 1: "What did you do yesterday?"

Apprentice 2: "I went to the movies."

☐ STEP 4   FLUID COMBINATIONS OF THE THREE VARIANTS:

As children become more skilled in these simple conversation sequences, begin chaining them together.

☐ STEP 5   TELLING, ALONG WITH TELLING AND ASKING:

Eventually try and combine all three in a more natural manner.

Variations:

This is a good time to practice getting off topic, so that children can recognize the difference. Practice all three frameworks in a manner where children are deliberately venturing off topic. After a while, you can play a game where children try and function as a "tricky partner" and deliberately get off topic, to see if their partner will recognize it.

Obstacles/Opportunities:

Some children may have difficulty generating their own topics or responses. At this stage it is perfectly acceptable for the Coach to provide the material. However, in order to progress to Level III, children will have to learn to introduce their own variations.

LEVEL II, STAGE 7, ACTIVITY 80

Anticipation

ACTIVITY HIGHLIGHTS
- ° Learning to anticipate your partner's actions
- ° Basing your actions on anticipated partner actions

Summary:

When I (Steve) was writing this activity I couldn't get the old Carly Simon lyrics, "Anticipation. It's making me wait," out of my thoughts. And for some reason I kept picturing bottles of Heinz ketchup. Oh well. This exercise is not about making people wait. On the contrary it is about being able to take a brief look into the future and figure out where your partner is going to be next. Now children are learning to coordinate their actions with future, not-yet occurring actions of their social partners. The best example we could come up with is that of the "lead pass." We are most familiar with the concept in sports such as soccer, football and basketball, but it is equally applicable to baseball. When there is a man on base and his teammate hits a long fly ball, both the fielder and the base runner are playing the game of Anticipation and trying to gauge their actions based on their assumptions of what the other is going to do next. Anticipation is a critical skill to emphasize as we leave Stage 7 and move to Stage 8, with the addition of loads of variations and unpredictability that will be introduced by peer partners.

Participants:

Coach and two children.

Getting Ready:

All you need are appropriate balls, two drums and some masking tape.

Coaching Instructions:

There are two activities involving movement and music. Make sure that the child enacts each role in both activities.

■ ACTIVITY 1   ANTICIPATING MOVEMENT:

To practice this, we often begin with a simple back-and-forth catch (or rolling back-and-forth). Tape a four-foot line (shorter for younger children), with two squares at either end of the line. One child will walk back and forth between the two squares. The other child stands several feet away and has to throw (roll) the ball to the square where his partner is headed and deliver it just when he reaches the destination. After partners have mastered this, they practice a more fluid version where the child in motion practices moving back-and-forth between the two squares and receiving the ball at each square. As the children become proficient, first remove the line and then remove the boxes. Children have to learn to "lead" their throw so it ends up where their partner is going to be.

■ **ACTIVITY 2   ANTICIPATING MUSIC:**

The Coach plays a simple five-beat rhythm on her drum. Play the same rhythm a number of times until you are sure the children have learned it. When you are ready, begin the rhythm, but stop after the third beat. The two Apprentices should learn to finish the rhythm by supplying the fourth and fifth beats together.

Variations:

See how complex a rhythm you can use.

Obstacles/Opportunities:

It goes without saying that you will modify this activity based upon the motor skills, eye-hand coordination and age of the children. Make sure to use video replays and Self Instruction as you practice and perfect this exercise. In a later stage we will be practicing anticipation in "Two-on-two Soccer" and other small team activities.

7

STAGE 8: DUETS

Goals and Objectives

As you might expect from the name, this stage is the typical time for introducing matched peers to our program. When we introduce peers we have to be careful to begin with simpler activities than those that the Apprentice has already mastered with an adult guide. No matter how hard you have tried to simulate a peer, you will never present the same degree of challenge and unpredictability. So while we introduce a peer at this stage, we typically go back to earlier activities and replicate them prior to proceeding.

Activity Highlights

In Stage 8 we give Apprentices more of the responsibility for partnership, negotiation initiation, rules, roles, and coordination of their movements. They also have to take responsibility for referencing and evaluating their partner's level of enjoyment. In Stage 6 we systematically introduced predictable breakdowns. Now the breakdowns are unpredictable. By Stage 8 Apprentices should be old hands at managing constant breakdowns. They should know that relationship encounters are like an old boat that will only stay afloat through the patching and bailing efforts of the crew. Social encounters are continually being disconnected and will inevitably "spring another leak" just when you have finished patching the last hole. Repairs are constant but now partners have more patience and have learned much more perseverance. They are not detered by things that do not go well. They have developed memories to help them understand that usually, with enough effort and joint negotiation, things sort of work out.

This stage begins with peer partners reviewing several key activities that they have previously mastered, but will now need to learn to conduct with another child. We always make sure to move backwards for review a bit each time we introduce a new degree of complexity into the child's world. Then we move on to an activity that teaches the two Apprentices to use only non-verbal signals to complete their tasks, for example, obtaining the needed puzzle pieces from their partner. Then follows a series of activities that reinforce the value and enjoyment of maintaining connections with your peer partner. This is followed by another conversation exercise aimed at teaching peers the importance of maintaining their partner is curiosity in conversation. Finally, we introduce "Ball and Net," an activity that presages the next stage of Collaboration. Ball and Net is a game requiring the cooperation of a small team to keep the ball bouncing in the net without falling to the ground before the team wants it to.

Critical Tips

- Remember to return to simpler activities with peers until they are comfortable with one another.

- Spend enough time with Apprentices teaching them to practice observing their joint interaction so that they can regulate and make repairs without your help.

- Remember that you are no longer the center of attention, the Apprentices are!

- Make yourself less conspicuous. At times avert your gaze so that partners reference each other and not you.

- Do not intervene too quickly when Apprentices are a bit frustrated. Give them a bit of time to work things out.

- If they are available use Explorers and Partners as "Assistant Coaches."

Reviews for Duets

ACTIVITY HIGHLIGHTS
° Activities for beginning peer groups

Summary:
We began to describe activities for two peer partners at the end of the last stage. However, those are not the activities we use to begin our new peer dyads and small groups. We selectively pick those activities our Apprentices have previously mastered with adults and recycle them as a means to making our partners feel comfortable in getting adjusted to one another.

Participants:
Coach and two children.

Getting Ready:
Apprentices should be well matched and should both have previously prepared by mastering prior activities.

Coaching Instructions:
Children practice the following activities together:

- Build a Mountain
- Rhyming Words
- Too Far to Whisper, Too Close to Shout
- Ice Cream Happiness
- Two-Ball Toss
- Crashing Cars
- Activity Transformations
- Rule Changes
- Unexpected Jokes
- Role Reversals
- Transforming Rhythms

Obstacles/Opportunities:
Make sure not to skip this step. Children need time to get to know one another and feel comfortable together. These already learned activities provide a space that allows the partners to focus on each other, rather than on learning new activities.

LEVEL II, STAGE 8, ACTIVITY 82

Find Me

ACTIVITY HIGHLIGHTS

° A coordinated game that peer partners can learn independently

Summary:

This activity uses the avenue of darkness as a conduit to magnify excitement. The seeker does not simply walk away but uses his voice and light to find the hidden person, who may call out to be found. Repair is crucial for this game and both partners must work hard to bridge the gaps.

Participants:

Coach and two children.

Getting Ready:

You will need one flashlight, ten beanbags and an interior space that excludes light.

Instructions:

The activity begins with the room set up. Together throw beanbags around the room creating a chaotic appearance. The child who is designated as the "hider" uses the flashlight to locate a hiding place while the other child stands outside the door and counts to 20. Upon reaching 20 the "seeker" enters the room and shouts, "Where are you?" The "hider" responds, "Find me." This continues with the "seeker" moving through the darkness until he finds his friend. They celebrate the finding. The "hider" gives the flashlight to the "seeker" and roles are reversed.

Variations:

If necessary, you can also supply the "finder" with a small "pinpoint" flashlight. We are fortunate to have space that can be made extremely dark. Many people do not have this capability. Using paper bags, it is possible to produce a similar feeling of wariness. Simply place paper bags or pillowcases over a child's head, making sure he can breathe but cannot see and replicate the game. Scarves tied so that they cover the eyes work equally well.

Obstacles/Opportunities:

This is an opportunity for children in a dyad to take responsibility for maintaining their play together. They are now able to think about another person when that person is outside their visual range. For children who are phobic of the dark, this game can produce such intense fear that it may not seem worth the effort. That will be for you to decide. Our approach has always been that it is by facing our fears that we achieve bravery, not through our foolhardy lack of wariness.

Drumming Duets

ACTIVITY HIGHLIGHTS
° Collaborative rhythms
° Enhancing the feeling of connection of peer partners

Summary:

Music is a great way to cement a feeling of unity and connection between new peer partners. At this stage, we may begin each meeting with a short period of synchronized drumming,

Participants:

Coach and two children.

Getting Ready:

Children should have extensive experience of playing drums.

Coaching Instructions:

The activity has three steps:

☐ STEP 1

Begin by playing a simple rhythm on your drum (long, long, short, short). Children are asked to match the rhythm. After they are successful, demonstrate a simple variation and ask one child to carefully add the variation to the pattern (long, long, short, short, short). All three of you now match the new rhythm. Now demonstrate and teach the other child a third rhythm (long, short, short, long, short, short). All three drummers match the new rhythm. Practice this until all of you know your distinct rhythm and can play it without any help.

☐ STEP 2

Now take turns with each player playing his variation and the other two partners matching it. Go from one variation to another, using a head nod to signal when it is time for the children to begin their variation.

☐ STEP 3

Now, fade out of the interaction and teach the children to vary their rhythms without your participation.

Variations:

You can perform many variations of this exercise on drums.

Obstacles/Opportunities:

There is a strong temptation to urge or allow children to improvise their own variations and to make this a true "jam session." Try and hold off on this until they are very proficient in the initial exercise and are ready to move into Level III, which does teach improvisation, but in a careful systematic manner.

LEVEL II, STAGE 8, ACTIVITY 85

Are We Connected?

ACTIVITY HIGHLIGHTS
- ° Evaluating the coordination of actions as a unit
- ° Observing your own level of coordination

Summary:

In this exercise, Apprentices learn to evaluate their actions and judge their degree of coordination as a unit. We encourage the Apprentices to work together to modify their actions and function as a more synchronized unit. As part of teaching Apprentices to be more aware of their coordination we have them practice being slightly non-coordinated and then making corrections.

Participants:

Coach and two children.

Getting Ready:

You will need a video camera and monitor.

Coaching Instructions:

This activity has two steps:

☐ STEP 1

Children perform activities where they are purposefully out of synch with one another. For example, practice walking side by side. After a few steps, provide a signal to one child to begin walking ahead of, or behind the other. Continue this activity with each child purposefully walking behind, or ahead of his partner. Have a game of catch, where children initially throw in a careful manner and make sure that their partner can catch it. After a short while, signal children to throw the ball too high or low. Make sure to videotape these activities.

☐ STEP 2

Now, play the video of the chosen activities. Have the children pause the tape, as soon as soon as they notice that they are no longer coordinated. Ask them what they would do to become more coordinated.

Variations:

It is fun to do a similar exercise with sound only. Use a cassette recorder to teach children how to catch themselves when they strat talking out of rhythm with one another.

Obstacles/Opportunities:

It is crucial not to rush through this exercise. When children develop an "eye" for the moment when their actions are not coordinated with a partner, they are able to take much more responsibility for the regulation of social encounters. The increase in their confidence and poise is remarkable.

LEVEL II, STAGE 8, ACTIVITY 84

Mixed up Puzzles

ACTIVITY HIGHLIGHTS
° Using non-verbal signals for problem solving
° Shifting attention between tasks and social partner
° Collaborating with a partner to reach a mutual desired goal

Summary:

In this exercise, children must coordinate their non-verbal signals in order to complete their activities. It is another good activity where you can work on de-emphasizing words and increasing the importance of visual referencing. It is also very good practice in shifting attention between communication and task actions.

Participants:

Coach and two children.

Getting Ready:

Make sure that the Apprentice is familiar with using head nods, headshakes and pointing for communication. Use two puzzles that are twelve pieces or less.

Coaches Instructions:

Take the jigsaw puzzles and mix them up into two piles, making sure that half of the pieces of each puzzle are in different piles. Place each pile at opposite ends of a table and out of the potential "grabbing" distance of partners. Seat children at each puzzle, with the puzzle "frame" in front of them. Explain that there are two different puzzles, but they are all mixed up so that they each have some pieces from the other puzzle. They have to finish their puzzles, but they are not allowed to talk to each other and are not allowed to get up and/ or grab anything from their partner's pile.

Variations:

There are many work-related projects that can be done in this manner. Try digging a hole together without talking, or planting a garden.

Obstacles/Opportunities:

This is another great activity for our overly verbal children. This exercise may also motivate you to try many other collaborative projects that can be done without a word.

LEVEL II, STAGE 8, ACTIVITY 86

Partner Pretend Play

ACTIVITY HIGHLIGHTS

° Symbolic pretend play

Summary:

Pretend play has now developed to the point where children can use representational figures to interact with each other. Roles are carefully controlled and characters tend to stay within frameworks. Many children have reached a point where they anticipate things that may cause confusion and avoid them prior to their introduction. While in this play the figures "talk" to one another, we want the children to continue to observe their partners' facial expressions for the inherent satisfaction that is so basic to this play. Language is more important now, though the child does not have to be verbally fluent to succeed. A few crucial words and phrases will suffice, as long as they are delivered in context and with enthusiasm. Participants rely on words to keep their pretend figures in character and to maintain theme and framework. Constructing a zoo is interesting to children and provides a setting for working on contingent language. Children build the zoo but then become the characters that move in a train around the facility.

Participants:

Coach and up to three children.

Getting Ready:

You will need a white board or similar large surface. You also need a container of animals, a container of natural wood blocks and one small train. Place the white board flat on the floor. Coach and children sit across from each other, each having one full side of the white board. They make a map on the white board as an architectural design for the zoo they will construct together.

Coaching Instructions:

Children select five animals each and place them evenly across the front of the white board. The magic marker is passed around and each draws a cage around his animal. Blocks are placed in the center of the white board and children construct cages for their animals by placing blocks on top of the lines they have drawn. Once the animals are safely locked inside their cages, the children work together to make a track around the white board for the zoo train. A train is placed on the track and small figures are placed on top of the train. The children move the train around the track in tandem with each participant responsible for his or her character's comments about the zoo. For example: in a deep voice like a father one could say, "Look honey, there's an elephant, I believe it's from India." Then in a high voice to mimic a child another could say, "Oh Daddy, can I pet the elephant." Then again in a low voice, "No honey, elephants are wild animals and we must respect their space. That's why they're in the zoo."

Variations:

While one child moves the train around the perimeter of the white board, the other sits inside and pretends he is part of an "animal family" visiting the moving zoo (the zoo train) and the other child is "on display" in the moving zoo. For example, the mother elephant says to her baby, "Look honey, there they go again, always in the same car, always in circles." The baby says, "Mommy why don't they get dizzy?" Mommy replies, "I don't know honey. I think they are different from us."

Obstacles/Opportunities:

This is an opportunity for children to comment on the same stimulus from a different perspective. Different characters have different tones of voice and different ideas, as well.

8

LEVEL II, STAGE 8, ACTIVITY 87

Partner Role-Plays

ACTIVITY HIGHLIGHTS

- ° Coordinating more complex role-plays
- ° Making transitions from solo to social activities
- ° Re-connecting with a peer after short separations

Summary:

Now we approach shared role-plays that have a new level of complexity. Roles are more fleshed-out. Characters have their own distinct activities – their own areas of separate attention – in addition to their shared "scenes." During the role-play, the characters have periods where they separate and then have to rejoin and re-connect emotionally and behaviorally with each other.

Participants:

Coach and two children.

Getting Ready:

Children should already be proficient in the simpler forms of role-playing that we have presented in prior activities.

Coaching Instructions:

There are six steps to this activity. We have provided a sample script for a "Parent–Child" role-play at the end of the exercise description. Feel free to write your own script and tailor it to the age and interests of the children.

☐ STEP 1

The children are assigned their roles. Depending upon their sex, one is assigned the role of a daddy or mommy and the other plays a son or daughter.

☐ STEP 2

The children practice their simple structured scripts with you, prior to working together. While the actors are going through their roles, make sure they narrate their actions out loud using the "present tense" form of Self Talk.

☐ STEP 3

Now practice each small segment of the role-play. Make sure that you have mastered a segment before you move on to the next one.

☐ STEP 4

Combine a few segments together, before practicing the entire play. Pay special attention to the segments where children have to transition from carrying out a solo activity, such as working in the office, to a joint activity, such as having dinner together.

□ STEP 5

Now practice the entire role-play. Keep working at it until the children can enact it fluidly.

Variations:

Add variations to the basic theme such as; "the child is feeling sick and goes to the office where he calls the parent to come and get him." Try out a few different scenarios. It is fun to videotape a role-play after it has been mastered for the children's enjoyment, as well as to show to others.

Obstacles and Opportunities:

Children who insist on adding too much "real-life" material will not be successful in this activity. They have to agree to perform a fictionalized, simple version of a role-play and not the actual moment-to-moment recounting of what they may experience daily. This activity also provides an opportunity for a slightly more proficient peer "Coach" to assist the children in successfully carrying out the activity. The "Assistant" Coach can be an "Explorer" who is himself working within Level V. The major requirement is the patience to work slowly and carefully and the knowledge that it is more important for the children to discover how to make the activity work by themselves, than it is for the Coach to make sure that they get it "right" by over-helping. One of the most important skills to be learned by the Assistant Coach is how to wait and give Apprentices the time to struggle and even get frustrated, when he already knows the solution.

Sample Script for Role-play

The parent wakes up and says, "It's time to wake up (the child)" and goes to the child's room to wake him/her up.

The child wakes up.

The parent tells the child to get dressed and says, "I am going to the kitchen to make breakfast."

The parent goes to the kitchen and makes breakfast, while the child pretends to get dressed.

The child walks to the kitchen and sits at a table with the parent and they eat breakfast together.

Then they get in their car and the parent drives the child to school.

After the child gets out of the car, the parent drives to work.

For a short time, the child pretends to be at school and performs a simple scripted activity, while the parent pretends to be at work similarly doing a pre-arranged simple activity.

When given a cue, the parent looks at his/her watch and says, "It's time to go pick (child) up from school."

8

The parent gets in his/her (pretend) car, drives to the school, picks up the child and takes him/her home.

In the car, they talk about what they did today using "Telling and Asking."

This particular activity can end when they get home, with each asking the other, "What are you going to do next?" or it can continue all the way to bedtime.

LEVEL II, STAGE 8, ACTIVITY 88

Curious Conversations

ACTIVITY HIGHLIGHTS
° Learning to have curious conversations
° Remaining on a shared conversational topic

Summary:

With this exercise we return to working on elements of reciprocal conversation. The one thing that makes conversations work is the perception that the other person is genuinely curious about what you are saying. In this exercise, children learn the meaning of having a curious conversation.

Participants:

Coach and two children.

Getting Ready:

You will need one container of matchbox cars or similar small objects. Two or three cars should be of similar color – three red cars that are different models, three blue cars that are different models and so on. You will also need two chairs, a table and an optional mailing tube.

Coaching Instructions:

This activity contains six steps:

☐ STEP 1

Remind children of their previous work on conversations and practice some of the basic formats like "Telling and Asking." Now explain that we will use the pictures in our minds to have a conversation and that we will stay on the same topic.

☐ STEP 2

Practice with one child at a time. Take a car but keep it hidden from the child. Make sure he is gazing at you and say, "I like the red Jeep. Do you know which car I am talking about?" The red Jeep is then placed on the table and the Coach asks, "Is this the car you thought I liked?" Now it is the child's turn. He removes a car from the container without displaying it and tells you, "I like the blue Jeep? Do you know which car I mean?"

☐ STEP 3

Now gradually include both children with you in this activity. When they seem to be proficient, move yourself out and let them proceed on their own.

☐ STEP 4

As the activity progresses, make sure that from time to time you purposefully "misunderstand" each of the children. When asked, "Is this the car you thought I liked?" you might respond, "No, I thought you said the blue Chevrolet."

☐ STEP 5

The next phase of this activity centers on a similar script but one that lacks important information and concrete details. Each partner's job is to be curious about important details. Remove a car from the basket, hold it beneath the table and say, "I like the yellow car." Note: The make and model are not identified. "Do you know which car I mean?" If the child guesses correctly, respond with, "Yes, I was thinking about the yellow race car." If the guess is incorrect counter with, "No, I don't like the Oldsmobile, it is too big. The car I like is a really fast car." If the child guesses the school bus, respond, "No, I don't want all those kids in my car. The car I like is a really fast car." If the child still guesses incorrectly, produce the car. Prolonged guessing will only be discouraging. Now have children practice this same framework with each other.

Variations:

See if the activity can proceed in a reciprocal manner without providing concrete objects.

Obstacles/Opportunities:

Children who become overly focused on the object, in this case the car, and neglect their partner present one obvious obstacle. Be sure to substitute less competitive objects if this happens. Another problem can occur if children do not understand that the purpose of the activity is to help their partner to guess correctly and not to stump them. This is a conversation and not a "win–lose" activity.

8

LEVEL III: CHALLENGER

Introduction

Summary

Challengers primarily relate within groups of two. Like very young children, they still have trouble initiating and maintaining their relationships in larger groups, without being disrupted by others. Dyadic relationships with a matched partner seem to create a space in which the relationship can develop. Success in Level III can be thought of as mastering the balance of Co-Regulation and Co-Variation. These relationships are a mixture of comfort and spice. The more there is comfort, the more we can safely add spice.

This is the level where children learn how to add variation while maintaining coordination with a peer partner. Ritualized activity evolves into spontaneous actions. Common frameworks are established. Then new elements are added. Partners can now change or even violate prior rules, upset expectations and use things in ways that they were not originally intended for.

Participants

Now our peer partners are taking more responsibility. The adults are becoming true Coaches taking a back seat roll to the unique excitement that children can only generate with one another. Both partners start by systematically adding variations.

Settings

In Stage 9 we are still primarily working in physical movement and action settings. However, such physical settings become much less important as we progress into the later stages of Level III. We still want to guard against the intrusion of other individuals and so we do not yet conduct these exercises in groups until a bit later in the initial stage. We also still make sure that objects and activities that are obvious temptations for departing from interaction do not tempt Challengers.

Language

In Level III, Challengers use language as a major interaction enhancer. We frequently hear interesting variations on words and phrases, made-up words and names, and improvised "silly" conversations, songs and sayings. Language is also put to work as a means of regulating encounters. It is used for explicitly introducing variations. It is also used to obtain agreement and check with social partners for their acceptance and appreciation. Because peers are constantly inputting novelty and variation, there is much greater potential for confusion and conflict. Language is employed for on the spot negotiations, checking for understanding, communicating confusion and making compromises. Finally language is used for Executive Functioning – to aid in reflection, planning and evaluation of actions.

Coaching Points:

- Remember to celebrate each of the Challenger's Co-Creations.

- Record Co-Creations in journals and photographs.

- Challengers will still require you to provide structure for negotiations and complex decisions.

- Watch out for the "need to win" at all costs. It will sabotage collaboration!

- Remember, you are still in charge of the pace and progression of activities.

- Certain objects can still distract the Challengers and cause them to stop referencing their partners. Be careful to limit objects that compete for attention.

STAGE 9: COLLABORATION

Goals and Objectives

Stage 9 marks the formal celebration of peers as interactive partners. While you as Coach are still present, you are truly in the role of a coach and no longer the primary interactive partner. Rather you assume the functions of a facilitator, referee, boundary keeper and limit setter for the peers. Challengers face the "challenge" of adapting their actions to their peer partner's reactions. They do this to maintain the balance between predictability and creativity, a hallmark of relational encounters.

Activity Summary

The stage begins with children learning to function as a coordinated team in various activities. Challengers learn the strength of uniting together to move objects from one place to another, face the darkness, overcome obstacles, support and encourage each other, defeat adversity and reach common goals. We take a brief detour in the middle part of the stage to practice a slightly more advanced form of Self Talk called Self Instruction. Following this, they practice reflection and planning. Towards the end of the stage we introduce competitive team activities. Challengers have to juggle their desire to win with their desire to function as a good team member and maintain a friendship with teammates and competitors alike.

Critical Tips

- This stage is a critical time to introduce Reflection and Planning.

- Collaboration takes place both for enhanced enjoyment and "strength in numbers!"

- Continue to stress non-verbal communication for language dependent Challengers.

- Make sure to continually assess readiness for this level. Be prepared to return to Level II if the level of demands for improvisation is too challenging.

- Be sure to emphasize the importance of encouraging and "cheering" for your partners.

LEVEL III, STAGE 9, ACTIVITY 89

Ball and Net

ACTIVITY HIGHLIGHTS

° Taking collaborative actions for common results

° Coordinating actions so you can work together

Summary:

"Ball and Net" could be considered a metaphor for conversation – keeping the ball in the air and sharing responsibility for doing so. Children love it because it's fun. Teamwork is a given and each person who participates in this game must participate with skill and attention.

Participants:

Coach and three children.

Getting Ready:

For "Ball and Net" you will need a mesh net approximately four feet by four feet. Each corner should have a handle for holding the net. You will also need three small air-filled balls.

Ball and Net Coaching Instructions:

Coach and Apprentices stand in the center of a room. Lack of clutter is important due to the activity level and possibility of breaking objects. Although the game was intended as one of increased challenges for keeping the ball in the air, children often enjoy knocking it off the net after a period of keeping it going. This provides a convenient endpoint to the game and has been incorporated into the basic rules. Each person holds a corner of the net in each hand. Place one ball in the center of the net. Agree to a reasonable goal such as five bounces without any of the balls falling off. Together all partners say, "Ready, Set, Go" and begin to raise and lower the net to bounce the ball in the air. If the ball falls to the floor, pick it up and begin again. Upon reaching the agreed upon goal, fling the ball as high as you can, assuming there is nothing fragile above you, and let it fall where it will.

Variations:

Balloons, different size balls or other objects can also be bounced on the net. Once competent, children can also learn to bounce it lightly, vigorously or gradually harder and harder. Balls can be rolled from side to side. Partners can walk or jump as they bounce the balls.

Obstacles/Opportunities:

"Ball and Net" is a game that becomes more challenging as it is played. But, keep in mind that success is a great motivator for this game. Information is gathered quickly when the game does not go well and strategies develop quickly during this exciting and vigorous game.

LEVEL III, STAGE 9, ACTIVITY 90

Lifting and Carrying

ACTIVITY HIGHLIGHTS
- ° Practicing cooperative effort towards a common goal
- ° Enhancing the perception of shared strength

Summary:

Working together to carefully move heavy objects is a simple everyday activity that is deceptive in its complexity, especially once you stop compensating and require children to keep their actions synchronized.

Participants:

Coach and two children.

Getting Ready:

Make sure to use objects that cannot be moved by one Apprentice. Objects should also require some delicacy in their transport, such as a shallow tray overflowing with small blocks.

Coaching Instructions:

Instructions are straightforward. Provide some reason why the object has to be carefully moved from one room or setting into another. Explain that the object is very delicate and that you will be the moving supervisor and make sure that nothing breaks or falls. Show children how to grasp the object firmly from different sides. Make sure they learn to coordinate their lifting actions. Once lifted, one child will walk forward followed by the other.

Variations:

If you would like to add an additional problem-solving element to "Lifting and Carrying," work on removing a drawer or shelf from an armoire or dresser and carrying it to another room. Variation can also be introduced by asking that heavy bulky objects be moved from one room to another. This will require opening a door.

Obstacles/Opportunities:

Small crisis points may occur when partners reach difficult places such as a closed door, hallways that require turns and furniture that is in their pathway. Initially remove such obstacles, but as they become proficient, provide them with time to see if they can solve the problem themselves. One major obstacle may be the tendency for partners to blame each other if the object is dropped. Prior to setting out, tell both children that this is a no-blame activity. If something goes wrong it is not anyone's fault. Make sure to practice responses to accidents before starting out on the real thing.

LEVEL III, STAGE 9, ACTIVITY 91

It's Dark!

ACTIVITY HIGHLIGHTS:
° Facing challenges together
° Overcoming fear by interacting with peer partners
° Collaborating for a common goal

Summary:

Based on an earlier game called "Find me," two children now face the unknown, relying only on the security of each other. This activity remains a favorite because it touches the edge of excitement by introducing a twinge of anxiety or fear. And in truth, one reason we work so hard at relationships has to do with our fear of facing the scary unexpected things of this world alone. This activity is structured to ensure that partners move together. They use each other's emotional reactions and physical actions to guide their ability to stay coordinated. Even tones of voice change during this exercise and the range of verbal expression involves whispers and squeals.

Participants:

Coach and two children. You can also use four children playing in two teams, as long as each team is able to patiently wait its turn.

Getting Ready:

To do this exercise you will need to have access to a room that can be safely traversed in the dark without any fear of injury. Of course you will also need to make sure the room can be dark enough so that the activity is exciting. In addition, you need two flashlights and some beanbag chairs.

Coaching Instructions:

Begin by going into the room by yourself with the lights on, making sure there are no hazards and taping "clues" in various locations on the walls. Clues can be pictures or words that provide hints about where you have hidden some small treasure. Place at least four clues on the wall. Increase the number based on the age and ability of the children. A number, such as one, two, three or four, should cover each clue so that the number must be lifted to read the clue. Each team must accumulate all the clues in the correct order to solve the puzzle. We prefer that the "clues" are actual puzzle pieces that can be put together to reveal an object which shows where the treasure is located. Spread out five beanbag chairs in different locations around the room. Now hide the flashlight under one of the beanbag chairs, walk to the door and turn out the lights. The children should be waiting outside. Explain that the purpose of this game is to locate a flashlight hidden in a darkened room and use it to find the clues. There are special clues on the wall, but to see the clues, they must first find the flashlight. To play this game, the two children must stick together and hold hands the entire time they are in the dark room, except when one of them is going to read the clue. You may have to demonstrate the game a number of times, before children understand it well enough to proceed.

Have the children hold hands. Stay right behind them and act as a "spotter" and guide, by placing a hand on each of their shoulders and maintaining it with gentle pressure. Now walk into the darkened room together. Make sure that the children are walking at a slow, careful pace and are not lifting their knees as they walk. If you think it will increase the excitement, as you walk you can talk about how you are scared and really want to find the flashlight. Make sure that children are carefully "probing" for objects with their feet as they walk. When the pair reaches a beanbag chair, instruct them to stop and look for the flashlight. Once they find the flashlight, it is time to discover the clue. Now they each take a different role; the flashlight "shiner" and the clue "finder." The "shiner" scans the room until clue number 1 is located. When it is found, the "finder" walks over, lifts up the number, removes the clue and returns to his partner. When both partners are back together, take the flashlight, step behind the partners to again act as a spotter and turn off the light. The team now has to make its way back to the door and outside. Once outside they can place the puzzle piece on a table, fit it together with the pieces they have already obtained and get ready for their next excursion into the dark room. As children get more proficient, you can allow them more freedom of movement and stay behind them without touching them. When they have retrieved all the clues, these will provide the location to a hidden treasure. Make sure they stay in role at all times and that the "shiner" does not become the "finder" until it is his turn.

Variations:

For older children, this game can be moved outside and played at night. This time, however, two children must hold hands in order to find two other hidden children who are also holding hands. This is the old favorite of Hide and Seek which carries its own built-in wariness. When discovered, the hidden children jump out and attempt to scare the seekers.

Obstacles/Opportunities:

Children can forget to hold hands during this activity and if this should happen, work on it prior to returning to the room. This exercise presents a great opportunity to create an emotional bond between two children who are just getting to know one another.

LEVEL III, STAGE 9, ACTIVITY 92

Buddy Baseball

ACTIVITY HIGHLIGHTS

° Cooperative team play
° Cheering for and encouraging others

Summary:

One year at our summer camp for young children, we found that some of our campers were unable to play the game of baseball, which we had played in previous years. So we developed the following game which became such a favorite that we added it to our regular activity repertoire in succeeding camps. This activity helps children know where to look, stay coordinated with a friend and competently take on every role associated with the game.

Participants:

Coach, Assistant Coach and six children.

Getting Ready:

You will need a small baseball diamond. It can be a temporary diamond and you can even use carpet squares as bases if you like. You will also need two paddle drums and some drumsticks.

Instructions:

Two children begin the game on the "pitcher's mound." Two children are at "home plate." Two sit behind home plate – they are the cheering section. To begin, the "drummers" on the pitchers mound hold their drums and drumstick. The drummers yell to the runners on home plate, "Are you ready?" They begin to drum and the children at home plate hold hands and run to first base, at which point the drumming stops. While they are running, the cheering section shouts, "Go guys go. Run to first base." When it is time to run from first to second, the drummers must visually make sure the runners are ready to go. They must then track them visually until they arrive at second base, at which time they stop drumming. The cheerers continue to shout and scream until the runners make it home. Rotations occur until everyone has had a chance to fulfill all roles.

Variations:

Following competence with this game, we often introduce kickball. The cheering team now has a dual role. They place the ball in front of the kickers, the drummer and kickers function as previously described and the game continues as before.

Obstacles/Opportunities:

The most difficult role is that of the cheering squad. They must watch with no real payoff. We have found that we have to spend more time developing this role than any other. Children can learn to become good observers as a result of this game. They track the game and movement, start and stop independently and those who are running learn to listen, look and shift gaze between themselves and the base.

LEVEL III, STAGE 9, ACTIVITY 93

Parking Garage

ACTIVITY HIGHLIGHTS
- Introduction to collaborative play for children
- Working together to run a parking garage/car wash

Summary:

The game "Parking Garage" is a transition into play that is somewhat unpredictable. The second activity, "Car Wash," which gets connected to "Parking Garage," is lots of fun because it provides play in which they can mess with water and mess...did we say mess? Using found items and previously used materials, children learn the potential for play, using objects outside the area for which they were intended. Creativity is explored within this imaginative structured framework.

Participants:

Coach and three children.

Getting Ready:

You will need three cardboard boxes, a mail tube, matchbox cars, play money, small box, large waffle alphabet blocks, a pan of water and towels. Objects are placed in a corner of a room.

Coaching Instructions for Parking Garage:

The children carry each of the three cardboard boxes to the area where they will construct the parking garage. Then they stack them to form four levels (the top of the highest box is used as the "roof" level of the garage). Next, four ramps are constructed from alphabet waffle blocks. The ramps are propped up, one per level. The children next work together to construct a road made out of blocks. One end of the mail tube is balanced against the "garage" structure, with the other end adjacent to the "block" road. Matchbox cars are lined up at the end of the road furthest from the parking garage

One child, the "driver," drives the first matchbox car to the parking garage and asks the "parking attendant" if he will park his car. The attendant asks, "What level?" and the driver replies, "Level 3." "OK, give me a dollar," says the parking attendant. He receives it and places the dollar in the small box. Now the third child, the "valet," drives the car up the appropriate ramp and parks it on the requested level. The driver drives at least three more cars to the parking garage and asks the parking attendant to park them, following the script above. After the cars have been parked, the driver returns to the parking garage. He says, "Parking attendant, will you get my blue Jeep?" The attendant asks, "Where is it?" "Level 2," says the driver. "Coming up," says the attendant. The parking attendant calls the valet and tells him which car is needed. The valet gets the car and places it in the tube. At the bottom of the tube the parking attendant retrieves it and drives it over to the driver. The interaction continues until all cars have been returned to the starting point. The children get a chance to play all three roles.

Coaching Instructions for Car Wash:

The car wash is set up on the road leading to the garage. The driver selects a car and pushes it along the road toward the carwash. As he approaches the attendant stops him and says, "Stop. What do you want?" The driver answers, "I need my car washed." The attendant says, "OK, give me some money." Provide either $1 for a car that isn't very dirty, or $20 for a filthy car. The car washer then washes the car and both attendant and car washer towel it dry. Once dry the attendant becomes the parking attendant and asks the driver if he wants to park his car. Now they proceed to the Parking Garage game.

Variations:

One of our favorite variations substitutes zoo animals for cars. There are few differences, although the initial approach is now to a "zoo keeper" and the request is for a cage, not a parking space. When leaving the zoo area, the animals usually ask to go back to the jungle or back to the circus. You can also instruct the driver to insert subtle changes into the play. For example, the driver might choose to take only three cars home, leaving the fourth for a reason that will introduce humor into the script. For example, the driver could say, "I'm not taking the other car tonight. My cat will probably pick it up later."

Obstacles/Opportunities:

Some children have great preference for one role over another. Upset can usually be avoided by assigning the preferential role to the child last. You may also find it helpful to structure the sequence of this game visually. We have found post-it notes to be a good resource for doing this. We write down each role on a post-it note. If one child really likes to be the "car washer" best, his favorite role will be third in a line of post-it notes. He can clearly reference the notes to reassure himself that he will get to play his favored role.

LEVEL III, STAGE 9, ACTIVITY 94

The Beltway

ACTIVITY HIGHLIGHTS

- ° Introduction to children's collaborative play
- ° Collaborating on a joint building activity
- ° Working together to create a symbolic link between partners
- ° Preparation for joint attention activities

Summary:

In this activity, children work together to construct a highway, the "beltway," that provides a link for them to travel to the important places in their lives. Pretend people drive their cars faster and slower, and there are pauses that provide time for reflection and planning.

Participants:

Coach and up to three children.

Getting Ready:

You will need building blocks, cars that fit on the blocks, pretend telephones, play houses and some trees and similar objects. The children are seated on a floor with materials initially placed next to you.

Coaching Instructions:

This exercise has four steps:

☐ STEP 1

Explain that the children will construct a road together that is similar to a local highway in your area that connects important places. We will call our highway the "beltway" because it will be in the shape of a belt. The beltway will make it possible for us to visit each other for birthday parties, picnics and just to play or hang out together.

☐ STEP 2

Now the children take turns selecting blocks and under your supervision, construct a belt shaped highway that is wide enough to accommodate two of the cars "driving" side by side. After the road is finished, each person should select a model house to represent his or her home. Houses should be placed on opposite ends of the circle, next to the beltway, separated only by a two-block-wide driveway that connects the beltway to the house. They can each have several trees and similar objects, but not so many that building the house and yard becomes the center of attention. Place each child's selected car in a designated driveway area connected to the beltway. Place a play telephone next to each house. Finally, place some kind of structure midway between each house that will serve as a convenient meeting place for the children. Give the structures a visual label such as "Gas Station," or "Main Street." Place one or two more structures somewhere along the Beltway that can serve as a destination point. Give them visual signs such as "Mall," or "Movie Theatre."

☐ STEP 3

Now, one child calls the others on the phone and they decide to meet so that they can drive on the beltway together. They pick a designated landmark to meet at. They each take a car out onto the beltway and drive until they meet at the designated place. They each go off the beltway into the driveway of the meeting place and exchange greetings.

☐ STEP 4

In the final step, they decide where they are going to go for their drive and begin driving together. Initially, limit choices to one of their houses for a special event such as a birthday or holiday, or the "destination" structures that have not yet been visited which can be to such as an ice-cream parlor, a movie theatre or a mall. Another choice is to go "cruising" together, side by side down the beltway,

9

pointing out the sights they see to one another. The only rule of "cruising" is that the partners have to stay alongside each other as they drive. As the game progresses you can add new diversions and stopping points for the partners to drive to.

Variations:

Of course, once this sort of play is introduced, the variations are limited only by the children's ability to manage varying materials while maintaining their focus on the relationship and keeping ideas within the agreed upon framework

Obstacles/Opportunities:

This game is good preparation for peer interaction and can be used by speech pathologists for group speech work. It is one of the early games we use to transition children from working with a Coach to interactive play with several peers.

LEVEL III, STAGE 9, ACTIVITY 95

Self Instruction

ACTIVITY HIGHLIGHTS
° Using Self Instruction for regulating actions
° Using Self Instruction to review and modify actions
° Using Self Instruction for planning actions

Summary:

The key to remaining synchronized in complex social environments is to be both a careful observer and a rapid adaptor, as circumstances require. Self-Instruction is a special kind of Self Talk that is essential in directing ourselves to take adaptive actions. In this exercise we teach Apprentices to use Self Instruction.

Participants:

Coach and two children.

Getting Ready:

Children should be versed in using Self Talk from prior exercises.

Coaching Instructions:

Once again use simple activities that have already been practiced. You can use drums, Moving and Falling, or any similar activity. There are three steps in this exercise:

☐ STEP 1

Use Self Instruction to prepare. This step entails children translating instructions for an upcoming action into their own words. For example, if you say, "This time we are going to run halfway and then walk slowly until the endpoint," the child would translate this into, "I have to run half the way and then slow down." He should also include, "I have to stay next to [Coach]."

☐ STEP 2

Use Self Instruction for rapid adaptation. As you change elements of the framework, the Apprentice learns to use Self Talk to translate the necessary change into his own words. For example, "Now we have to go slower," or, "Now we wait till we count to four.'"

☐ STEP 3

Use Self Instruction for correction. The Apprentice accepts feedback from you and translates it into self-instruction targeted at how to improve, for example, "I went too fast. I have to slow down."

Variations:

We like to use Self Instruction for rehearsal prior to entering any new situation, or any setting where the child has previously had difficulty. The child rehearses potential difficulties and the alternative behavioral strategies that he can employ. Afterwards, he reviews the success of his rehearsal.

Obstacles/Opportunities

Self Instruction is a key element in the development of Executive Functioning. It opens the door to useful reflection, self-evaluation, preparation and planning. Be sure to model your own Self Instruction out loud.

9

Replays

ACTIVITY HIGHLIGHTS

° Reviewing completed activities

° Spotting the need for corrective actions

Summary:

In the last activity, children practiced using Self Instruction to translate the Coach's feedback so they could modify their actions. In this activity, they learn to rely on their own observations and evaluation to provide feedback to guide their future actions.

Participants:

Coach and two children.

Getting Ready:

You will need a video camera and a monitor to play back the video. Remember to set up your camera so that you can capture the critical elements of the activity you are recording.

Coaching Instructions:

This is a simple activity. Make sure the camera is running and begin the activity. After several trials, stop and playback the video. Pause the replay at critical moments, so children can observe themselves acting out of "synch." Practice using "we" language, when it is clear that children need to take an action such as slowing down, moving closer, or counting together. Remember to incorporate the lessons learned from the previous Self Instruction activity. The combination of video feedback and Self Instruction becomes a powerful method of developing Executive Functioning skills. To practice this exercise, return to three previously practiced movement activities. They are the easiest to observe in terms of making corrective actions to become more coordinated:

° Two-Ball Toss

° Moving and Falling Together

° Crashing Cars

Variations

If you would like, you can begin using regular video feedback as a routine part of working on many of our activities.

Obstacles/Opportunities:

Children who are perfectionists may have trouble watching the video without an emotional reaction. Try to keep framing the issue in terms of corrective actions and not problems.

Musical Variations

ACTIVITY HIGHLIGHTS
° Learning to stay connected while adding variations
° Reviewing the evolution of a final product from a series of variations
° Creating activity variations for your social partner's amusement

Summary:

In prior musical activities, you have been largely responsible for the introduction of variety and the framework of the composition. In this activity the children begin to take responsibility for the composition. Excitement is generated from the ability to work as a team and from the increased complexity of the composition. A feeling of kinship and unity should mark the progression of the work. This activity is an exercise in how to appropriately influence others and accept influence yourself.

Participants:

Coach and two children.

Getting Ready:

You need one drum per person, a container with additional instruments and a cassette recorder. Participants sit facing each other on carpet squares. Each child begins the activity with the drum he chooses. The entire session should be recorded for future use.

Coaching Instructions:

☐ STEP 1

Play a simple six beat rhythm on a drum: "Hard/slow, hard/slow, hard/slow soft/fast, soft/fast, soft/fast." Narrate the rhythm as you drum. Repeat the rhythm four times. Instruct the children not to change the basic six beats of the rhythm. What they will be doing is co-varying within the six-beat framework.

☐ STEP 2

Now teach several variation choices and allow the children to choose from among them. The variation choices are as follows:

- Soft/slow, soft/slow, hard/fast, hard/fast, hard/fast, hard/fast
- Hard/slow, hard/slow, soft/fast, soft, fast, soft/fast, soft/fast
- Soft/fast, soft/fast, soft/fast, soft/fast, hard/slow, hard/slow

☐ STEP 3

After learning to play these variations the children take turns choosing a variation and then playing it. The drumming should gradually become more fluid, as children become more proficient in the three choices. Continue taking your turn

9

233

playing the same basic rhythm without variation. It is the children who will do all the variation.

☐ STEP 4

If the children can master Step 3, allow them to add their own variations, as long as they stay within the framework of the six-beat rhythm.

Variations:

You can include other instruments. We enjoy bells and feel they are usually a good complement for the drums.

Obstacles and Opportunities:

It may be difficult for some children to remember the basic framework and stay within it. This type of organizational problem may require additional practice. Providing visual structure, such as a symbol to represent the different rhythm combinations, may also help the child. As the children become more flexible and appreciative of the ideas of others, there will be increased opportunities for them to participate in many creative peer activities.

LEVEL III, STAGE 9, ACTIVITY 98

Buddy Walkers

ACTIVITY HIGHLIGHTS
° Careful synchronized movement
° Develop cooperative negotiation and communication

Summary:

The challenge of "Buddy Walkers" is that two people must move in tandem in order to reach a common goal. This is extremely difficult but fun. You must pay attention and react to each other's emotional states, which can range from mildly to highly frustrated. The elation that results from mastery is exhilarating to say the least.

Participants:

Coach and two children.

Getting Ready:

Buddy walkers consist of two wooden skis. Each ski has two ropes, one in the front of the ski and the other at the mid-way point of the ski. The skis are parallel to each other. The partner in the front places his left foot on one buddy walker and his right foot on the other. The partner at the back places his feet behind his partner's on the same buddy walkers. Once partners are on the buddy walkers, they pick up the ropes and must figure out how to move together to reach their goal.

Coaching Instructions:

This task screams for you to intervene frequently and provide instruction, but the value of the exercise comes from the children's ability to negotiate their synchronized movement on their own, with minimal help from you. In some cases the children may have to spend upwards of 15 minutes trying to coordinate their first step together. A range of emotions usually exists during this time and the activity may initially be rife with argument and accusation. As with any difficult task, however, the accomplishment produces exhilaration. Clearly they have accomplished and achieved a difficult goal. High tens and cries of "we did it" justly complete the activity.

Variations:

"Buddy Walkers" can be done with partners facing each other, requiring one of them to face backwards while the other faces forwards. While this is obviously more difficult in one way, it provides the advantage of face-to-face contact, which dramatically increases the ability for accurate social referencing.

Obstacles/Opportunities:

The desire to "win" or reach a destination can easily overpower the enjoyment of working as a team. Be prepared to stop the activity immediately if it becomes too goal focused. On the other hand we want the partners to develop the desire to work together to reach their goal, as long as the inevitable problems along the way are not dealt with through blame and acrimony.

9

LEVEL III, STAGE 9, ACTIVITY 99

Relay Race

ACTIVITY HIGHLIGHTS

° Cooperate with a peer partner in a competitive activity

° Maintain the priority of shared enjoyment over the need to win

Summary:

This particular relay race is easily taught, lots of fun and can be used with several children or a group. The activity teaches children to know where to look and to think on their feet, literally. As a child runs from place to place, he must consistently look at his partner to see where he is to go and what he is to get. This activity does have winners so it also is an opportunity to learn the importance of supporting one another when a loss occurs, and other elements of good sportsmanship. A high ten and an exuberant, "Congratulations, man, you were awesome," is expected.

Participants:

Each team consists of two children. Once learned, larger groups can play although a dyad will remain the primary unit.

Getting Ready:

For each dyad that plays you will need four plastic containers, one basket, one tissue box, one carpet square, red, yellow, blue and green construction paper, and 12 colored cubes; three each in red, yellow, green and blue. A carpet square for each "communicator" is placed next to one wall. Next to each carpet square, a basket is placed for the "finder's" objects. Four plastic containers are placed randomly around the room. Each contains three 6" x 2" colored papers. By example, the first container will hold three red papers if one dyad is playing the game but twelve red papers if six dyads are playing the game. The second container will hold three green papers, the third three blue papers, and the fourth three yellow papers. A tissue box is placed in front of the carpet square. It contains 12 small blocks: three red, three blue, three yellow, three green.

Coaching Instructions:

The finder of each team faces the communicator, standing several feet away. When you signal the beginning of the race, the communicator reaches into the tissue box and holds up a block. (A tissue box was chosen because its construction makes it difficult for the communicator to see the blocks inside.) He holds the block in the air while the finder runs quickly to the container with matching paper, selects the same color and quickly returns to the communicator. The communicator hands him the block and the finder runs back to his starting place and places block and paper in the team's basket. Now the finder waits, while the communicator selects a new block and the game continues. Midpoint through this game, signal a brief pause in the game and announce a role change between communicator and finder. The first team to finish stands on their carpet square and shouts, "We did it, we did it." The game stops immediately. The other teams shout, "Congratulations" then turn to each other and say, "I liked playing with you."

Variations:

A number of variations can make this an even more exciting game. Each communicator can assemble a tissue box full of items that his teammates must locate. Rather than one finder, children can work as "buddies" and run through the house or neighborhood to locate items. This makes a nice birthday party game. Use of items rather than colors adds variety to the game. Hiding objects around the room or in a field, rather than in clear plastic containers, adds an element of chance to the game. Using facial expression rather than words will reduce bossiness, and ensure visual referencing.

Obstacles/Opportunities:

The reason that the game stops immediately rather than playing out to second and third place winners has to do with the difficulty many children will have playing this game. The purpose is to give them a framework within which to enjoy teamwork not to make them feel incompetent. One bonus is that they will also learn to handle winning or losing well. Bossiness, disorganization, problems with visual referencing, and an inability to lose or win graciously can all surface as obstacles during this game. Each should be addressed but not necessarily in a pat way. For example, if only one team had problems with disorganization, you would help that team process the problems it encountered privately. However, if this was a problem for everyone, you might work on organization skills with the entire group. Bossiness should be analyzed child-by-child and deficits targeted individually. Winning and losing graciously lends itself to group work and a review of their expectations.

9

Shark and Fishermen

ACTIVITY HIGHLIGHTS:
° Working together to overcome shared threats
° Functioning as allies

Summary:

"Shark and Fishermen" is an exciting activity, where children band together to save the "crew" of their fishing boat from a "child-eating" shark that happens to be roaming around a carpeted floor. The children learn to rely on each other as faithful allies, who make sure that no child is lost to the shark.

Participants:

Coach and up to four children.

Getting Ready:

You will need about eight to ten beanbag chairs and a platform that can easily and safely be accessed by the children. Lay the beanbags out on the floor in a random pattern. But make sure that one beanbag is close enough to the platform for children to climb from beanbag to platform.

Coaching Instructions:

Explain the game to the children. You are the shark and will roam around the floor, looking for something to eat. The beanbags are islands and the shark cannot eat you if you are on an island. But if you venture off the island you can be eaten. All of the children except one begin the activity on the beanbag chairs farthest from the platform. One child plays the role of fishing boat captain and begins the game on the platform. The other children are the crew of the fishing boat. The crew fell off the boat and the captain is trying to get them back on board before the shark eats them. The captain can signal to different crewmembers when it is safe to move to the next island. When the crew person gets to the nearest beanbag, the captain will help him climb aboard. Now start the game. Roam around proclaiming that you are a starving shark and "just miss" the children as they leap from beanbag to beanbag. One by one the crew is rescued and makes it safely back on board. Make sure there are some scary "close calls." Rotate the role of captain. Children often want to take on the role of shark. That is fine, as long as they can play the role appropriately.

Variations:

Fishermen can become fish who need to be caught and saved before the shark eats them.

Obstacles/Opportunities:

The captain will typically need lots of coaching to coordinate his leaping crew persons and keep them from being eaten. This activity when done properly builds a great sense of team unity.

LEVEL III, STAGE 9, ACTIVITY 101

The Monster Again

ACTIVITY HIGHLIGHTS

° Learning the strength of mutual support
° Triumphing together against adversity

Summary:

When approaching this activity, it is important to remember that it is our vulnerability when we are alone that pushes us to work hard for acceptance into groups and involvement in relationships. While this activity is contrived, a basic truth is explored. Through friendship we learn that the "monsters" of loneliness and anxiety are best addressed most successfully through meaningful supportive relationships.

Participants:

Coach, Assistant Coach and three children.

Getting Ready:

You will need about eight beanbag chairs, one large table, two tablecloths, a plastic fork and spoon, and a small bag of talcum powder. The room or area should be set up to imitate a camp scene. One beanbag is in the center of the room symbolizing a pretend campfire and the table is turned on its side. A cloth is stretched over it representing the tent. You can use an actual small tent if you prefer. The second tablecloth is used as a covering to turn the Coach into a monster. The monster carries a fork in one hand and a spoon in the other. He can even carry a bottle of mustard for extra seasoning. The remaining beanbags can be used to construct a hiding place for the group.

Coaching Instructions:

This activity has five steps:

9

☐ STEP 1

The Assistant Coach begins the group meeting by telling the children that he has heard about a monster that lives somewhere in the area. This monster only eats those who go off by themselves, never people who stay together and collectively fight him off. You can tell the monster is in the area when you hear him beating his drum. When you hear the drumbeat you must fight him off together. If you do not work together the monster will defeat you and eat all of you.

☐ STEP 2

Now begin a pretend campout. The Assistant Coach tells the story of the monster which goes like this: "There was a monster that loved to eat people who were easy to catch because they did not understand how important it is to be a good friend. He lives somewhere around here and watches to see if anyone is not part of a group or team." The Assistant Coach continues with the story, "This monster never lives in your house or any other building – only here. He is very big and wears some kind of cloth covering. He is always prepared with a fork and spoon to have a tasty "children" meal. There is only one thing that works to scare the monster away. If three children can chant the special chant from a hiding place and the monster cannot see them, he will run away."

☐ STEP 3

Now the different roles are described. One child must be a lookout who will listen for the monster. This lookout will be right outside the door, or very nearby. There also needs to be a hideout and one of the children must build it. When the lookout hears the monster coming, everyone should run into the hiding place and they must all scream the chant to defeat the monster. Finally, someone has to keep saying the special chant, so that the group can remember it. The chant can go something like, "Oogabooga monster man, go back to monster land." The chant should be complex enough to be challenging but at the same time easy enough so that the three children can actually remember to say it. Each of the children is now assigned a role in preparing for the monster. The lookout should be provided with some type of signaling device like a gong or bell. The builder should begin constructing the hideout. The chant "rememberer" begins to dance around the campfire, repeating the chant over and over so that the group will remember it. Conduct periodic "Monster Drills" so that the team can practice their routine of rapidly going to their hideout and saying their chant in unison.

☐ STEP 4

Now it is time for the monster's approach. The monster begins to beat her drum softly, as though from a distance. As the Monster approaches, she beats the drum louder and louder. The lookout sees the monster and rings the alarm bell. Hopefully, the three children carry out their routine to perfection. If not, the monster growls and grabs one of them, saying, "I'm hungry. I'm going to eat this one." If this happens, the Assistant Coach can hold onto the child that has been caught and yell, "We need to save him. If we all pull together we can rescue him." When the other two children help, all it takes is a light tug to free their captured comrade. Now they are free, but the monster has spotted them. Quickly the Assistant Coach produces some talcum powder and blows it at the monster. The monster screams in agony and retreats out of sight and back to his lair. The Assistant Coach explains that luckily he had some magic powder that drove the monster away. Unfortunately, it can only be used one time. The next time the monster comes, they must make sure that none of them is caught. The team will need to work together to defeat the monster.

☐ STEP 5

Team members gather again around the campfire to tell the story of their recent adventure. Then two of them pretend to sleep in their tents, while one goes back to guard duty. The play continues as before.

Variations:

If children are too upset by the notion of a monster you can use an alternative figure. For example, they can pretend to be sheep that have to work together to fight off a wolf that wants to eat them. Try to find some representation of a common enemy that can only be defeated through their joint efforts.

Obstacles/Opportunities:

Group building often takes a form such as this in a natural setting. Watch a playground and you will see children pairing up and fighting off pretend threats as well as challenges from other peer groups. Usually, children will know that the monster is the Coach. But, because of the excitement and thrill involved, do not be surprised if children still desire to believe that the monster is real.

Map Reader and Scout

ACTIVITY HIGHLIGHTS
- Simple collaborative problem solving
- Experiencing the power of team-work
- Practicing skills of joint attention

Summary:

Map-reading and forms of "treasure hunting" seem to lend themselves to learning collaborative teamwork. In this exercise, the children work together to reach their destination. They follow a map from marker to marker until they arrive at a "treasure." One child, the "map reader" holds and "reads" the map, the other, the "scout" looks for markers and retrieves them.

Participants:

Coach and two or four children (one or two teams).

Getting Ready:

Materials include hand-made maps of a designated area which has been chosen based upon age and map-following abilities. Colored markers are needed to signify when a specific area has been reached. Carefully construct maps that are as simple, or complex, as the ability of the children to follow them.

Coaching Instructions:

There are four steps to this exercise:

☐ STEP 1

Children may first need instruction in how to use a map as a representation of an actual area of physical space. This is a crucial organizational skill in its own right. Take as much time as you need to teach this.

☐ STEP 2

Once children have sufficient map skills, provide them with a map that has colored points on it. Each point signifies a colored marker that you have placed along the route. Make sure they understand how to use the map to retrieve all the markers and bring them back.

☐ STEP 3

Designate and teach the two role assignments. One child is given the job of map reader. Only he is allowed to read the map. The other is the scout who accepts the directions of the map reader and is the only one allowed to retrieve the markers.

☐ STEP 4

Practice a structured format for managing the shared journey. Upon reaching a new location and retrieving a marker the scout must ask, "Where do we go next?" and wait for the map reader to indicate the direction using words and gestures. The map reader and scout must make sure they understand one another before the scout goes off on the next phase of the mission. While the scout is scouting, the map reader remains at the prior location. When the scout spots the next marker, he calls out, "I see it" and the map reader then moves to join the scout.

Variations:

As children become more adept at this activity, allow them to walk together from marker to marker. You can also increase distances between the markers. Markers can be "landmarks," such as a specific piece of furniture, that have clues taped to them, making this a true treasure hunt. The children can also learn to go on a walk and make a map together as they walk along. They can then use this map to construct a treasure hunt with markers that other persons have to follow. Finally, the children can work together to make their own map of a particular area, prior to beginning the game.

Obstacles/Opportunities:

It is important to emphasize to children that the goal of this activity is not winning or reaching the treasure. Like many of our activities, this exercise has the potential for becoming primarily a means to an end, with children focusing more on reading the map correctly, than on functioning together as a team.

9

STAGE 10: CO-CREATION

Goals and Objectives

In Stage 10, Challengers experience the excitement of acting as partners in a creative process. Together they produce something can only result from their collaboration. Peer partners experience an intense pride in what they accomplish as a team. They desire to frequently reflect on their accomplishments, photograph and record their new creations. The products they create are solely for their own enjoyment, not for an external source. They do not particularly care if anyone else appreciates them.

Activity Summary

Stage 10 begins with activities that gradually familiarize children to the excitement of Co-Creation. Choices are still structured and limited by the Coach. Creations begin with simple rhythms and songs. In the "Art Car" activity, Challengers receive their first taste of a tangible joint creation that can be displayed and admired by others. In "Co-Created Games" partners produce a lively new version of a game that provides the first opportunity they may have had to teach something new to a peer. "Our song" introduces children to the unity we feel when we have our own special "alma mater." Co-Creation progresses to language and role-plays, jokes and building activities, as Challengers practice Co-Creation in different media. Coaches still make sure that neither partner dominates the activity.

Critical Tips

- Make sure to record the partners' creations.

- Work in as many different media as you can think of.

- Carefully watch to make sure peers retain a 50/50 partnership.

- Do not become personally invested in the product. All that matters is that the peer partners enjoy it.

Created Rhythms

ACTIVITY HIGHLIGHTS
° Jointly creating unique rhythm patterns
° Increase feelings of unity

Summary:

Our first activity in this stage presents the characteristic elements of all of our Co-Creation exercises. It begins by presenting a basic framework. Children choose their own distinct variation from limited choices. The choices are integrated with a little help from you (as little as possible) into something new and unique. Children name their creation, celebrate it and return periodically to remember it.

Participants:

Coach and two or three children.

Getting Ready:

Children can provide their own drums if they would like.

Coaching Instructions:

There are six steps in this exercise:

☐ STEP 1

Each child chooses his own rhythm on the drums. Make sure that each rhythm selected is different and simple enough. Make sure that you record each rhythm so that you can all remember it.

☐ STEP 2

After they have each chosen their rhythms, children play them in succession as a single piece. They can also try playing the rhythms together.

☐ STEP 3

Now they jointly agree on a final rhythm which is used to complete the piece. Once again, record the rhythm so that it can be duplicated.

☐ STEP 4

You should add some simple connecting beats to tie the piece together.

☐ STEP 5

The children practice playing their simple piece until they can replicate it. They make a final recording.

☐ STEP 6

As a final step they give their composition a distinct name and the piece is saved for future reference. Following the naming, lead the children in a brief celebration of their accomplishment. Remember to play it periodically for them so they can reminisce about their accomplishment.

Variations:

Once the children have the hang of this co-creation process, give them opportunities to create many different distinct rhythms to add to their "album." Also, once experienced, allow them to choose and combine longer and longer rhythms. Try and gradually eliminate your role and see if they can "bridge the gaps" in a piece with their own efforts. Remember to let them struggle a little. Make sure you periodically play their "oldies" so they can reminisce.

Obstacles/Opportunities:

While we refer to this stage as Co-Creation, we are not yet ready to give the children unlimited creative license. The key to this stage is learning to share a creative event with a partner. Make sure that neither of the children's creative desires dominates or becomes the center of attention. The key is that neither child is interested in creating a specific thing or the "right" thing. Rather they can't wait for the surprise of finding out what their shared efforts will create.

LEVEL III, STAGE 10, ACTIVITY 104

Art Car

ACTIVITY HIGHLIGHTS:
° Great experience of group creation
° Creating group pride

Summary:

Each year the International Houston Festival features an Art Car parade, which is the highlight of the two-week festival. Art Cars are wonderful, weird "Junkers," each with its own unique theme and style, produced by devoted teams of artists, who have slaved over their creation for months. A recent entry belongs to a family near our office. Our children often take a field trip to visit it. A small car, it is aptly named the "Bug." It is completely covered with plastic bugs, small dinosaurs and Mardi Gras beads.

Participants:

Coach and up to four children.

Getting Ready:

Purchase toy autos that are at least one foot in length. Choose materials depending upon the children's ages and abilities. The group decorates them cooperatively as they please.

Coaching Instructions:

Collaborate on one car at a time. There are six steps in this activity:

☐ STEP 1

First the team chooses the type of car they are going to use, from several possible models. Provide several choices but do not go overboard. Make sure not to choose any car that is too distracting for a particular child. This in itself is an important activity for learning to negotiate and compromise.

☐ STEP 2

Once the car is chosen, the children are ready to select the theme for their car. Have them choose from several simple themes, such as the following:

- "Writing Car" decorated with writing implements like pens, pencils, paper, erasers.

- "Computer Car" decorated with keyboards, monitors, hard drives, etc. (remember these do not have to be real).

- "Baseball Car" decorated with baseball paraphernalia.

☐ STEP 3

Make sure that the children are equal partners in working on the car.

☐ STEP 4

When the auto is finished the children must decide on the name of the car together.

☐ STEP 5

Now take photographs of the children posing with the car.

☐ STEP 6

It is time for the celebration. Create a pretend parade in which they can display their art car to the screaming crowd. Videotape the parade with the art car as the main attraction. Finally place it in some special display area. Make as many art cars as you would like. The more cars you make, the better the parades. Cars can also turn into parade floats. Add some toy people and other related objects if you would like to give the parade a bit more "oomph."

Variations:

Why not make an "art plane," "art boat," or "art house"? In Houston we have two houses that are tourists attractions One of them has been almost completely covered with orange related products, the other with aluminum cans. Does this give you any creative ideas?

Opportunities/Obstacles:

Be careful to monitor the children's need for the car to turn out a certain way. One child's intense desire for perfection can spoil the fun for everyone.

LEVEL III, STAGE 10, ACTIVITY 105

Created Songs

ACTIVITY HIGHLIGHTS

° Creating your own novel songs

° Using familiar lyrics to integrate contributions

Summary:

People have made up their own unique version of popular songs from time immemorial. It is a great way of fostering a feeling of comradeship. In this activity, children take elements from familiar songs and use them to Co-Create a completely new version.

Participants:

Coach and up to four children.

Getting Ready:

Practice this exercise yourself prior to trying it out on the children. Make sure that you have pre-selected several songs that children are familiar with.

Coaching Instructions:

This exercise has six steps:

☐ STEP 1

Present several simple "standard" songs and have each child pick the one they like best. Make sure that the song is a simple one and not a modern hit.

☐ STEP 2

Each child chooses a line of words from their song. Your job is to help partners to pick a line that will not be too difficult to integrate into the final product.

☐ STEP 3

Children make this selection three times, until they each have picked three song lines.

☐ STEP 4

Now type the lines on a computer and have the children fit each other's lines together to make a song. Allow the children some poetic license to change words, make them sillier and take more "ownership" of them, as long as all are happy with the changes and no one dominates. Provide help when absolutely necessary to eliminate or modify a particular word.

10

☐ STEP 5

Now supply the children with a choice of two or three melodies, none of which is from the songs that have been chosen. The children then agree on the melody they will use for their new co-created lyrics.

☐ STEP 6

The final job is to shape the lyrics to fit the song. This will typically entail some editing efforts by you. Take one line of music and lyric at a time and fit lyrics into the music. When children are satisfied with a line, you should record it. When you are done with all six lines, have the group sing the song and make a final recording.

Example:

This is a mixture of two American classics, "She'll be Coming Round the Mountain" and "Home on the Range" sung to the tune of "The Yellow Rose of Texas" (yes, we just had to throw in some Texas chauvinism!):

She'll be Home on the Range

She'll be home, home on the range, when she comes, when she comes.

She'll be home, home on the range, when she comes, when she comes.

She'll be coming round the mountain, where the deer and antelope play.

Where seldom is heard a discouraging word. She'll ride six white horses when she comes.

She'll be home, home on the range, when she comes, when she comes.

She'll be home, home on the range, when she comes, when she comes.

Variations:

The obvious but more difficult variation is to have children each pick out a melody from a song and combine melodies and then use the words of a third song. Give it a try and see what happens.

Obstacles/Opportunities:

Like all of these exercises, you will only see real benefit from multiple trials of co-creating songs. Although you will have to help in a significant way, do not get hung up on producing a quality song to the point where you become the central figure in the composition. If the children do not see the piece as their creation, you have defeated the purpose of the exercise.

Our Song

ACTIVITY HIGHLIGHTS:
° Creating a group/tribal song
° Developing group unity

Summary:

Now that the children have had experience creating songs, they are ready to create their own theme song. As children develop a sense of unity, chants, songs and shared history become the glue of relationships. The "We-go" begins to have equal status with the "Ego." The creation of a club song is a step in this direction.

Participants:

Coach and three or four children.

Getting Ready:

You need a CD player and alma maters from local colleges or high schools.

Coaching Instructions:

This activity has four steps:

☐ STEP 1

Children choose the name of their club. The name can be based on shared interests of the participants. For example children who all like model cars and really enjoyed the "Art Car" exercise, can be named the "Drivers."

☐ STEP 2

Each child chooses a special "club name" that is only shared with other club members. In the Drivers Club each child can choose a special car.

☐ STEP 3

With your help, children begin by choosing the words for their song. The main theme of the song comes from the club name and the individual members nicknames.

For example, the Drivers Club has three members and their nicknames are Lamborghini, Mitsubishi and Corvette. Their song begins as follows:

Sam was a Chevy. Now he's a LAMBORGHINI

Sharon used to be a Ford. Now she's a MITSUBISHI

James use to be a Saturn. Now he's a CORVETTE

10

☐ STEP 4

The main verse is always followed by a short refrain. The refrain should be slow and soulful and composed of simple words that describe how members of the group feel about each other:

> I am your friend, you are mine
>
> We drive through life together.

☐ STEP 5

Now introduce the music. Play several alma maters from local high schools and/or colleges. The children choose one to be the melody for their song.

Variations:

See if the group can develop simple "code words" that only they know. This is sure to solidify feelings of mutual closeness.

Obstacles/Opportunities:

The creation of a group song will provide an instant identity for future members who join the "club." A new member will influence or change the dynamics of the group as well. As members leave or join, the song will include this information, such as, "Now he's in college," thus documenting the group's on-going history. It is also possible that the group identity will change from the "Drivers" to the "Dixie Chicks." Unlike other alma maters, this one is a fluid, living document.

LEVEL III, STAGE 10, ACTIVITY 107

Created Phrases

ACTIVITY HIGHLIGHTS:
° Creative use of language
° Creating a sense of unity and shared secrets

Summary:

In an earlier exercise we practiced silly combinations of rhyming words. Now we get to make up meaningless words and play with combining them into ridiculous phrases.

Participants:

Coach and up to four children in two teams of two. The children must be capable of reading and writing words to do this exercise.

Getting Ready:

You will need a set of rhyming words similar to those used in an earlier exercise. You will also need some small, blank index cards, markers and a set of same-sized square or rectangular blocks. Finally, you will need several cards with nonsense words already prepared. We have provided a short list of nonsense words below.

Coaching Instructions:

The children should take turns laying out a block. Each time they lay out a block, they should place one of the rhyming word cards on the block. Make sure that the blocks are laid out in pairs as the children move across the table or floor. When all the words have been used, go back to the first pair and either pick a nonsense word, or have them make up their own word to substitute for one of the other words. Then go to the next pair and have the other child do the same with one of the words. When you have completed all of the pairs, return again to the first pair and this time remove the second "real" word and substitute a meaningless word for it. Continue down the line. Now you should have several pairs of meaningless words that sound funny. Continually say the phrases out loud and gradually join the various two-word meaningless phrases together into meaningless sentences. Eventually the sentence becomes the "code phrase" that must be kept secret.

Variations:

Another variation is a guessing game. You can start with any two letters that would be easy to make a work from, like "U" and "N". Now each child takes turns drawing a letter from the bag and says, "My letter makes a word that you use with hotdogs." This is a point game but the points are awarded to the group as a whole. If a child gives a good clue and the other children can respond adequately, they cheer and the team gets a point. Usually, there is a world record that is to be beaten or a record from a previous time that must be surpassed.

Obstacles/Opportunities:

An inability to monitor laughter can be an obstacle for some children. They enjoy the laughter so much that it becomes unrelated to their joint creation. In this regard, they laugh too long and too loud with little regard for their peers' enjoyment. We often allow children to type their ideas on a computer, rather than spew them forth. This gives them a little more time to think and we have not noticed that it impairs their enjoyment.

- Amsy	- Loopen
- Boodoo	- Plip
- Mully	- Pote
- Droppeyboo	- Spatch
- Howten	- Blootch

10

Sample Meaningless Words:

These were turned into a chant, jointly contributed by two seven-year-old children. The first eight are repeated rapidly at the same tempo. The last two are said slowly and powerfully.

LEVEL III, STAGE 10, ACTIVITY 108

Created Games

ACTIVITY HIGHLIGHTS
° Jointly creating inventive new games
° Gaining popularity through creativity

Participants:

Coach and two children.

Getting Ready:

You will have to choose the particular game genre that you wish to start with. Be prepared to pursue this activity with many different types of activities.

Coaching Instructions:

This exercise has eight basic steps:

☐ STEP 1

The children each pick one of their favorite games within a specific genre. Initially you should select the genre from which they will both choose, such as card games, chess/checkers type games, or simple board games.

☐ STEP 2

Each child must tell you, or write down, three important elements of the game they have chosen.

☐ STEP 3

The children take turns with each presenting one element from their game until there are a total of six elements, three from each game. You should record the elements on a list.

☐ STEP 4

Now you will jointly create a new game that combines the six elements that have been selected. Modify any elements that would make the game unworkable or too complicated.

☐ STEP 6

Now children give this game a new name, which typically is some combination of the old names. For example, Chess and Checkers could become "Cheskers."

☐ STEP 7

The children play the game. Make modifications as necessary to ensure that the game is fun.

☐ STEP 8

As a final step, help the children make a short "documentary" video demonstrating how to play the game.

Variations:

Try the same exercise with movement oriented activities like soccer, basketball, baseball, hide-and-seek, tag, dodge ball etc. How about ping pong pool?

Obstacles/Opportunities:

If either of the children chooses a game they believe they have unusual expertise in, they may feel the need to leave the game intact. Make sure to choose games that participants are not overly invested in. What is great about this activity is that if children are successful, and you aid them in creating a game that really is fun, they can teach this new hybrid game to different peers and gain some respect for starting a new fad.

LEVEL III, STAGE 10, ACTIVITY 109

Created Role Plays

ACTIVITY HIGHLIGHTS
° Practice in creating unique role-plays
° Creative collaboration with teammate

10

Summary:

Now we are ready to turn our new Co-Creators into budding playwrights.

Participants:

Coach and up to four children.

Getting Ready:

Children should be familiar with taking on role-play characters and coordinating their actions to make the play work.

Coaching Instructions:

There are six steps in this exercise:

☐ STEP 1

Practice several simple role-plays such as "Mommy and Daddy," "Doctor and Patient" and "Teacher and Student." Each role-play should have two distinct characters that do not appear in any other play. That will create six characters to choose from.

☐ STEP 2

Each child chooses one character from the prior role-plays that he will portray in the new play. Make sure that the characters are from different plays, for example, mommy and teacher.

☐ STEP 3

Now choose a script for the play. The script can be from the play in which no characters were chosen, such as, "Mommy and Teacher go to the Doctor."

☐ STEP 4

Write a simple script for the new play, by varying the chosen script enough to make sense of the new characters. Add some absurd, comic elements to liven it up. Make sure that the children give it a title.

☐ STEP 5

Now practice and enact the play, making sure to videotape the final version.

☐ STEP 6

Videotape the play and provide "screenings" for friends and loved ones.

Variations:

See if children can add brand new characters into the play without creating too much confusion or conflict.

Obstacles/Opportunities:

This is another activity where a child's perception of needing to get it "right" can interfere with the enjoyment and thus the purpose of this activity. We care not at all that the play is enacted with any skill or technical prowess, just as long as it leaves the partners in stitches.

Joke Factory

ACTIVITY HIGHLIGHTS:
° Jointly created humor
° Enjoying wacky improvisation

Summary:

In this exercise, we decided to provide a simple "Joke Factory" that children can tap into as a team to create novel pieces of humor. Each person picks from a short list of choices. Then they combine their choices into a joke that makes absolutely no sense. Once again we emphasize that the point of jokes is laughter and shared silliness and not "getting it right."

Participants:

Coach and up to four children, in two-children teams.

Getting Ready:

Make sure that the children have experienced prior activities where we practiced absurd, meaningless but funny jokes.

Coaching Instructions:

Tell children that you want them to help you develop a Joke Factory. This will be a computer program that can produce endless numbers of jokes. They will try out the factory by testing it with three basic joke formats:

° Why did the ___?
° What do you get when you mix a ___ with a ___?
° How do you make a ____? You ____.

Examples of each format are presented at the end of the exercise. One child works on the first line and the other child does the second line. Then they practice telling the joke together in a coordinated manner. Make sure to laugh uproariously.

Variations:

There are an unlimited number of joke structures that you can set up in this very way. See how many different ones you can come up with.

Obstacles/Opportunities:

The children can learn to be really creatively funny after they practice this exercise. It has a great effect of providing enough structure to feel safe, so that children can explore their creative sides.

10

Joke Factory Structures

1. Why did the *(name an animal)* _____?

- Elephant
- Rhino
- Ant
- Skunk
- Alien
- Dinosaur

(Name an action)

- Cross a Road
- Pick blueberries
- Hop on One Leg
- Run around in circles
- Wear a cabbage on his head
- Swim in spaghetti
- Wear a bathrobe
- Swim the backstroke

Because he *(add a reason)* _____

- Just took a bath
- Was very hungry
- Wanted to eat
- It was on sale
- Wanted to go home
- Had to blow his nose
- Had to scratch his toes

2. What do you get when you mix a *(animal)* _____ **with a** *(animal)* _____?

- Elephant
- Rhino
- Ant
- Skunk
- Alien
- Dinosaur

You get a _____

- Mixed up creature
- Whoknowswhatasaurus
- Headache
- Mess
- *(Add your own)*

3. How do you make a *(animal)* _____ *(action)* _____**?**

> *Animals*
> - Elephant
> - Rhino
> - Ant
> - Skunk
> - Alien
> - Dinosaur
>
> *Actions*
> - Do the backstroke
> - Cross a road
> - Eat a pickle
> - Go to sleep
> *(Add an action)*

You *(action)* _____

> Put a cabbage on his head
>
> Count to three and close your eyes
>
> Twirl him around and hope for the best
>
> Tell him there's a McDonalds down the street.

LEVEL III, STAGE 10, ACTIVITY III

Created Structures

ACTIVITY HIGHLIGHTS
° Using collaborative effort to create new structures
° Participating in a group creative process

Summary:

Blending your perceptions together to create something entirely new, is one of the greatest thrills of early friendships. We now ask children to work together and create a brand new structure that reflects their joint contributions.

Participants:

Four children can participate in two groups of two.

10

Getting Ready:

All you need are sufficient building materials.

Coaching Instructions:

There are three simple steps:

☐ STEP 1

Provide each team with one set of building materials. Tell them that they are going to work together as a team. Each team is going to work together to build one thing. First they have to choose what they are going to build. Initially limit choices to a house, a school, or a police station.

☐ STEP 2

Allow each team several minutes to decide. After they have made their choice, ask the team to choose a strategy for how you are going to work together. They can choose one of three strategies: They can take turns adding a piece, they can each work on a different part, or one can be the builder and the other the architect. Make sure that each child understands the meanings of the roles they have chosen.

☐ STEP 3

Let the teams get started. When they are finished, make sure that each team creates a unique name for their structure. Additionally, they should take a photo of their finished product, place it into their "Partner Journals" and add a paragraph to describe the process and product.

Variations:

After each team has completed their structure, you can ask the two teams to "merge" their structures into one single structure. This will take some re-building and movement, but it is an exciting activity both in terms of reinforcing flexible thinking and in strengthening the partners' perceptions of their ability to work as part of a cohesive, successful team.

Obstacles/Opportunities:

Many of our activities are conducted in dyadic-paired units. If you have a way of keeping pairs together, they can strengthen their emotional connections if you help them keep a "team journal" which chronicles shared travails and triumphs.

LEVEL III, STAGE 10, ACTIVITY 112

Created Sculptures

ACTIVITY HIGHLIGHTS
- Learning how to make an enjoyable variation
- Communicating the reasoning for your actions
- Staying coordinated in the face of unexpected variation
- Accepting and showing appreciation for your partner's contributions

Summary:

While on the surface, this may seem like a turn-taking activity, in actuality its main focus is on learning how to add variations while maintaining related to your social partners. It is also an important exercise in learning to acknowledge and appreciate the contributions of others.

Participants:

Coach and up to four children.

Getting Ready:

You will need a large set of multi-shaped, natural wood building blocks. If you want, you can substitute other building materials. Make a small deck of cards with the words "Connected" on half and "Variation" on the other half. You will also need a white board and markers, on which you should write the four ways to stay connected and the four acceptable variations. Children sit around a circle. The blocks are in a container in the center, but closer to you.

Coaching Instructions:

There are two steps to this activity:

☐ STEP 1

Tell the children that they are going to build a sculpture out of the blocks. They will take turns picking a card which will tell them if they should make a "Connection" or a "Variation." Then they will choose a block and add it to the project. If they pick a "Connection" card, they have to make sure that their idea is connected to their partner's. They have to stay connected. But, if they choose a "Variation" card they must make sure they have added something new to the structure. They have to add a variation. The children must use one of the following choices for their connections and variations. These should be provided in writing on the white board, so the partners can reference them.

Ways to Stay Connected:

1. I used the same shape block.

2. I used the same size block.

10

RELATIONSHIP DEVELOPMENT INTERVENTION WITH YOUNG CHILDREN

3. I kept going (in the same direction).

4. I put my block next to yours.

Variations:

1. My idea makes it larger.

2. My idea makes it taller.

3. My idea makes it wider.

4. My idea makes it stronger.

☐ STEP 2

Pass the basket of blocks around the circle. Each child picks a card, makes sure he can read it and then takes one block from the basket and makes his contribution. After each child places his block, he must explain which of the four ways he has chosen to either remain connected with actions before his, or vary the structure. He is asked to explain his contribution by saying either, "This is my idea. The way my idea is connected to yours is ___,"or, "The way my idea changes the sculpture is ____." Do not accept any variations that are not listed in the choices above.

☐ STEP 3

The other children are encouraged to complement each contribution by acknowledging that they see how the sculpture has stayed connected or has changed in a positive manner. You should take your turn, the first few times this exercise is practiced, in order to model the process.

Variations:

Cardboard sculptural kits with beautiful colors and shapes are available in gift shops and toy stores. These may be used to co-create sculptures.

Obstacles/Opportunities:

Some children simply can't accept that their ideas are being changed as part of the on-going process. We have had some children break down and cry without consolation because an idea was changed. While this exercise is difficult for these children, they are clearly in the most need of these skills.

STAGE 11: IMPROVISATION

Goals and Objectives

Now Challengers are ready to operate as partners in environments where things are constantly transforming, much like real life settings. This stage introduces Challengers to the demands of peer play and conversation, where topics, themes and movements may change on a moments notice. Challengers have now become the major contributors to these "on-the-fly" changes which are made without stopping to discuss or negotiate. This requires rapid referencing, regulating and repair skills.

Activity Summary

The stage begins with exercises aimed at preparing children to rapidly introduce their own ideas in a coordinated manner. The children learn flexible thinking, rapid adaptation and alternative ways of using familiar materials and actions. Practice in improvisation expands over a number of different areas, including rhythms, music, song and movement. The children learn to emphasize the fun of their joint activity over the concept of reaching any particular endpoint. The joint creativity of this stage comes to full fruition when partners improvise their own role-plays, jokes and poems.

Critical Tips

- Remember to stay with simple materials.

- You may have to work individually with Challengers who have difficulty coming up with their own contributions.

- Begin each activity by providing a simple framework that serves as a base for later improvisation.

- Once again, remember not to get caught up in the quality or meaning of an improvised product. What is important is the peer partner's enjoyment, not whether they produce something that you think is worthwhile.

LEVEL III, STAGE 11, ACTIVITY 113

Improvised Activities

ACTIVITY HIGHLIGHTS:
- ° Learning the joy of improvisation
- ° Flexible thinking
- ° Rapid adaptation to other's ideas

Summary:

With this activity we move full force into the area of improvisation. The children are given some basic materials and they improvise together to create a new activity. They are successful because by now they have a storehouse of activity ideas and can re-combine the elements of the many activities they have already mastered.

Participants:

You can do this with several pairs of children if you wish.

Getting Ready:

Select materials that you believe will be simple and familiar enough so that they will not become the focus. We like to begin with some of our "veteran" materials such as beanbag chairs, balloons, balls and blocks. Typically, by this stage, our children can use these few materials to make quite an assortment of activities.

Coaching Instructions:

The activity has three steps:

☐ STEP 1

Lay out the materials that the partners are going to use. Tell them that you want them to use the materials to make up their own game. They can make up any game they like, as long as they both agree and it is fun for them.

☐ STEP 2

To provide a reference source for them, visually display the names and photographs of many of the activities that they have already mastered. Often this review is enough to get the team going. If not, you can have them enact several activities and pick the parts they want to use in their own creation.

☐ STEP 3

If you see the team getting stuck and running out of ideas, take one of the materials and say, "Let's see. Here are some beanbag chairs. What are some ways that you like to use beanbag chairs? Will any of those uses work now?" If partners are still having trouble, you can make a list of different ways they can use each material. For example, blocks can be bowling pins, obstacles, houses, forts, or roads.

Variations:

Practice a very different form of improvisation. Tell partners that you want them to do a certain activity, but do not provide the usual materials needed. Rather, require them to improvise from materials that would not normally be used. For example, tell them to make up a game of tennis, but do not provide rackets or a net. Instead, provide several cardboard cylinders, a pile of beanbag chairs, some scotch tape, several plastic plates and some sheets of paper. Do this with as many activities as you can think of and you will be surprised at how quickly children develop flexible and divergent thinking skills.

Obstacles/Opportunities:

The need to have it "my way" is the biggest obstacle in this activity. Another obstacle can be the lack of imagination that some of our children demonstrate. These are both good reasons to keep working at this exercise.

LEVEL III, STAGE 11, ACTIVITY 114

Improvised Structures

ACTIVITY HIGHLIGHTS:
° Flexible thinking
° Rapid improvisation

Summary:

Quite frequently, in typical children's play, themes will suddenly change without warning. A scenario where two children are spacemen fighting aliens abruptly changes into one where two doctors are operating on a wounded lion, with only a brief suggestion by one of the partners triggering the transformation. In this activity we practice this type of thematic improvisation in a more gradual format. The children take turns adding new features to their co-created structures. Periodically they pick a card that allows them to change the entire framework into something else.

Participants:

Several teams of two children can participate along with you.

Getting Ready:

You can use any type of construction materials that you like. We prefer to use simple building blocks. Provide a number of pretend "props" that might be associated with different types of structures like airports, fire stations, schools,

11

garages, shopping malls etc. You will need to construct a deck of cards that has two types of cards; one that says "keep the same structure" and the other that says, "change the structure." The deck should contain two "keep the structure" cards for every one "change the structure" cards.

Coaching Instructions:

Explain the two types of cards to the children. They will take turns making additions to a basic structure. Each time it is their turn, they pick a card from the deck. If they pick a "keep the structure" card, they should make an addition that does not change the structure. For example, if you are building a house, add a door, a window, a chimney or some other part of a house. However, if you pick a "change the structure" card, this means you must turn it into something else. If you are building a house, then you could add some props that will change it into a garage or an airplane terminal. You choose the initial building theme for the children. It should be something simple like a house. There is one more rule. When you choose a "change the structure" card and make a change, you must check with your partner to see if they are enjoying the change. If they do not like the change, you must try another change, until you find one your partner enjoys. Supply enough "change the structure" choices, so that children who cannot think of their own changes will have ones to choose from.

Variations:

The corollary to this activity is to turn one prop into another without varying the basic structure of what you are building. For example, if you are building a house, if you pick a "transform" card you could take the chimney and transform it into a satellite dish. Make sure to require partners to check with each other for enjoyment, prior to completing their turn.

Obstacles/Opportunities:

Concrete, literal thinking can be an obstacle in this activity, but this also represents a great opportunity to improve cognitive flexibility.

Improvised Rules

ACTIVITY HIGHLIGHTS:
° Increased flexibility
° Ability to adapt rules as needed

Summary:

Our children tend to be very rule-oriented. Rather than viewing rule variations and changes as exciting novelty, they often perceive them as disruptive. This activity emphasizes the potential excitement we can feel when together we change the rules of a game so that we never know what is going to happen next. In this exercise, the children play a board game where each partner has to change one of the rules in order to move their piece.

Participants:

Several teams of dyads can participate.

Getting Ready:

Use a simple board game such as Candy Land. You take turns picking a card from the deck. The cards have either one colored square, two squares of the same color, or an illustration of one of the special places on the board (like Ice Cream Mountain). You move your piece along the "road", proceeding to the square that corresponds to the color or symbol on the card you have selected (you move to the second red square if you get two reds for example). The first player to get from one side of the board to the other wins.

Coaching Instructions:

Explain to the children that you are going to play a familiar game in a brand-new way. Children will take turns. They will roll the dice, or pick a card, and then move their pieces, just as they always do. But, there is a big difference. When it is your turn, before you pick a card, you have to make one change in the rules of the game. The change cannot be one that favors you. Rather, the change must be one that makes the game more fun and interesting. At the end of this description, we present several possible changes using the example of Candy Land. Prepare a list of possible changes that partners can use, if they cannot come up with any of their own.

Variations:

Of course you can do this activity with any game or physical activity.

Obstacles/Opportunities:

This is another great opportunity to learn flexible thinking and rapid adaptation. It is a great way to help children focus on their fellow players rather than winning the game.

11

Possible Candy Land Variations:

° You must move backwards

° You must skip every other space

° Roll the dice instead of picking a card to see how many spaces you move

° Each partner picks a card for someone else

° Before you get to move, you have to spin around three times and say your name backwards.

Improvised Rhythms

ACTIVITY HIGHLIGHTS

° Reviewing the evolution of a final product from a series of variations.

° Creating activity variations for your social partner's amusement

Summary:

This is an exercise in how to influence and accept influence. In prior musical activities, you have largely been responsible for the introduction of variety and the framework of the composition. In this activity Challengers begin to take responsibility for composition. Excitement is generated from the ability to work as a team and from the increased complexity of the composition.

Participants:

Try this with up to four children.

Getting Ready:

You need one drum per Challenger, a container with additional instruments, carpet squares, a video camera and a cassette recorder

Coaching Instructions:

This activity has five steps:

☐ STEP 1

Play a simple five beat pattern on a drum. "Hard/slow, hard/slow, soft/fast, soft/fast, soft/fast." Narrate the pattern as you drum. Repeat it as many times as you need to so that the children can learn it and play it along with you.

☐ STEP 2

Provide variation choices to the children who are free to choose from among them. The choices are as follows:

- Soft/slow, soft/slow, hard/fast, hard/fast, hard/fast
- Hard/slow, hard/slow, hard/fast, hard/fast, hard/fast
- Soft/slow, soft/slow, soft/fast, soft/fast, soft/fast

☐ STEP 3

After learning to play the variation choices, the children take turns choosing a variation and playing it. You should continue to take your turn playing the basic pattern without variation. It is the children who play the variations.

☐ STEP 4

When all the children have mastered Step 3, allow them to add their own variations, as long as they stay within the framework of the five-beat rhythm.

Variations:

You can include other instruments. We enjoy bells and feel they are usually a good complement for the drums. As participants become proficient with this exercise, you should allow them more leeway in introducing their own rhythms and begin to move from a structured turn-taking format into a more fluid and "natural" one.

Obstacles and Opportunities:

It may be difficult for some children to remember the basic framework and stay within it. This type of sequential organizational problem may require additional practice. Providing visual structure, such as symbols to represent the different pattern combinations, may also help the child with this problem. As children become more flexible and appreciative of the ideas of others, there will be increased opportunities for them to participate in many creative peer activities.

LEVEL III, STAGE 11, ACTIVITY 117

Improvised Music

ACTIVITY HIGHLIGHTS:
° Making up your own shared musical contribution
° Rapidly adapting and enjoying your partner's changes

Summary:

Work with instruments has been leading up to the ability to freely express oneself while maintaining synchrony with other participants. This, of course, is difficult for accomplished musicians and without the structure of notation a concerto would never begin. Using the various themes introduced in the last activity, and building on previous instrumental interactions, participants are now able to play in a more improvised manner. Physically and emotionally they have learned not only to self regulate but also to allow space for other participants' contributions. Visual checking in is extremely necessary if the music is not to disintegrate into a mass of slamming noise. Nonverbal signals are used to cue solo activity and create the space necessary for doing so. Recordings made from each session allow participants to critique and improve the music they make together.

Participants:

Coach and up to three children.

Getting Ready:

The children take turns playing the drum, the keyboard and the set of bells. Construct a set of picture cards that portray simple scenes, such as a butterfly on a flower, a thunderstorm, or a picnic.

Coaching Instructions:

Each participant is given one instrument. You will begin by playing the keyboard and the other members are given simple percussion instruments. Begin by removing a card from a box. For purposes of demonstration, it will say butterflies and flowers. Start by banging the keyboard and producing an atonal uninteresting sound followed by a softer, more melodious tune. A short discussion should take place to identify, which sounded more like a butterfly and which like a flower. Play again, but now play the butterfly and flower piece. Nod for the drummer to join in, followed by the bell player. As they play together, you should nod for the drummer to become silent. Now it is the bell player's turn to perform a solo. Using the same facial expression, bring everyone back into the song and finish it up. Now, turn the keyboard over to the most capable child. Continue to improvise, using cards for the thematic framework and continue to rotate instruments. Other instruments should be available as well, although you will need to monitor their inclusion. Too many, lead to an inability to improvise in a coordinated manner.

Variations:

Replicating other pieces along with movement can also be fun. Integrating physical movement with musical presentation is great but should be approached with care due to on-going difficulties with over-stimulation and self-involvement.

Obstacles/Opportunities:

Both musical ability and lack of musical ability can interfere with coordinated improvisation. The desire to express oneself musically can lead to a solo presentation. While not bad in and of itself, the goal for this activity is to make something as a group that cannot be performed individually. Children who are already competent on an instrument may lack enthusiasm for the musical ideas of others. If bossiness gets to be a problem, we would make him sit with us and learn to watch.

LEVEL III, STAGE 11, ACTIVITY 118

Improvised Songs

ACTIVITY HIGHLIGHTS
° Experiencing the joy of jointly improvising
° Creating new songs

Summary:

People have always obtained enjoyment from taking familiar songs and improvising new words that make them sillier, even when the new version is not particularly meaningful to anyone other than the song creators. Now, our Challengers are ready for this new type of creativity. We use a familiar song format from the prior stage but add the improvisational element so that the new creation is unlike anything previously sung.

Participants:

Coach and two children, or two teams of two.

Getting Ready:

It helps to tape record the productions and type the lyrics as partners go along, so they can keep track of their production.

11

Coaching Instructions:

This activity has three steps:

☐ STEP 1

Begin by asking the partners to select a familiar melody from among several you have chosen for them.

☐ STEP 2

Once the melody is chosen, provide lyrics to at least three other songs in an easily readable format. List them in a "phrase-by-phrase" basis, so that partners can easily select the particular song phrases they wish to add.

☐ STEP 3

Now tell partners that their job is to create new lyrics to the melody they have chosen. They have to take turns picking lyrics from each of the other three songs to add to their new song. The only rule is that each time lyrics from one song are chosen, the next partner must choose lyrics from one of the other songs for the next phrase. Practice this along with the children, until you are sure that they understand. Then back off and allow them to begin the creative process. At this point, your job is to ensure that partners follow the rules and to help tweak the chosen phrases slightly, so that they better fit into the melody.

Variations:

As children become proficient, allow them more leeway in choosing their own melodies and lyrics, as long as they do not present too difficult a challenge. Try reversing the procedure. Take a set of lyrics from one of the songs. Now have the children blend the melodies from the other songs, picking up a melodic phrase from a different song on each turn and blending them together. This can turn out even more hilarious than the original exercise.

Obstacles/Opportunities :

Do not be surprised if the products have no meaning whatsoever. The goal of the exercise is met as long as the partners have fun and enjoy their joint improvisational process. Children who insist on the lyrics making sense are demonstrating that they are not yet ready for this activity. Similarly, those who attempt to control the creative process should go back and work on earlier collaborative exercises.

Improvised Movement

ACTIVITY HIGHLIGHTS
° Learning freedom of movement
° Increased body and movement awareness

Summary:

Moving in synch with others and the physical presentation of our bodies in space are basic to our everyday ability relate to other people. In this exercise, the partners begin some type of movement, taking turns with one in the lead and the others following.

Participants:

You can try this with a small group.

Getting Ready:

The children should be made to feel comfortable with moving in an improvised manner.

Coaching Instructions:

This exercise has five steps:

☐ STEP 1

Explain that this game will require that children make up their own movements and then rapidly change them when you hold up a "change" card. One partner is in the lead at all times and the other partners follow his lead. The children change the lead each time you hold up a "change" card and additionally, they have to change and perform a completely new movement.

☐ STEP 2

The next step is for all the children to feel comfortable with improvised movement. Begin by introducing movement in a very low light. You should introduce cards that have various themes you would like them to act out in movement only. Examples are; bubbling soup, molasses, butterflies and clouds at night.

☐ STEP 3

Begin this step by playing soft drum rhythms and having participants move around the room in any direction, reflecting the pattern suggested by the drumming. Beginning with strong loud beats. Bang slowly at first then faster; abruptly changing to a ringing of the bell, then a rain stick.

☐ STEP 4

As children begin to improvise their movements the card game can be used differently. Placing all cards in a box, each participant draws one card and acts out

11

273

his own rhythm. For example, one participant might have a card that says molasses, another popcorn and yet another, butterflies in the garden. As participants move and watch these very diverse expressions, they will come to bring different movements into their enactment.

☐ STEP 5

Now you are ready for the partners to take over the game. Have one start an improvised movement and make sure that the other partners follow it. Every 30 seconds or so you should hold up a change card with a new partner's name on it. Now it is his turn to improvise a movement and have everyone follow it. Continue the activity in this manner until you can introduce changes in a rapid, fluid manner.

Variations:

After they have completed the basic activity, partners should be asked to contribute their own ideas for "movement enactments." Initially, these can be simple such as "railroad trains," "thunderstorms," or "dinosaurs." Gradually work with the partners so that they can contribute more complex concepts such as "optimism," and "triumph."

Obstacles/Opportunities:

Reluctance to enact movements in front of others is a major obstacle. Typically, this can be overcome if we choose movement enactments that are not embarrassing to the participant. We are not wedded to any particular enactment, so do not hesitate to modify them to increase the comfort and enjoyment of the activity.

LEVEL III, STAGE 11, ACTIVITY 120

Improvised Role-Plays

ACTIVITY HIGHLIGHTS:

° Practice in more natural fluid role-playing
° Rapid flexible thinking and adaptation

Summary:

Typical children's play is a completely improvised event. Role-plays rarely stay with a theme for very long. Plots interweave. Characters are abruptly added and deleted. Even if characters remain, their roles may change dramatically. In this activity, partners learn to enact fluidly improvised role-plays, choosing from a selected cast of characters, themes and events.

Participants:

Two or more children.

Getting Ready:

If you are working with four children, ask a team of two participants to be the "watchers," and alternate watchers and "players." Your major job is to prepare the raw materials from which the participants will improvise their role-plays. Select a number of different characters and add brief descriptions for each. Provide different props for each character, such as hats, glasses, fake noses, diaper, baby bottle, stethoscope, police badge, mailbag, computer, computer repair tools, jackets and other distinguishing characteristics. Next, make a list of simple plot lines. These should be no more than one or two simple sentences in length. Finally, tape-record a number of sample silly voices using exaggerated high-pitched, low-pitched, nasal, and other silly voices. Three sets of props are basic to this role-play.

1. *Props for parents and child:* for example, for two boys, dress-up clothes will be geared toward a father and grandfather. Other props will include bottles, diapers and dolls.

2. *Props for patient and doctor:* these include white coat, doll, stethoscope, bandages, rubber gloves and a pretend needle.

3. *Good guys, bad guys:* here we use police costumes. We usually also include pirate gear for the bad guy.

Three large containers holding props for each role-play are on a counter. Then children will most likely be overwhelmed by choice of role-play and choice of objects so the coach will narrow the choices and roles in the beginning. As the children become more masterful and better able to make choices as a team, objects for all three role-plays can be made available.

Coaching Instructions:

This exercise has five steps:

☐ STEP 1

Practice with participants to make sure that they know how to enact each of the basic characters in their "non-improvised" forms. Review each of the characters and their related plot elements so that participants understand each one. Review the different available props. Review the different silly voices that participants can use.

☐ STEP 2

Now begin the basic role-play by asking partners to each choose roles that fit together easily, like mother and father, or teacher and student.

11

☐ STEP 3

When participants have had a bit of time to get into their roles, stop the action. Ask both of the players to choose a new character, a new voice, new props and a new plot line. Tell them to make sure that the new characters and plots fit together.

☐ STEP 4

Now, stop the actions more frequently and have partners switch characters and plot lines. This time make sure that, along with matching characters and plot lines, they also choose voices and props that are unexpected and make their characters really silly, like a baby with a deep voice, or a policeman wearing a diaper with a badge pinned onto it. Tell them to surprise each other with the voices and props that they choose. Stop the action frequently and tell them to switch voices and props but continue in character and with the same plot line. Make sure that they continue to identify who they are to each other to avoid confusion.

☐ STEP 5

As a final activity, have partners surprise each other by choosing characters, props and voices without consulting each other. Then they have to collaborate on a plot line that will be enjoyable for them.

Variations:

Other role-plays from life include, waitress and diner, fireman and home owner, airline pilot and passenger. Once children have become competent with role-play and role reversal, they are often able to take on dual roles using various props. Usually the competence expands on its own when children are ready to play in this way. The premature introduction of dual roles will overwhelm children if they are not ready to play like this. Gradually allow participants to introduce their own characters and plot lines. They are always welcome to insert new voices and props.

- Postman
- Policeman
- Computer repairman
- Talking computer
- Mother
- Father
- Child
- Teacher

- Student
- Robber
- Doctor
- Invisible patient
- Baby
- Pet dog
- Pet cat

Obstacles/Opportunities:

You know you are doing this exercise correctly if all participants are frequently falling to the floor with laughter. Videotaping the role-plays really heightens the enjoyment. Keep your eyes on the mutual referencing for shared joy during playbacks of these hilarious videos. Some children have spent so much time in front of TVs, computers or video games that they are almost incapable of interacting in a fluid manner when props such as these are introduced. In the beginning, the Coach may have to spend some time helping them think about what each of the characters does, and how they talk, walk and look. This should be minimal and consist of short sequences with plenty of time for practice and independent expansion of ideas. The ability to role-play helps lead the children into comfortable experiences with typically developing children. When we have had the opportunity to work with very young children, we find that they begin to approach dress-up corners in classrooms and independently at home. Certainly, cousins and siblings will enjoy this play with the child. Older children, who have done this have been able to revisit and target childhood deficits. They will also have the added benefit of good planning and following through on their plan, reflecting on their plan and, working on the videotape until it is presented as they want it to be.

Sample Characters

Sample Plot Elements

- I am a postman and I have to deliver an important message.
- I am a person at home waiting for a message to see if I won the lottery.
- I am trying to catch a robber.
- I am a robber, trying to rob a bank.
- I am trying to fix a computer.
- I am a computer who is refusing to work until I get fed.
- I am a mother telling my child to go to sleep.
- I am a child who doesn't want to go to sleep and is sneaky.
- I am a mother preparing dinner for the father.
- I am a baby crying in my crib.
- I am a doctor who is trying to examine an invisible patient.
- I am an invisible patient who is trying to get the doctor to help me with my tummy ache.
- I am a dog who wants to catch a cat.
- I am a cat who wants to scare the dog, so he will stop bothering me.

11

LEVEL III, STAGE 11, ACTIVITY 121

Improvised Jokes

ACTIVITY HIGHLIGHTS
° Appreciation of improvised humor
° Emphasizing shared enjoyment over scripted joke-telling

Summary:

As you can already see, we love to use humor in our exercises. When children develop a good improvised sense of humor, both as a co-creator and appreciative audience, they immediately become attractive to their peers, despite any other limitations they may have. We all love someone who genuinely laughs at our jokes and comes up with zany additions to our ideas.

Participants:

Two children, or two pairs of two.

Getting Ready:

Remind children of the simple joke frameworks that they used in the "Joke Factory" exercise. Make sure to review this exercise to refresh their memories. The three basic joke-types that we used were:

- Why did the _____?
- What do you get when you mix a _____?
- How do you make a _____?

Coaching Instructions:

There are three simple steps:

☐ STEP 1

Teach children to use three additional joke frameworks

- What did the _____ say to the _____?
- What is the capitol of _____?
- What is the national [food, bird, animal] of _____?

Provide enough examples of each, so that all participants are proficient in using these frameworks.

☐ STEP 2

Now the real fun begins. Participants use a round-table format, where they rapidly go around with each partner having a turn beginning a joke and one of the other participants volunteering a ridiculous ending. Make sure to emphasize that they are not to care whether the joke makes sense or not, as long as it makes everyone laugh. You may participate as part of the round-table and model ridiculous endings, so that everyone feels comfortable using this framework and does not worry about getting it "right."

☐ STEP 3

Stay on one framework for a while before changing to another one. If everyone is comfortable, try to initiate a more fluid process where each child picks a framework and the group then uses it for their jokes. Try to gradually withdraw participation and become a highly appreciative audience.

Variations:

Have each participant bring in one new joke format each time you meet together. Allow children to provide some examples of the format. Then incorporate them into the improvisational mix.

Obstacles/Opportunities:

As you might expect, the biggest obstacle is a child's unwillingness to accept the nonsensical nature of jokes as they rapidly change and "morph" into new entities. This is a sure sign that we have to backtrack to earlier stages. As we stated in the summary, this type of practice will payoff in immediate benefits in the world of peer relations. The reason for this is that this exercise reinforces the essential truth that the key to humor is not the need to get it right but to have fun and make sure your partners are having fun too. All you have to do is study the totally improvised and oftentimes nonsensical humor within the Marx Brothers films to know that this is so. If you stopped to analyze them, you would have no idea why their jokes were funny, but that does nothing to keep you from rolling on the floor with laughter!

11

STAGE 12: RUNNING MATES

Goals and Objectives

In this, the last stage of this book, Challengers begin to perceive of their relationships in a more self-conscious manner. The child at the close of Level III is aware about needing to act in a way that will be attractive to peers. He knows that other children will not tolerate a cheater, or a sore loser, nor will they want to be with someone who does not find ways of compromising and collaborating with them. He also knows that to keep a friend, he must provide something that is meaningful to them. By this stage he knows that communication will not always be effective. He is actively checking for misunderstandings and seeking to correct them.

Activity Summary

This stage begins by exploring the relationship between emotional expressions and their internal feeling states. Children learn that their feelings emanate from within them and not from another person. They learn to be accurate "readers" as well as "senders" of emotional expressions. We practice non-verbal "conversations" where children learn the different components of non-verbal language and manage emotional expressions in a more deliberate manner. Children also learn to be more aware of their communication environment. They learn to choose their physical space carefully and regularly check for accuracy, understanding and topic connection. As the stage progresses, we teach several critical friendship skills; learning to be a graceful loser and joining in a peer's activity without interrupting and intruding. At the end of the stage we introduce Challengers to the work of Level IV, which is covered in a second book, by practicing two simple joint attention activities.

Critical Tips

- Remember to have everyone involved with the Challengers use similar emotion labels to avoid confusion.

- Learning progresses much faster if we all use Self Talk out loud regularly.

- Remember to continue to amplify your emotional expressions.

- Non-verbal communication must be practiced all day long. Practice should be part of a daily routine.

LEVEL III, STAGE 12, ACTIVITY 122

Emotions

ACTIVITY HIGHLIGHTS
- Understanding and appropriately using basic emotions
- Learning that emotional expressions emanate from internal feelings
- Identifying the non-verbal expression of basic emotions
- Meaningfully sharing emotions with social partners
- Linking feelings with their causes

Summary:

This is the first activity to directly work on understanding our emotions. We begin with four basic feelings: happy, sad, angry and scared. In this exercise emotional expressions are viewed as a meaningful communication of something you are experiencing. Do not be surprised if you spend months on variations of this activity. It is critical for further development and combines many different elements of emotional awareness and communication.

Participants:

Coach and up to four children.

Getting Ready:

In the initial phase, you will use "emotion cards" that have line drawings of faces, each making one of the basic emotions. Following this you should not need any props besides a mirror. Having a video camera and monitor is extremely helpful.

Instructions:

There are nine steps to this activity:

☐ STEP 1

Explain that we are going to learn about four expressions: happy, sad, scared and angry, and that we can show the expressions with our faces. Demonstrate the four expressions. Use line drawings for illustration. Practice the expressions in front of a mirror.

☐ STEP 2

Explain that we have expressions because something happens that causes us to have a feeling. When we have a feeling, the feeling turns into an expression. Move in front of a mirror and make the appropriate expression while speaking as follows:

> "I have this expression because I feel sad inside."
>
> "I have this expression because I feel happy inside."
>
> "I have this expression because I feel scared inside."
>
> "I have this expression because I feel angry inside."

12

☐ STEP 3

Now the children should practice making each of the expressions and relating it to a feeling, just as you did.

☐ STEP 4

Practice "passing" the emotion to one another. Sit in a small circle and take turns making an expression and sharing the feeling. After each child makes the expression and relates it to a feeling, he reaches out and gently places his hands on the cheeks of his partner to the left. This signals he is "passing" the same emotion to the partner. The person who has received the emotion makes the appropriate expression and states that they are having the feeling. Periodically signal when it is time to change expressions and begin passing a new expression.

☐ STEP 5

Once children master passing basic expressions, we work on linking emotions with some simple causes for these feelings. Explain that we have feelings because something happens to cause these feelings. Say, "We are going to practice having feelings and saying what makes those feelings." Use a whiteboard and write "1. Cause," "2. Feeling" and "3. Expression" on the board. Make sure that children understand this causal chain. Demonstrate this chain as much as needed and then pass the "chain" around the group. For example, you may say, "I played with my friends. Playing with my friends makes me happy. When I am happy, I have this expression." Continue this for all four emotions.

☐ STEP 6

The activity becomes more fluid, as children get to choose whatever emotion they wish and explain why they have it.

☐ STEP 7

Children practice guessing the emotions of their group members based upon their facial expressions.

☐ STEP 8

After guessing the expression and the related emotion, they practice responding in a caring manner. Insert some simple conversation as follows:

- Child notices sad expression: "Are you sad?" (Affirmative reply). "Why are you sad?" (Reply). "Is there something I can do to cheer you up?" (Reply).
- Partner notices a happy expression: "You look happy!" (Reply). "I am glad you are happy. I'm happy too."
- Partner notices scared expression: "You look scared." (Reply). "What are you scared about? (Response). "I get scared too sometimes."

☐ STEP 9:

Continue to regularly add emotions to this activity, until you have a large repertoire.

Variations:

Play a variation of the "pass the emotion" game. One partner picks an emotion and explains why he has it and then passes it onto the next one. The next partner must explain why he has the emotion, using a different but equally valid reason and so on, until you indicate a need to change emotions.

Obstacles/Opportunities:

This is a great opportunity for everyone closely involved with the child to use emotion labels in the same manner as the child is practicing. It helps greatly if those involved make an extra effort to narrate their own emotions and the simple reasons for their feelings out loud. It is also crucial to encourage children to use their new skills to query those close to them about their emotional expressions. Be careful not to minimize your facial expressions by saying things like, "I'm fine. It's no big deal." You may think you are protecting the child, but in reality you may be confusing him.

LEVEL III, STAGE 12, ACTIVITY 123

Talk Without Words

ACTIVITY HIGHLIGHTS

° Practice the different components of non-verbal communication
° Learn to have non-verbal "conversations."

Summary:

In this exercise we continue with the theme of non-verbal communication. Now, we break down the elements of "speaking without words" into two main areas; "Body Language" and "Sound Language." We practice each separately and then integrate them into more complex non-verbal "conversations."

Participants:

Up to four children.

Getting Ready:

You will need a video camera and monitor or TV for this exercise. Prior to starting you should choose a range of non-verbal expressions you wish the participants to practice. Make sure to clearly distinguish the different "body" and "sound" expressions that characterize each one. Make a videotape to illustrate each expression. Do not add any words for your sound portion of the tape, just

12

285

the non-verbal auditory accompaniments. You will also need to make a video-tape of two people having each of the non-verbal "conversations." Examples of these conversations are presented at the end of the exercise. Sample videotapes are also available from our website.

Coaching Instructions:

☐ STEP 1   LEARN TO READ YOUR PARTNER'S BODY LANGUAGE

First play the video without the sound on and have the children watch the body language in the different segments. If you have the ability, play the segment in slow motion and pause at critical points so you can capture important components. Carefully observe one segment at a time. Test each participant's ability to read the body language by playing different segments out of order and seeing if they can recognize the communication.

☐ STEP 2

Now ask each participant to enact a "body" communication. Stay with one at a time. After participants have accurately modeled all of the basic forms, quiz them by seeing if they can accurately recognize each other's body talk. Work with one pair of partners at a time, with the others acting as "watchers." Finally, have each participant practice reading body talk accurately without benefit of video playback.

☐ STEP 3   LEARN TO READ YOUR OWN BODY LANGUAGE

Repeat the procedure, but this time have each participant view their own video segments and learn to correctly identify their own body talk. Make sure that not only can they visually identify their body language but that they can also do so kinesthetically. Go back to each segment and have participants identify the changes they can feel in their face, their arms and their trunk, when they enact the different responses.

☐ STEP 4   LEARN TO READ YOUR PARTNER'S "SOUND" LANGUAGE

Repeat the procedure for step 1. However, turn off the video and just work with the audio portion of the tape. Make sure you do not use any words in the sound recording.

☐ STEP 5   LEARN TO READ YOUR OWN "SOUND" LANGUAGE

Repeat Step 2 and similarly just use the audio portion.

☐ STEP 6   USE ONLY BODY LANGUAGE TO HAVE A CONVERSATION

Now you are going to work with reciprocal expressions. These come in both "symmetrical" and "complementary" forms. Have participants watch the video and then practice their own simple "body" conversations. When they are ready, videotape the conversation and have them analyze it. When they have enacted all of the conversations, make sure that they can recognize each one without any hints.

☐ STEP 7

Use only sound language to have conversations.

☐ STEP 8

Use both body and sound language to have conversations.

Variations:

The possibilities for non-verbal conversations are endless. Watch your favorite movies with the sound off. Stop the action regularly and have participants guess the conversations that are going on.

Obstacles/Opportunities:

This is another opportunity for highly verbal partners to learn to rely less on their words. Practice non-verbal conversations at regular times in the day. Make it a part of the daily routine!

Elements of Body and Sound Language

- Sad
- Worried
- Angry
- Happy
- Curious
- Surprised
- Proud

Sample Non-Verbal Conversations

Symmetrical

- We are both members of a team that just won a big race.
- I am angry with you and you are angry with me.
- We are brothers who just had our pet dog get run over.

Complementary

- I am sad and you are wondering what is wrong.
- I am angry with you and you are confused about what you did to make me angry.
- I am feeling very worried and you are trying to make me feel better.

12

LEVEL III, STAGE 12, ACTIVITY 124

Can You Hear Me Now?

ACTIVITY HIGHLIGHTS
° Heightening awareness of personal space
° Learning the impact of physical position on communication effectiveness

Summary:

Many of our children are oblivious to the impact of their physical position on others. This activity provides an introduction to becoming aware of the effect of your position in space on the person you are interacting with. In this activity, children practice the dimensions of "too far away," "too close," "too soft" and "too loud."

Participants:

You can work in pairs or with three children, with the children rotating as the "watchers."

Getting Ready:

No materials are needed for this activity.

Coaching Instructions:

There are three steps to the activity: too far and too close, walking away while talking, and too loud and too soft.

☐ STEP 1

Tell children that this will be a lesson about being too far and too close from each other. When you are talking to someone, you can be too far away from them, so they can't hear you, or too close to them, so they feel uncomfortable. Start by practicing being too far away. Ask each person to stand far apart and try to conduct a conversation about what they see, while using a normal speaking voice. Tell them to keep moving back to determine when they can no longer accurately hear each other.

☐ STEP 2

Now tell children that they will practice how walking away while talking, may leave the other person unable to hear you. Ask two children to slowly walk away from each other while talking, again using a normal speaking voice. Have one child slowly walk out the door and continue talking while the other remains inside.

☐ STEP 3

Practice speaking too loudly and too softly. Have children practice talking very softly so that they cannot hear each other. Finally have them practice getting within normal speaking distance and talking too loudly to one another.

Variations:

An excellent real-life exercise is to walk down a fairly noisy street together, and walk either far ahead or behind your partner while talking about something that he absolutely needs to talk with you about. Hopefully he will be amazed at the number of communication breakdowns and misunderstandings. Contrast this with how much easier it is to communicate when you remain side by side while you walk.

Obstacles/Opportunities:

As the variation illustrates, this activity is an excellent introduction to the concept of "communication breakdowns" and the need for continual monitoring of accuracy. We will be continuing this theme in the next activity and in later stages, but, this activity certainly can be a strong example.

LEVEL III, STAGE 12, ACTIVITY 125

Pass It On

ACTIVITY HIGHLIGHTS

° Understanding the frequency of communication breakdowns
° Engaging in routine checking for accuracy and understanding of communication

Summary:

As we stated at the close of the last exercise, most children do not yet understand how common communication breakdowns are in normal conversation. Therefore, they rarely, if ever, check to see that their statements are understood, or whether they have accurately comprehended the speaker. Of course this leads to an even higher frequency of communication problems. This exercise is our variation of an activity that is as old as the hills. The goal is to provide an experience in how easy it is for any communication to breakdown, even when we are standing right next to the person who is communicating to us.

Participants:

Try this exercise with a group of four children.

12

Getting Ready:

Participants should have an awareness of how their body position can impact on the reception of communication. You need a whiteboard and markers for this activity. Everyone should sit side by side facing the board.

Coaching Instructions:

There are eight steps in this exercise:

☐ STEP 1

Begin the activity by writing down a sentence that will be shared with everyone. Tell the participants they are playing the game "Pass It On." In this game, when your partner whispers something, you have to pass it on to the next person in line. The last person in line says it out loud. You are not allowed to ask for the words to be repeated. Just try to remember it as best as you can.

☐ STEP 2

Now, begin the game by whispering a sentence to the person next to you. You can modify the sentence to make it more or less challenging, based upon the language processing abilities of the participants. Here is a sample, "Johnny went to the bakery to get his mother a loaf of wheat bread and four oatmeal cookies."

☐ STEP 3

When the last participant says the sentence out loud, write the initial sentence on the whiteboard in one color and the final sentence directly under it in another color. Group members compare the two. Make sure to point out the amount of change. Try this with several sentences. Make sure that you increase the complexity so that there are inevitable breakdowns. But do not make it so complex that it is impossible to pass along successfully when children stop and make sure they understand it.

☐ STEP 4

Now require each participant, when he hears the sentence, to ask the speaker to repeat it slowly, to make sure that he heard it correctly. Record your results and have the group analyze how much better they do.

☐ STEP 5

Next teach each participant not only to ask for repetition, but also repeat the sentence back to the speaker, to make certain he heard it correctly. Again, note for the group whether there is any improvement.

☐ STEP 6

Now go back to passing sentences, without any kind of repetition or checking, and have participants notice that the communication gets distorted once again.

☐ STEP 7

Use the activity to begin building the communication habit of "Checking." Explain to participants that in typical conversations, all of us must "check" all of the time, or else we will hear things differently than they were said to us. To illustrate this further, allow two children to talk to each other about a simple topic, like an interesting object that you set in front of them. Make sure to tape record the interaction. Wait until you have recorded a conversation breakdown. Now stop the conversation and have children listen to the taped segment of the breakdown. Ask the listener to stop and repeat back what he thinks he just heard the speaker say. Play back the actual communication on the tape recorder and compare the difference.

☐ STEP 8

Now continue the simple conversation and ask participants to stop and check, each time they are not absolutely sure they heard the speaker correctly. Do the same "Stop the Action" and compare the accuracy of the listener to the speaker.

Variations:

As a corollary, try and repeat this exercise using non-verbal communication. Have participants pass along a simple non-verbal message and illustrate how frequently the message becomes distorted. Teach participants to engage in frequent non-verbal "checking."

Obstacles/Opportunities:

This exercise is a good introduction to monitoring communication. However, we are only addressing the issue of accuracy of content and not making sure that the listener understands the speaker's intention or meaning. That will be the work of later stages.

LEVEL III, STAGE 12, ACTIVITY 126

Wordless Drawings

ACTIVITY HIGHLIGHTS:
° Non-verbal collaboration
° Creative communication for problem solving

Summary:

In this exercise we illustrate that non-verbal communication can be used not only to express emotions, but also to reach a common goal. This is a very simple exercise and we provide it only to open the door for many other activities that you can practice without words.

12

Participants:

Teams of two children.

Getting Ready:

You will need a white board, two different color markers and one eraser. The children stand side by side facing the board. Place one marker on one each side of the board with the eraser in the middle.

Coaching Instructions:

Tell partners that the task is to use their markers to work as a team and draw one picture that they both really like. There can only be one picture on the board. They have to work together, but cannot talk to each other. They also have to have as much fun as possible working together.

Variations:

The world is full of examples of people using non-verbal signals for collaboration. You can find examples in the world of professional sports. A very interesting illustration is found in the world of professional baseball. There is a highly intricate language of non-verbal signals that players and coaches use to communicate with one another. Take the group to baseball games and see if they can learn to "break the code" and follow the signal system.

Obstacles/Opportunities:

The focus on how we use non-verbal signals for collaboration can open up a whole new world of meaning for children when they observe interaction around them. If you can find a videotape of a crowded elevator or subway, you can study the intriguing world of non-verbal signals employed in those settings.

LEVEL III, STAGE 12, ACTIVITY 127

Connected Conversations

ACTIVITY HIGHLIGHTS:
° Practicing remaining on topic
° Practicing conversation "repair" skills

Summary:

Back in Level I we introduced the concept of connected and disconnected topics to Novices. A good deal of work has already been undertaken to help children maintain connections with their peers, without which this particular exercise would have little value. Now we enact a much more sophisticated version of the earlier activity. This time, the children have to make up their own statements and questions and use them in the proper, connected manner.

Participants:

A group of up to four children.

Getting Ready:

Each participant needs one blue, yellow and red card with their name on each card. "Good Idea" is written on the blue card alongside their name. Similarly, "Connected" is written on each yellow card by each name and "Disconnected" is written on each red card by each name. A post-it note is attached to each of the blue and yellow cards.

Coaching Instructions:

This exercise is taught in four steps:

☐ STEP 1

Maintain control of all the cards and explain their meaning through demonstration. Place your blue card in the center of the table and say, " I have a good idea." Choose a fairly broad but definable category so that participants will clearly understand the activity. For example, say, "I want to talk about birthdays." Now write "birthdays" on the post-it note attached to your blue card. This is a visual reminder of the subject. We often begin with a simple topic such as birthdays because everyone has something to say about it.

☐ STEP 2

As each participant responds to the birthday idea in a connected manner, place his connection card on the table. Every time a participant says something that connects with the topic, a line is made on his connection post-it. Disconnections occur as follows: one child says, "For my birthday we went to McDonalds," then the next says, "I had pizza with pepperoni last night for dinner." In an exaggerated manner produce the last participant's red card and explain that he has "disconnected" and must say the following, "Uh oh, sorry," followed by a connected statement about the topic. Once the person makes a connection, the red card is removed and a connected mark is placed on the post-it on his yellow card.

☐ STEP 3

It is now time for the participants to have "good ideas." In the beginning any idea is acceptable.

☐ STEP 4

Once the exercise is understood, a final component is added. An idea presented by a participant must be agreed on before the connection/disconnection activity occurs. For example, a partner might say that his good idea is train whistles and ask, "Do you want to talk about train whistles?" If there is disagree-

12

293

ment, he will need to find another topic. By this juncture, the Coach is simply in charge of the cards.

Variations:

The cards should be used only in the initial, explanatory stages of this work. Participants should quickly be taught to produce and read facial expressions that signal that a disconnection has occurred.

Obstacles/Opportunities:

You may be surprised by the topics that lead to a long series of connections. A young man who said he wanted to talk about "train whistles" suggested one of our favorite examples. We assumed that the connected comments would last for about two rounds and in fact, we thought this would be an opportunity to do a small lesson on selecting topics that might also be of interest to others. In the end we had to bring his idea to a halt because there was no stopping the flow of information that this group of individuals with Asperger Syndrome brought up about train whistles.

LEVEL III, STAGE 12, ACTIVITY 128

Learning How to Lose

ACTIVITY HIGHLIGHTS
° Learning how to lose gracefully
° Regulating your emotional reactions to losing
° Prioritizing relationship over winning

Summary:

People hate a sore loser – someone who always has to win to feel good. Learning to have friends also means learning how to lose gracefully and without ruining the enjoyment for your partners.

Participants:

Coach and up to four children.

Getting Ready:

You need a simple game, such as checkers, which has winners and losers, and can be conducted very rapidly.

Coaching Instructions:

There are four steps to this exercise:

☐ STEP 1

Tell participants, "Every time you play a game with a friend you are really playing two games. One game is the game in front of you. The other game is the Friendship Game. Which game is more important? Of course, it's the Friendship Game! When you play with a friend, winning the Friendship is much more important than winning the game. Let's see if you can learn how to win the friendship and lose the unimportant game."

☐ STEP 2

The children play a game and purposefully try to lose. Say, "I want to see how fast you can lose without cheating. The faster you lose, the more points you get." This is a simple and enjoyable way to get children who have trouble with losing to learn to relax.

☐ STEP 3

Tell the children that they will play a simple game but this time, you will add a new element. Tell them, "Now you are going to play two games at the same time. There is the checkers game (or whichever game you are playing) and the Friendship Game. I want to see if you can win the Friendship Game. You get friendship points for each thing you do that makes you a good friend." There are five things that the children can do to get points:

1. Encourage their partner "You can do it!"

2. Compliment your partner i.e., "That was a good move."

3. Share good feelings i.e., "This is fun!"

4. Talk to yourself about losing, i.e.,"Friends are more important than winning a game. I can win the Friendship Game!"

5. There is a final thing they can do. If their partner wins they can congratulate them.

☐ STEP 4

Spend time practicing and role-playing all five of these skills. Once all children are proficient, it is time to incorporate the skills into the game. Tell the children that this time when they play, they can earn friendship points for encouraging others, complementing others and sharing good feelings, and bonus points for talking to themselves and congratulating their partner if they win. Finish by saying, "Let's see how many friendship points you can each get."

12

Variations:

Just like people hate a sore loser, they dislike someone who always wants to do what he wants to do and who doesn't seem to care about his partner's interests or desires. In this variation, the children practice doing things that are not particularly interesting to them, just because it makes their friend happy.

Obstacles/Opportunities:

This activity will take some practice for children with serious emotion regulation problems. If any of the children show any signs of distress, stop the action and request that they rehearse what their true goal is.

LEVEL III, STAGE 12, ACTIVITY 129

It Takes Two

ACTIVITY HIGHLIGHTS

° Experiencing the power of joint effort
° Learning to work as a team to overcome adversity

Summary:

In previous activities, the Coach has served as a mythical adversary in the guise of the monster. In this activity, the Coach comes out of disguise and enacts a semi-playful role as the adversary – the person who places obstacles in the path of the group which can only be overcome through joint effort. It goes without saying that your goal as Coach is for the group to defeat you. Just make sure you don't make it too easy, or they will never appreciate the challenge.

Participants:

Coach and a group of two or three children.

Getting Ready:

Make sure that all the children appreciate that you are enacting the role of the "mean" Coach. You will want to limit your appearance in this role and only take on the role at the appropriate times.

Coaching Instructions:

The goal of this activity is for the group, through their combined efforts, to defeat you. How much you have to cue the group to do this depends on the individuals. Initially, you may have to chant something akin to, "It takes three to open the door," before the group members fully realize that they will only reach their goal through combined action. We always start by being an obstacle to their shared goals. This is a very physical activity where we block the children from getting what they want, or going where they want to go, and they must work together to physically move us out of the way. After a while, the group members may start having fun planning ways that they are going to defeat you. This should become a source of great "private" conversations that they pointedly exclude you from. There are three main ways that you are going to act as the "Mean Coach:"

Acting as an obstacle to a goal:

The group decides to get a game or object out of a drawer or closet. You block the way and say that they are not allowed to come through. The group is able to shove your dead weight out of the way without hurting you, but only through their combined effort and after a significant struggle.

Challenging them to an activity and trying to defeat them:

Play soccer against two or three of the children and let them know that you will defeat them if they cannot play together as a unit. For some reason the Coach should always lose at the last moment.

Interfering with an activity:

This is the very last way that we function as the "Mean Coach" as it is the most difficult to interpret accurately. The group is playing a game and you sneak up and snatch an object that is crucial for the game. For example, if two children were playing Chess and you would sneak up and knock over their pieces. In this case the group would win by finding some place where they can create a barrier to stop you from entering. They will have escaped from your meddling by finding or making a refuge, and will then be left alone to pursue their relationship in peace.

Variations:

We have had a number of experiences where two Coaches have challenged a group of children to Baseball and Soccer tournaments. Week after week the team competed against us, both winning and losing some close games, with the championship and trophy of our tiny league at stake. Each game brought an increase in suspense and a closer bonding of team members as they united against their persistent foe. Just when it looked like they were going to be defeated, something happened through their combined efforts and they pulled out victory from the jaws of defeat.

Obstacles/Opportunities:

Once again we emphasize that we always check to make sure that the Challengers feel safe when we change roles into the "Mean Coach." The trick is to walk the tightrope and not terrify them, but at the same time create enough excitement and uncertainty that defeating the Coach has real meaning to the team.

LEVEL III, STAGE 12, ACTIVITY 130

Joining In

ACTIVITY HIGHLIGHTS

° Learning effective strategies to join activities

° Learning to be a good observer of others

Summary:

In this exercise, the children practice simple strategies for joining in an activity. They are taught simple methods for trying to join and also for inviting another person to join in as well. The key elements practiced here are observing, narrating what the peer is doing, approaching, and trying to join. In a later stage we work on the more complex aspects of joining in.

Participants:

You can try this with up to three children, with each taking turns playing the role of a joiner, a watcher and an actor.

Getting Ready:

The only materials needed are those the actor will use, for example, some simple blocks.

Coaching Instructions:

This activity has five steps:

☐ STEP 1

To begin with one child is given the role of actor, another is the joiner and the third is the watcher, but the children should switch roles often. The actor is given some blocks, or similar simple materials to play with. The actor's role is simple. The joiner has to practice four steps: Getting Ready, Narrating, Approaching and Joining.

☐ STEP 2   GET READY

During the initial phase, the actor waits for the joiner to make the first move. The joiner first practices moving to observing distance – close enough to see what his peer is doing, but not so close as to bother him. Joiners will require practice determining the correct distance for observing. The actor is to act interested in his building task and not to notice the joiner unless he comes too near.

☐ STEP 3   NARRATE

Once he has figured out a good spot for observing, the joiner stops and briefly narrates what his partner is doing. He should already possess this skill from prior activities.

☐ STEP 4   APPROACH

After narration, the next step is to approach to joining distance. Practice how to physically approach in order to get near enough to indicate interest, but not to interrupt the actor.

☐ STEP 5   JOIN

The actual "joining" act entails four simple steps. First, the joiner compliments the actor with a phrase like, "Hey that's a great thing you are building." The compliment is immediately followed by a simple curious question such as, "What is it?" The actor is instructed to answer accurately with a neutral manner but not to invite the joiner to join him. Then the joiner enacts the third step and asks to join in saying, "Can I help?" In this initial simple version, the actor accepts the request and allows the joiner to join in. After this is successful, we insert a fourth step. Prior to asking to help, the joiner asks, "Mind if I watch?" After this is agreed to, the joiner sits down near the actor but not so near as to interfere with his actions and remains there for several minutes. He should practice making non-verbal comments to indicate his interest and admiration for the "Actor's" efforts. Only after this should he ask, "Can I help?"

Variations:

A second version of the exercise involves the actor behaving in a more inviting manner. The activity begins the same way. However, when the joiner moves into joining distance, the actor briefly narrates his current activity and then invites the joiner to play with a phrase such as, "Hey, I'm building a _____. Would you like to do it with me?"

Obstacles/Opportunities:

The inevitable question to be asked here is, "What about rejection?" This is an important concern, as we know that in typical children's play, about half of all attempts to join in with peers are rejected. While having a simple strategy like the one in this exercise should reduce rejections, it certainly will not eliminate them.

12

Discovery Boxes

ACTIVITY HIGHLIGHTS
° Introduce the excitement of sharing perceptions
° Practice the essential steps of joint attention

Summary:

We all love to share surprises with one another. This activity is a great way to teach the excitement of sharing a new discovery. This is one of our first perception sharing activities. The children learn how to show objects in order to share the emotions they feel. We like to make this a very dramatic affair. The "sharing" partner learns how to build suspense by taking a few seconds to pick an object and then assumes an exaggerated facial expression to draw out the tension, before showing it. In this activity we practice the three essential steps of joint attention: "discovering" a new perception "showing" it to your partner and "sharing" the excitement of the discovery. We also add a variation of "asking" to this basic format.

Participants:

Begin with two Coaches and two or four children. After a short initial trial only one Coach will be needed. Allow the partners to take turns being the "Shower" after you have practiced and believe they are ready. After participants learn the basic framework of joint attention in this activity, the next activity should be simple to teach with only one Coach.

Getting Ready:

Use a container with a top that is wide enough to allow you to reach in and pull out a small object. A large tissue box can suffice. A second container acts as the "finished" box. It is where objects are placed after they are shown. Use six small objects suited to the age of the participants. Objects should be interesting such as a piece of quartz, a plastic spider or a foreign coin, but ones that will not distract attention from the main objective of the activity.

Coaching Instructions:

The process of showing and being shown should initially be broken down into a series of four small steps. Coaches should take each step in a deliberate manner and make sure that children model their actions with appropriate emotional display.

☐ STEP 1

Initially, each Coach sits next to a child, with the pairs at about a 45° angle from each other and about two to three feet apart. Explain that the name of this game is "Asking and Showing." Model the activity and then gradually guide the children, until they understand and can enact their role independently. They must learn to enact both the actions of "showing" and "asking" as well as Self Talk and emotional expressions.

☐ STEP 2

One Coach takes on the role of the "Shower" and chooses an object to show his partner. The other Coach is the "Asker" and requests that he or she be shown an object. The job of the "Shower" is: (1) To reach into the box and pick something out without knowing what it is, (2) To become excited by the discovery. (3) To share it with his partner. The "Shower" has to choose an object purely by feel without looking into the box. Only the "Shower" can touch the object. Only an "Asker" can start the game, by asking to be shown something.

☐ STEP 3

Instruct the children that the "Shower" and "Asker" have to do exactly what you do. At each step, make sure to narrate each of your actions out loud, using very simple words. Sample self-narration is indicated in parentheses:

> *Asker:* "I want to see what you have in the box. Please show me!"
>
> *Shower:* Removes an object by feel, without looking into the box ("I feel one! I can't look inside!"). Glances at it briefly ("wow" or "cool"). Draw attention to your emotional reaction to the object, as if you are making an exciting discovery.
>
> *Shower:* Hold the object out at eye level and make sure the asker can see it, "Can you see it?" If there is no response, continue saying with an amplified facial expression, "Wow! Can you see it?"
>
> *Asker:* Alternates between "Yes I can! Wow! It's a _____" and "Yes I can. What is it?" Then after several successful trials says, "No I can't see it very well."
>
> *Shower:* In response to this new question the shower says, "Here, let me move closer to you. Can you see it now?"
>
> *Asker:* "Yes. Thank you."

☐ STEP 4

When you believe children are ready, hand one of them the box and say, "Now it is your turn to be the "Shower." You are going to show _____ (the other partner)." You should then sit behind the partner who is showing and coach as little as possible. When both partners can perform their initial roles without coaching, it is time for role reversal.

Variations:

A simple variation is to eliminate the initial asking part of the script and begin with showing. This adds a new element to the shower's role as he must first make sure that the asker would like to share the perception, for example by asking, "Do you want to see something?" prior to showing. Another natural variation is for partners to make their own activity boxes and bring things with

12

them to surprise each other. This can be a natural bridge to an early conversational activity such as "Asking and Telling" where the "Asker" practices asking something simple like "What is that?" and the "Shower" practices simply answering the question.

Obstacles/Opportunities:

Make sure that the "Shower" is focused primarily on his partner and not the object and is communicating with enough animation and invitation. Make sure that the objects are interesting enough to be shown and admired but not so compelling that they distract attention from the relationship. Objects are there to enhance the relationship not compete with it. Finally, make sure that the children know that emotion sharing is the most important part of the activity. As a final note, this is a great activity for our hyper-verbal partners in learning how to get the maximum emotional impact using the fewest words.

LEVEL III, STAGE 12, ACTIVITY 132

What Do You See

ACTIVITY HIGHLIGHTS

° Practicing all five steps of complex joint attention
° Learning to monitor and repair breakdowns in perceptual coordination

Summary:

This is a variation on the classic activity, "looking out my window," that all children enjoy. In fact when the Connections Center was located in an office high-rise, we often looked out of an office window, onto a busy freeway below, to do this activity. In this exercise, the children practice taking turns pointing out what they see and making sure that their partner sees it too. This is another excellent introduction to learning how and why we love to share our observations with our social partners.

In the prior exercise, participants practiced the first three steps of true joint attention – Discovery, Showing and Sharing. In this exercise we expand the skill and use a new five-step format we call Complex Joint Attention, – Asking, Telling, Checking, Repairing (if needed) and Sharing. We introduce the new concepts of "checking" your partner's attention to make sure that it is directed to the same place as yours and taking "repair" actions if you observe that your perceptions are not coordinated.

Participants:

Coach and one or two pairs of children.

Getting Ready:

Make sure the partners are proficient in the first three steps of joint attention – Asking, Showing and Sharing. You can use any interesting setting for observation. It could be a window overlooking a highway, or a detailed picture book like Richard Scarry's *Big Book of Animals* or *Trucks*. Make sure that whatever setting you use, it is not so distracting that the partners are unable to make rapid attention shifts.

Coaching Instructions:

This activity has two steps:

☐ STEP 1

Begin by explaining the activity in a manner similar to that used for "Discovery Boxes." There are the same two roles of "Shower" and "Asker;" however, this time, instead of showing something in the box, we will be showing something we see outside the window, or on a page of a book. Practice joint attention just as in the discovery box activity, but now with the new materials that you have selected.

☐ STEP 2

Next, introduce participants to the five steps of complex joint attention:

Asking: "What do you see?"

Telling: "I see a red truck."

Asking: "Where?"

Telling: (Pointing) "There it is."

Checking: "Do you see it?"

Telling: "Yes or No."

Repairing: If the answer is "No" they should try another method to get their partner to see it.

Sharing: When the answer is "Yes," both partners turn away from the object and share the excitement, both exclaiming "We saw the red truck!"

Children may need extensive practice to integrate all five steps in a fluid manner. With some you may decide to take a preliminary step of working on asking, telling, checking and sharing and make sure that they are mastered prior to adding the need to repair the shared attention.

Variations:

When we feel that the children have mastered all five stages, we can add more complexity to this activity by providing each of the partners with their own perceptual stimulus and teaching them to take turns sharing what they see. For example, each participant can be stationed in front of a different window and

12

take turns being the "Teller" and the "Asker. "Or, each can have his own discovery box and take turns sharing what he has picked from the box. Remember that they must both turn from their windows, or their objects, when it is time to share their excitement.

Obstacles/Opportunities:

Most of our children know how to look out a window and tell what they see even prior to this exercise. It is critical to distinguish this "looking and telling" skill, from a true perception-sharing experience. In perception sharing, the most important part of the activity occurs when partners share their non-verbal emotional reactions by shifting their gaze from the object of attention, back to each other's faces.

LEVEL III, STAGE 12, ACTIVITY 133

Conversation Photo Book

ACTIVITY HIGHLIGHTS
○ Introduction to perspective taking
○ Taking actions that help social partners share perceptions.
○ Learning to ask relevant questions

Summary:

This is our initial exercise in learning to take the visual perspective of your social partner into account. It is also our first foray into sharing what is meaningful in your life in a representational format. The children compile photo albums of important people and places in their lives. They learn to turn the pages of their album and actively reference to make sure that their partner can see the photo. They also practice asking and answering questions about the photos.

Participants:

Coach and four children.

Getting Ready:

Each child first compiles a small photo album, beginning with five or six personal photographs of persons or places that are important to him or her. The Coach also compiles an album with similar photos. Initially, participants are seated at enough of an angle and distance from one another that they cannot see each other's photos, unless the "Shower" physically turns the album so that the photo is in his partner's line of sight.

Coaching Instructions:

There are six steps to this activity:

☐ STEP 1

Open your photo album, turn to the first picture, look at it briefly and make a noise indicating interest. Then say, "Would you like to see my picture?" After receiving a "Yes" reply, turn the photo in a slow deliberate manner so that your partner can clearly see the picture. In a very slow deliberate voice say, "This is my house. Can you see it?" Point in a slow, exaggerated manner to the house, then turn the photo away and shift your gaze to the child's face, again using an animated, exaggerated manner. Use a positive, excited tone of voice, exaggerated facial expressions and gestures. Remember not to use more than a few words! After you have succeeded in sharing enjoyment with the child you can move to the next step.

☐ STEP 2

Now reverse roles. The child opens his photo album, selects a photo and looks at it with exaggerated interest and excitement. Next he asks you if you want to see the photo. He practices turning the book so that you can easily see the photo and pointing to where he wants you to look. Make sure that he asks if you can see the photo. During this phase, always affirm that you can see it, unless he is clearly not turning the book in your vicinity.

☐ STEP 3

Now you will insert "checking" and "repairing" into the activity. When your partner shows you his picture and asks if you see it, pretend that you cannot see it very well. Make sure that he views your reply as meaningful and adapts his showing to attempt to improve your view of the photo.

☐ STEP 4

Now have two children practice "showing" and "looking" with each other.

☐ STEP 5

The children practice "checking: and "repairing" their own interaction. Each is quietly instructed to pretend they cannot see the picture well, requiring the other child to modify their actions.

☐ STEP 6

Add one of our beginning conversational structures from "Asking and Telling" to the exercise. After being shown the photo, one partner asks a relevant question about the photo of the other. The children may need significant instruction in determining what are important and unimportant questions to ask. For example, asking about minor details in the picture is unimportant. They should be taught to ask "who, what, when and where" questions and then given

12

the choice of whether to ask who the person is (unless it is clearly the other partner), what they are doing, when the photo was taken and where the photo was taken.

Variations:

The children should continually update their photo albums by entering photos that recount their daily lives and special experiences. They can also add some silliness to the activity by bringing in a photo that is clearly not about them – such as a picture of a robot – and sharing it as a surprise "visitor" to their album.

Obstacles/Opportunities:

Choosing photographs can be a collaborative endeavor. Pictures should be rotated frequently to avoid boredom. Remember, this is not the time to get into extensive conversations, nor, is it a place to review details. The fewer words the better!

LEVEL III, STAGE 12, ACTIVITY 134

Barrier

ACTIVITY HIGHLIGHTS
° Introduction to perspective taking
° Coordinating different perceptions.

Summary:

This is a fun exercise to begin our work on teaching how to integrate another person's perspective with the child's own. The children cannot see each other over the barrier. Nor, can they see what the other one does. They must depend upon their communication to adjust their actions. The activity is simple. The children are on opposite sides of a barrier and must coordinate getting a ball from one side into a basket on the other side.

Participants:

You can try this with two teams, where one team is always taking the role of "watchers."

Getting Ready:

Find or buy a cardboard barrier that is tall enough to block the view of the children while they are seated. You also need five soft, small balls and one medium size basket. Make sure the size of the basket and balls is such that the game will not be too simple, or too frustrating, for the participants given their motor abilities. Do not place the barrier on the floor between the two partners yet. Seat both partners in the same positions they will take when the barrier is placed between them. Provide one child with the balls. Provide the other with the basket.

Coaching Instructions:

There are three steps in this exercise:

☐ STEP 1

Explain that the goal of the game is to work together to get as many balls into the basket without hitting the ground. One partner will be the thrower and the other the catcher.

☐ STEP 2

Practice the activity without any mention of a barrier. Only move on to the next step when the children are coordinating their actions to successfully get the balls in the basket without an obstacle between them. You can also use this step to decide how far apart children should be from one another to make the game exciting, but not impossible.

☐ STEP 3

Now explain that since they are now such experts you are going to let them try the advanced version of the game. Place the cardboard barrier between them. Tell them that the game is the same except for one thing. In this version, because of the barrier between them, the thrower must rely on the catcher to tell him where to throw, because he can no longer see the basket himself. After each throw, make sure that the partners provide each other with feedback and make adjustments.

Variations:

There are many variations of this game, which also is a great beginning for cooperative learning. When children master Step 3 you can add another level of complexity. After each throw, move the basket to another spot so that extra communication is needed. This is a good game for teams to play against each other as well, if the partners can positively manage the extra stress of competition.

Obstacles/Opportunities:

The desire to win can become an obstacle that can interfere with the fun of this activity. Children with emotional regulation problems may get frustrated and start blaming themselves and others. If you suspect or notice this, stop the activity immediately.

12

LEVEL III, STAGE 12, ACTIVITY 135

Our Stuff

ACTIVITY HIGHLIGHTS:
- Binding friendships using shared emotional memories

Summary:

This is not an activity per se, rather it is a reminder to Coaches of the importance of binding initial friendships with shared memories. Often, we become so focused on the next challenge or task that we do not take the time to reflect on our prior accomplishments. Developing shared emotional memories is a critical part of relationship development. In every Level we work on emotional memories in different ways. By the end of Level III, children who have been practicing our activities together have spent a good deal of time looking back at their shared triumphs and joyful moments. We try to provide them with many reminders of their time together, such as photographs, videotapes and journal entries. We are careful to make regular time for reminiscing and are excited when we see children beginning to initiate this type of memory sharing.

One of the ways that we use objects to bind children together is to save their co-created activities in a special area. When a small group creates their own version of a board game, we make sure that the game is placed in a special container or drawer that will only be used to store their created items. We place their photographs, videos and other shared creations in the drawer as well. They quickly learn that "Our Stuff" is in a special place that is jointly owned and that only contains the products of their united effort, their "We-go" creations. Children will return time and again to their special area to jointly reminisce with "Our Stuff." Each time they do so, you will notice a deepening of their connection.

LEVEL III, STAGE 12, ACTIVITY 136

Clubhouse

ACTIVITY HIGHLIGHTS
° Developing ownership in a group
° Increase group cohesiveness

Summary:

People of all ages enjoy a place to meet that is their own special place. As a child I (Rachelle) lived in a neighborhood bordered by an unkempt city park, trees and litter. The boys built one clubhouse after another complete with "No girls" signs. We wrecked them by stealing another neighbor's tomatoes and smashing them into the floor when they were not there, only to have a new construction emerge at a later date. All children enjoy the sense of privacy and camaraderie fostered by the construction of their own space. The construction of a clubhouse also creates an arena for legitimate problem solving: How does one keep it from falling down? How do we protect unwanted intruders from entry?

Participants:

This is a group activity. The size of the group may vary.

Getting Ready:

The following minimal list suggests materials that might be used for participants of different ages. Young children may use beanbags, a tunnel, a table and a table-cloth. Older participants may manipulate scraps of lumber in conjunction with more permanent structures such as tables or trees..

Coaching Instructions:

Planning will most likely be minimal and construction tends to be without architectural design, more "learn while doing." What is lost in aesthetics is gained through group problem solving. Materials are discussed as well as the relevance of permanence and tear down/construction time. Signs fortify the insiders against the outsiders. Photographs and videos document the evolution of design and enjoyment that occurs within the walls of the clubhouse.

Variations:

At one school, the "clubhouse" is actually their entire campus. However, there is one special room called the Beanbag Room because it contains only beanbag chairs, over 40 of them, one for each community member.

Obstacles/Opportunities:

Because participants are working as a group to create a structure that must support their entrances and exits, there is a good likelihood that they will become easily frustrated, anxious or bossy – perhaps all three. You should facilitate thinking sessions for the group or individual watching sessions for individ-

12

ual children. Keeping perspective on the goal – to build a house with friends for a secret private place – will often be incentive enough for emotional management. If upsets continue, provide the person who is upset with self-calming techniques so that he can re-enter the building process.

LEVEL III, STAGE 12, ACTIVITY 137

What's More Important?

ACTIVITY HIGHLIGHTS
- Examining your behavior from a friend's point of view
- Finding ways to make visiting friends feel important
- Taking responsibility for determining which objects distract from attention to friends
- Using methods that increase the feeling of control over the success of social encounters

Summary:

Parents often tell me how they work so hard to arrange a "play-date" only to have the desired child come over and be ignored, because their son or daughter became too focused on a video, computer game or similar activity. In this activity, children practice keeping their primary focus on a friend, while being tempted by some object or activity that is very compelling to them.

Participants:

Four children can participate in this activity.

Getting Ready:

Carefully select the objects and activities that will be used as "temptations" to pull partners away from their friends. Make sure to have several options, in case one is too powerful and you need more practice to work up to it.

Coaching Instructions:

This exercise has five steps:

☐ STEP 1

Explain to children that they are going to practice how to make a friend feel important. Explain about how people feel when they are ignored.

☐ STEP 2

Use Self Talk to demonstrate how you might feel when you come to your friend's house and he ignores you in favour of something or someone else.

☐ STEP 3

Have all the children role-play coming to a friend's house and being ignored. Make sure that everyone gets to experience both roles.

☐ STEP 4

Sometimes children do not ignore their friend completely, but they may still make him feel like he is not very important. Perform role-plays where a person is not totally being ignored, but he is made to feel less important than some activity. An example of this is watching a video together and being told to be quiet when one of the children makes some comment about the movie. Then role-playing how that child might be made to feel more important.

☐ STEP 5

Have the children each pick activities that make it either easier to put their friend first, or harder, and try them out. The children should experiment with different activities and gradually compile lists of activities that are "friend friendly" and "not friend friendly."

Variations:

The natural extension of this exercise is for children to take more responsibility in pre-planning activity choices when they have a friend coming over. If a friend insists on an activity that is on the "not friend friendly" list, make sure that the child has a good excuse for declining to do the activity.

Obstacles/Opportunities:

This is a crucial exercise in teaching children that they have to take part of the responsibility for managing some of their own problems. We want them to learn to be aware of those aspects of the environment that are difficult for them and to take actions, whenever possible, to minimize environmental obstacles. Carefully considering which activities will distract too much attention away from a friend, is one critical step in this process of "Ownership."

LEVEL III, STAGE 12, ACTIVITY 138

Friendship Maps

ACTIVITY HIGHLIGHTS
° Learning basic definitions of friendship
° Learning how to make good friendship choices
° Practicing early friendship skills

Summary:

Many children initially have little understanding of the definition of friendship. For some, anyone whose name they know is a friend. For others, someone who will play or work at their side qualifies. This activity introduces children to the concept of friendship at a very basic level.

Participants:

This activity is suitable for a group of four.

Getting Ready:

Make up a series of cards with the different attributes of a good friend on one side and the lack of this attribute (a negative attribute) on the other side. Attributes are provided at the end of the activity description.

Coaching Instructions:

There are seven steps in this exercise:

☐ STEP 1

Tell children that they are going to learn about what makes a good friend. Ask them if they can tell you who their friends are and why they believe that those people are friends. Often, at this stage, children cannot tell us very much about why someone has received the designation of "friend."

☐ STEP 2

Take out a set of friends cards for each partner. Have them place the cards in a stack. Go through each of the eight cards. After you read the card, provide a brief role-play demonstration of what the card means.

☐ STEP 3

Now the children should participate in simple, structured role-plays that illustrate the positive sides of each of the eight attributes. Clearly identify which attribute you are working on. Continue role-plays until you are sure everyone can perform all eight elements without any prompting.

☐ STEP 4

Now tell the children that you are going to practice how not to get chosen as a friend. See if the group can generate eight "bad friend" cards that correspond to the initial friend cards. Place each bad friend attribute on the flip side of the corresponding positive attribute. Now have participants role-play each of the bad friend attributes. Continue until you are certain that they fully understand each one.

☐ STEP 5

Mix up positive and negative attributes when taking on the role of either good or bad friend. One participant serves as your friend for the exercise. The others have to observe carefully and "Stop the Action" when they see you doing either one of the good or bad friend attributes. After stopping the action, the child holds up the card he believes corresponds to your behavior and/or says out loud:

1. Whether you are being a good or bad friend.

2. Which of the attributes he believes corresponds to your behavior.

☐ STEP 6

After each person has had success in recognizing the attributes, gradually substitute participants for yourself and have them enact the different attributes without telling each other in advance which they are doing. Rotate participants through this role.

☐ STEP 7

About four weeks later, ask children to again talk about their friends. Determine if they have generalized the concepts enough. If not it is time for a refresher course.

Variations:

We like children to learn some structured ways of remembering how each of these attributes works for them in real life. We often ask them to add a short journal entry of what they did to be a good friend following every extended peer encounter. We also encourage repeated rehearsal of these attributes prior to a "play-date" with a peer.

Obstacles/Opportunities:

Some children at this stage may not have a clue about what makes their social partners smile and laugh. They may require some additional "tutoring" in observing what makes others laugh and what does not, even though the "initiator" may think what he says or does is funny. The key is learning to reference their partner's reactions and then recording what worked.

Good Friend Attributes

Good Friends:

1. Show that they are happy to see each other.

2. Know how to make each other smile and laugh

3. Want to find the same things to play together

4. Do not act bossy when they play together

12

313

5. Play fair and do not ever cheat

6. Check often to see if their friends are having a good time.

7. Do not walk away in the middle of play and leave a friend

8. Act like friends are more important than things

9. Care more about a friend, than winning or getting their way.

Appendix A

Progress Tracking Form

Use this form to set your initial objectives and also to track your progress. In the first column on the right place an "M", "W", "D" or "N" next to each item, along with the date, to indicate whether it has been mastered, it is partially or inconsistently in place or whether the skill needs to be developed. Choose your initial activities based upon the earliest in which you have placed a W or D. Every few weeks return to this form and rate your progress along with the date.

Ratings Key

M = Mastered: (1) Performs the skill for the purpose of increasing the level of coordination, emotion sharing and mutual enjoyment with social partners. (2) Performs the skill independently over 80% of the time. Initiates without help, prompts, or rewards. (3) Performs the skill at a frequency expected in typical development. (4) Initiates the skill with different adults and peers (where indicated) and in different, appropriate settings.

W = Working: (1) Performs the skill solely for the purpose of increasing the level of coordination, emotion sharing and mutual enjoyment with social partners. (2) Performs the skill independently less than 80% but more than 20% of the time. (3) Performs the skill in a majority of situations where appropriate, but at a frequency less than expected in typical development. (4) Does not frequently perform the skill with different adults and peers (where indicated) but does so in a variety of settings.

D = Developing: (1) Initiates the skill some of the time, to obtain some goal or reward that is unrelated to the social interaction. (2) Performs the skill independently less than 20% of the time. (3) Does not yet initiate the skill with different people or in different settings

N = Not Yet: Does not perform the skill. Or, performs the skill only to obtain some reward or goal, unrelated to increasing coordination and shared enjoyment of social partners (e.g. get a treat, getting to watch TV).

(This is an abbreviated version of the full RDI Progress Rating Form. Complete Forms can be purchased at our website, *www.connectionscenter.com*)

Rating Periods: Date 1: _____   Date 2: _____
                       Date 3: _____   Date 4: _____
                       Date 5: _____

	Rate each item with an M, W, D or N	1	2	3	4	5
	Level I					
	Stage 1					
1	Makes eye contact and smiles at you, inviting you to share the excitement and joy					
2	Obtains your attention before communicating					
3	Pays attention to your facial expressions and words while you are communicating					
4	Enjoys your attempts at simple pretend play					
5	Shares excitement , when you act in a playful manner					
6	Communicates in a positive manner to invite you to participate in a joint activity					
7	Communicates appropriately to end or pause a joint activity					
8	Communicates excited anticipation during pauses in shared activities					
9	Shifts gaze to maintain focus on two different social partners, during joint activities					
	Stage 2					
10	References your facial expressions and gestures for comforting and reassurance					
11	Stops actions in response to your facial expression of disapproval					
12	Looks to your facial expressions and other non-verbal signals, to obtain approval					
13	References facial expressions and other non-verbal signals to know what action to take					
14	Follows your pointing to determine where to look to find something					
15	Follows your facial signals like head nods, head shakes, smiles and frowns to determine where to look for something					

16	Keeps track of your whereabouts during interaction and even when not interacting					
	Stage 3					
17	Communicates pride when he/she complies with your instructions as a helper					
18	Matches your actions to imitate, when learning a new skill or activity					
19	Observes to make sure actions are at the proper speed and degree of care					
20	Readily accepts your coaching to guide actions					
21	Matches simple emotional expressions with you					
22	Accepts changes in activity schedule without becoming upset or resisting					
23	Stops activities and makes a change without becoming upset or resisting					
	Stage 4					
24	Regulates timing and matches your actions, in a number of different simple coordinated activities					
25	Shares face-to-face expressions of enjoyment, after coordinating actions with you					
26	Uses your facial expressions to coordinate his/her behavior with yours in joint activities					
27	Enjoys shared, coordinated pretend play and role plays when led by an adult partner					
28	Synchronizes actions with you in a number of face-to-face coordinated activities					
29	Coordinates movements with your guidance to alternate standing and moving face-to-face, back-to-back and side by side with you at a rapid pace of change.					

	Level II					
	Stage 5					
30	Matches sounds and words to produce playful, nonsense sound and word combinations					
31	Enjoys activities more, when you add variations to familiar activities					
32	Adapts his/her behavior to match your actions, after you introduce activity variations					
33	Shares enjoyment, after successfully adapting behavior to match your variations					
34	Does not add any variations, or changes to joint activities without your permission					
	Stop here if rating a child under three years of age					
35	Demonstrates awareness of the effect on communication of moving out of another person's line of sight or moving too far away					
36	Accurately perceives and appreciates degrees of improvement					
	Stage 6					
37	Enjoys gradual changes you make, that transform a familiar activity into a novel one					
38	Enjoys the surprise of an activity transforming into its opposite, through a series of variations you introduce					
39	Enjoys activities where you unexpectedly change rules and add other "surprise" elements into familiar activities					
40	Enjoys activities where you introduce new functions for familiar objects					
41	Accurately expresses and shares expressions of happiness, anger, sadness and fear					
42	Recognizes and responds in a sensitive manner when social partners express feelings					
43	Uses words in an opposite meaning, or nonsensical manner, for shared humor					
44	Appreciates humor used in a non-scripted manner					
45	Enjoys pretend play and role-plays where the emotional state of the characters changes, based on rapid, unexpected plot changes you introduce					

	Stop here if rating a child under four years of age					
	Stage 7					
46	Recognizes and matches six different emotional expressions					
47	Initiates communication of six basic emotional expressions					
48	Demonstrates awareness that emotional changes occur in relative increments, not in an "all" or "none" fashion					
49	Effectively uses non-verbal expressions and words to tell you what is wrong					
50	Remains at your side, while you are walking together in everyday settings					
51	Signals to a peer that he/she is ready to begin an activity and waits for a response					
52	Waits for peer partner to signal that he/she is ready before starting an activity					
53	Modifies behavior to coordinate actions with a peer, in simple coordinated activities					
54	Prefers activities where peers constantly adapt their behavior to remain coordinated					
55	Communicates appreciation for a peer partner's novel contributions to joint activities					
56	Synchronizes timing and role actions with a peer to function as a "joke team"					
57	Pays attention to listeners emotional reactions when telling a joke					
58	Communicates that sharing laughter is the main point of telling a joke					
59	Stays highly focused on a peer partnerÆs responses during simple conversation					
60	Maintains a shared topic with a peer during simple conversation, for three "turns"					
61	Uses simple reciprocal conversation structures					
62	Participates in structured, mutually curious conversations with peers					

	Stage 8					
63	Uses self-talk to translate directions and instructions into his/her own words					
64	Uses self-talk to plan an action he/she intends to take					
65	Uses self-talk to review an action just taken					
66	Recognizes that having a specific feeling does not lock you into taking a specific action					
67	Does not automatically blame other people when upset or things don't work out					
68	Prefers activities where peer partners take turns adding variations					
69	Demonstrates anticipation of a peer partner's movements (e.g. kicking a ball to the location where your partner is heading, rather than his/her current location).					
70	Invites peers to participate in activities, even when a partner is not necessary					
71	Communicates to determine activities that are preferred by peer partners					
72	Communicates with a peer to coordinate beginnings and endings of joint activities					
73	Communicates effectively with a peer to agree upon and plan choice of activity, rules and roles before beginning an activity					
74	Communicates for clarification when confused about his/her role in an activity					
75	Immediately stops, or modifies actions when a peer is confused, annoyed or bored					
76	Functions as an equal, enjoyable partner in structured pretend play and role plays					
77	Deliberately adapts behavior in an attempt to increase the enjoyment of peer partners					
78	Frequently checks to make sure peer partners are happy with his/her actions					

	Level III					
	Stage 9					
79	Explores an unknown, or mildly fearful setting or activity with a peer partner					
80	Effectively uses non-verbal signals to collaborate with a peer in multi-step activities					
81	Enjoys activities where each of two peers takes a different activity role (e.g. builder and architect) and integrate their actions to reach a common goal					
82	Checks to make sure that peer partners agree with actions and ideas before proceeding					
83	Prioritizes shared enjoyment with peers, even when faced with competitive goals					
84	Uses effective methods to compromise, when partners disagree or have different ideas					
85	Supports and encourages peers when working and/or playing together					
86	Operates as an unselfish teammate to further team goals					
87	Plans actions specifically with the hope that they will lead to approval of peer partners					
	Stage 10					
88	Enjoys teaming with a peer to create new activities, songs, games and role-plays					
89	Ensures that teammates make equal contributions to creative efforts					
90	Communicates appreciation for creative ideas of peers					
91	Communicates that working as a team is preferable and more fun than working alone					
92	Prefers to obtain the contributions of peers, rather than just relying on his/her own					
93	Engages in joint planning and evaluation with peers when working on creative activities					

	Stage 11						
94	Enjoys improvising with peers, to create unexpected changes to familiar activities						
95	Enjoys improvising with peers to create funny variations of familiar songs and jokes						
96	Enjoys improvisational role-plays, where partners produce amusing, unexpected changes in the play and remain coordinated						
97	Checks to see if actions are understood and enjoyed during improvised activities						
98	Takes necessary repair actions, during improvised activities, when actions are not connected with partners and/or not mutually enjoyable						
99	Acts genuinely curious and excited when peers point out interesting perceptions and share objects, photos, sights and sounds with him/her						
100	Shares face-to-face excitement after gazing at common objects with a peer						
101	References a peer's line of sight to perceive a shared stimulus as intended						
102	Initiates simple joint attention with peers						
103	Shares joint attention, when peers point out an interesting stimulus						
	Stage 12						
104	Engages complex joint attention with peers						
105	Checks to see if peer partner accurately perceives shared perceptions						
106	Modifies physical position to better see or hear an object that a peer is trying to share						
107	Connects emotions with different events that might cause them						
108	Tries to determine simple causes for feelings he/she is experiencing						
109	Conducts simple conversations with peers using seven different emotions						
110	Communicates interest and concern for feelings of peers and familiar adults						

111	Provides help and comfort when peers display hurt or upset reactions					
112	Checks to make sure that listeners accurately understand what he/she is saying					
113	Checks to make sure that his/her topic is related to the other person in conversation					
114	Effectively joins into a peer's play activities, using simple strategies					
115	Wants to have friends for the following reasons: they treat you fairly, share with you, like the things you do, try to make you feel good and act like you are important					
116	Greets friends with happiness and excitement, even in an unexpected encounter					
117	Finds ways to quickly make friends feel comfortable when they visit his/her house					
118	Chooses topics that he/she knows are interesting to friends					
119	Chooses joint activities based upon a friend's preferences					
120	Treats friends in a fair manner, at least as well as he/she treats him/herself					
121	Does not try to cheat or win over a peer when playing games and competitive activities					
122	Does not act bossy or controlling with friends					
123	Offers to help, when friends are having difficulty performing some activity					
124	Does not ignore a friend for an activity. Pays more attention to a friend than an activity					
125	Acts as a graceful loser and makes the winner feel good when playing games					
126	Remains calm after making mistakes and re-groups to continue on with an activity					
127	Acts in a compassionate manner when friends make mistakes or have accidents					

Topic Index for Activities

Topic	Level	Stage	Activity number	Activity (superscript indicates number of children)	Objectives (see Appendix A for list)
Apprenticeship			31	Assistant[1]	17
	I	3	32	Bill Ding[1]	17
			33	Matching[1]	18
			34	Guiding[1]	19,20
Attention			1	My Words are Important[1]	3
	I	1	5	Unexpected Labels[1]	3
			16	Beanbag Medley I[1]	1,2,5,6,7,8
Attunement			7	The Tunnel[1]	1,5,
			8	Climbing and Jumping[1]	1,3,5,9
			9	Affection Sharing[1]	1,2,3,5,6,9
			11	Swing and Fly[1]	1,2,3,5,9
	I	1	13	Push/Pull, With Sound Effects[1]	1,2,5,6,7,8
			14	Fast-Paced Actions[1]	1,2,5,6,7,8
			17	Simple Participation[1]	1,2,5,6,7,8
			18	Beanbag Medley II[1]	1,2,5,6,7,8
			15	Jack-in-the-Box[1]	1,2,5,6,7,8
Collaboration	II	8	86	Partner Pretend Play[2]	76,77,78
			87	Partner Role Plays[2]	76,77,78
		9	97	Musical Variations[4]	82,83,84,87
	III	10	109	Created Role-Plays[4]	88-93
			110	Joke Factory[4]	88-93
			111	Created Structures[4]	88-93
			112	Created Sculptures[4]	88-93
		11	113	Improvised Activities[4]	94,95,97,98

Collaboration			114	Improvised Structures[4]	94,95,97,98
	III	11	115	Improvised Rules[4]	94,95,97,98
			116	Improvised Rhythms[4]	94,95,97,98
			117	Improvised Music[4]	94,95,97,98
			118	Improvised Songs[4]	94,95,97,98
			119	Improvised Movement[4]	94,95,97,98
			120	Improvised Role-Plays[4]	94-98
			121	Improvised Jokes[4]	94-98
	I	4	40	Vegetable Delivery[1]	24,25,26,28
			41	Store[1]	27
			46	Cars and Ramps[1]	24,25,26,29
	II	8	82	Find Me[2]	68,69,75
			83	Drumming Duets[2]	68,69,70,72,74,75,77,78
	III	9	93	Parking Garage[4]	81,82,83,84
			94	The Beltway[4]	81,82,83,84,87
Cooperation	III	9	98	Buddy Walkers[2]	80,82,83,84,85
Communication	I	1	3	Unexpected Sounds and Actions[1]	1, 3
			4	Chant[1]	1,2,5
		4	54	Rhyming Words[1]	30
	II	5	61	Too Close, Or Too Far[1]	35
	III	12	124	Can You Hear Me Now?[6]	112
			125	Pass it On[6]	112
Conversation	II	7	79	Conversation Frameworks[2]	59,60,61
		8	85	Are We Connected?[2]	80
			88	Curious Conversations[2]	62
	III	12	127	Connected Conversations[6]	113
Cooperation		9	102	Map Reader and Scout[4]	80-87
	III	10	103	Created Rhythms[4]	88-93
			104	Art Car[4]	88-93
			105	Created Songs[4]	88-93
			107	Created Phrases[4]	88-93
			108	Created Games[4]	88-93

Coordinating Actions	I	4	38	Beanbag Mountain[1]	24,5,26
			39	Breaking the Chain[1]	24,25,26,28
			42	Stop and Go[1]	24,25,26,29
			43	Start and Stop[1]	24,25,26,29
			47	Crashing Cars[1]	24,25,26,29
			48	Two-Ball Roll[1]	24,25,26,29
			49	Ropes[1]	24,25,26
			50	Drums[1]	24,25,26
			51	Patterns[1]	24,25,26
			52	Position[1]	24,25,29
			53	Connections[1]	24
	II	5	55	Degrees of Change[1]	31,32,33,34
			56	Car Crash Variations[1]	31,32,33,34
			57	Number Crash[1]	31,32,33,34
			58	Ball Variations[1]	31,32,33,34
			59	Drum Changes[1]	31,32,33,34
			60	Walking Changes[1]	31,32,33,34
		6	72	Transforming Rhythms[1]	37
		7	73	Are You Ready?[1]	51,52
			75	Synchronized Rhythms[2]	51,52,53,55
			76	Tricky Partner[2]	51,52,53,54,55
	I	1	13	Push/Pull, With Sound Effects[1]	1,2,5,6,7,8
			14	Fast-Paced Actions[1]	1,2,5,6,7,8
			17	Simple Participation[1]	1,2,5,6,7,8
			18	Beanbag Medley II[1]	1,2,5,6,7,8
	II	7	80	Anticipation[2]	69
		8	81	Reviews for Duets[2]	51,52,53,54,55
Creativity	III	10	103	Created Rhythms[4]	88-93
			104	Art Car[4]	88-93
			105	Created Songs[4]	88-93
			107	Created Phrases[4]	88-93
			108	Created Games[4]	88-93
			109	Created Role-Plays[4]	88-93
			110	Joke Factory[4]	88-93
			111	Created Structures[4]	88-93
			112	Created Sculptures[4]	88-93
		11	113	Improvised Activities[4]	94,95,97,98
Curiosity	I	1	15	Jack-in-the-Box[1]	1,2,5,6,7,8

Emotion	I	3	37	Expression[1]	21
	II	5	62	Degrees of Happy[1]	48
			63	The Sound of Excitement[1]	48
		6	70	Morphing Emotions[1]	45
	III	12	122	Emotions[6]	107,108,109
Executive Functioning	II	5	64	Getting Better[1]	36
		7	74	Talk to Yourself[4]	63
	III	9	95	Self Instruction[4]	63,64
			96	Replays[4]	65
Flexibility	I	4	54	Rhyming Words[1]	30
	II	5	55	Degrees of Change[1]	31,32,33,34
			56	Car Crash Variations[1]	31,32,33,34
			57	Number Crash[1]	31,32,33,34
			59	Drum Changes[1]	31,32,33,34
			60	Walking Changes[1]	31,32,33,34
		6	65	Activity Transformations[1]	37
			66	Function Transformations[1]	40
			67	Rule Changes[1]	39
			68	Opposite World[1]	38
			69	Unexpected Jokes[1]	43,44
			70	Morphing Emotions[1]	45
			71	Role Reversals[1]	45
			72	Transforming Rhythms[1]	37
		7	75	Synchronized Rhythms[2]	51,52,53,55
			76	Tricky Partner[2]	51,52,53,54,55
	III	10	111	Created Structures[4]	88-93
			112	Created Sculptures[4]	88-93
		11	113	Improvised Activities[4]	94,95,97,98
	II	5	58	Ball Variations[1]	31,32,33,34
Flexible Thinking	I	1	5	Unexpected Labels[1]	5
	III	11	114	Improvised Structures[4]	94,95,97,98
			115	Improvised Rules[4]	94,95,97,98
			116	Improvised Rhythms[4]	94,95,97,98
			117	Improvised Music[4]	94,95,97,98
			118	Improvised Songs[4]	94,95,97,98
			119	Improvised Movement[4]	94,95,97,98
			120	Improvised Role-Plays[4]	94-98
			121	Improvised Jokes[4]	94-98

Friendship	III	10	106	Our Song[4]	88-93
		12	128	Learning How to Lose[6]	125
			129	It Takes Two[4]	115
			130	Joining In I[4]	114
			137	What's More Important?[6]	115-124
			138	Friendship Maps[6]	115-124
			135	Our Stuff[6]	115
			136	Clubhouse[6]	91-93
Gaze Shifting	I	1	6	Two Coach Approach[1]	5, 9
Humor	II	6	69	Unexpected Jokes[1]	43,44
		7	78	Synchronized Humour[2]	55,56,57, 58
	III	10	110	Joke Factory[4]	88-93
		11	121	Improvised Jokes[4]	94-98
Joint Attention	I	2	25	Follow my Eyes to the Prize[1]	13,14, 15
	III	12	131	Discovery Boxes[4]	99-106
			132	What do You See?[4]	99-106
			133	Conversation Photo Book[4]	99-106
			134	Barrier[4]	99-106
Non-Verbal Communication	I	1	2	I Lost my Voice[1]	3
			9	Affection Sharing[1]	1,2,3,5,6,9
	I	2	24	Non-Verbal Towers[1]	13
			26	Trading Places[1]	12,13
			27	Mother, May I[1]	12,13
			28	Silent Card Game[1]	12,13,15
Non-Verbal Communication	II	8	84	Mixed Up Puzzles[2]	80
	III	12	123	Talk Without Words[6]	109
			126	Wordless Drawings[6]	97-98,105,106
Pretend Play	I	4	45	Parallel Pretend Play[1]	27
	II	8	86	Partner Pretend Play[2]	76,77,78
Referencing		1	10	Now You See Me, Now You Don't[1]	1,2,3,5,
			12	Masks On. Masks Off[4]	1,4,5,8
			19	Challenge Course[1]	1,2,5,6,7,8
	I	2	20	Sneaky Partner[1]	16
			21	Sneaky Pete[1]	16
			22	Disappearing Coach[1]	16
			23	Save Me[1]	4,8,9,10,
			29	Stay Tuned to this Station[1]	13
			30	You Lose[1]	13

Role-Playing	I	4	44	Role Actions[1]	27
		6	71	Role Reversals[1]	45
	II	7	77	Synchronized Roles[2]	51,52,53,54
		8	87	Partner Role Plays[2]	76,77,78
	III	10	109	Created Role-Plays[4]	88-93
Team Cooperation			99	Relay Race[4]	83,85,86
			100	Shark and Fisherman[4]	80,83,84,85,86
			101	The Monster Again[4]	80-87
	III	9	89	Ball and Net[2]	80
			90	Lifting and Carrying[2]	80,82
			91	It's Dark![2]	79
			92	Buddy Baseball[4]	83,85
Transitions	I	3	35	Transition[1]	22,23
			36	Incomplete Completion[1]	22,23

Levels and Stages of the Complete RDI Program

Levels I – III are covered in this volume for young children and in the second volume for older children and adolescents. The second volume also covers Levels IV – VI.

Level I: Novice

Stage 1: Attend

Stage 2: Reference

Stage 3: Regulate

Stage 4: Coordinate

Level II: Apprentice

Stage 5: Variation

Stage 6: Transformation

Stage 7: Synchronization

Stage 8: Duets

Level III: Challenger

Stage 9: Collaboration

Stage 10: Co-creation

Stage 11: Improvisation

Stage 12: Running Mates

Level IV: Voyager

Stage 13: Perspective

Stage 14: Imagination

Stage 15: Group Creation

Stage 16: Emotion Regulation

Level V: Explorer

Stage 17: Ideas

Stage 18: What's Inside?

Stage 19: Conversations

Stage 20: Allies

Level VI: Partner

Stage 21: Shared Selves

Stage 22: Family Roots

Stage 23: Group Connections

Stage 24: Intimate Relations